METHOD AND IMAGINATION IN
COLERIDGE'S CRITICISM

Method and Imagination
in
Coleridge's Criticism

by

J. R. DE J. JACKSON

Associate Professor of English, Victoria College,
University of Toronto

HARVARD UNIVERSITY PRESS

CAMBRIDGE, MASSACHUSETTS 1969

Printed in Great Britain

Contents

Acknowledgments

In addition to the debts to others implied in the footnotes to this essay, it is a pleasure to record obligations of a more personal kind. Professors Kathleen Coburn and Barbara Hardy read the manuscript at an early stage in its development and gave me the benefit of detailed comments on it. The more recent advice of readers for the press has also been of use. Professors Kenneth MacLean and Carl Woodring offered encouragement at a time when it was much appreciated. The teaching of Professors G. E. Bentley and Louis A. Landa, given before this study was begun, has proved a lasting source of inspiration. I owe most to Professor George Whalley, who first introduced me to both Coleridge and criticism, and who has responded generously to appeals for advice ever since.

I am grateful to the Huntington Library of San Marino, California, for permission to quote from a manuscript in its possession, to the State and University Library of Lower Saxony, in Göttingen, for its hospitality, and to the staffs of the Department of Printed Books and the Department of Manuscripts of the British Museum for their unfailing courtesy and helpfulness.

I have been assisted by grants in aid of research from the Commonwealth Scholarship Commission, the Canada Council, and the University of Toronto. Victoria College provided for the typing of the final draft.

Key to Abbreviations

A to R	S. T. Coleridge. *Aids to Reflection in the Formation of a Manly Character on the Several Grounds of Prudence, Morality, and Religion: Illustrated by Select Passages from Our Elder Divines, especially from Archbishop Leighton.* London, 1825.
BL	——. *Biographia Literaria; or Biographical Sketches of My Literary Life and Opinions.* London, 1817. 2 Vols.
CL	——. *Collected Letters,* ed. Earl Leslie Griggs. Oxford, 1956– 4 Vols.
C of Pure R	Immanuel Kant. *Critique of Pure Reason,* trans. Norman Kemp Smith. London, 1956.
EOHOT	S. T. Coleridge. *Essays on His Own Times forming a Second Series of the Friend,* ed. Sara Coleridge. London, 1850. 3 Vols.
Everyman	——. *Biographia Literaria,* ed. George Watson. London, 1956.
F	——. *The Friend: A Series of Essays, in Three Volumes, to Aid in the Formation of Fixed Principles in Politics, Morals, and Religion, with Literary Amusements Interspersed.* London, 1818. 3 Vols.
F (1809)	——. *The Friend; a Literary, Moral, and Political Weekly Paper, excluding Personal and Party Politics, and the Events of the Day.* Penrith, 1809–10.
LR	——. *The Literary Remains,* ed. Henry Nelson Coleridge. London, 1836–39. 4 Vols.
MC	——. *Miscellaneous Criticism,* ed. Thomas Middleton Raysor. London, 1936.
N	——. *The Notebooks,* ed. Kathleen Coburn. New York, 1957– 2 Vols. (double).
NOED	——. *Notes on English Divines,* ed. Derwent Coleridge. London, 1853. 2 Vols.
PL	——. *The Philosophical Lectures,* ed. Kathleen Coburn. London, 1949.

PW   S. T. Coleridge. *The Complete Poetical Works*, ed. Ernest Hartley Coleridge. Oxford, 1912. 2 Vols.

SC   ———. *Shakespearean Criticism*, ed. Thomas Middleton Raysor. London, 1960. 2 Vols.

Shawcross   ———. *Biographia Literaria*, ed. J. Shawcross. London, 1907. 2 Vols.

SM   ———. *The Statesman's Manual; or The Bible the Best Guide to Political Skill and Foresight: A Lay Sermon, Addressed to the Higher Classes of Society, With an Appendix Containing Comments and Essays Connected with the Study of the Inspired Writings.* London, 1816.

TM   ———. *Treatise on Method as Published in the Encyclopædia Metropolitana*, ed. Alice D. Snyder. London, 1934.

TT   ———. *Specimens of the Table Talk*, ed. H. N. Coleridge. London, 1835. 2 Vols.

UL   ———. *Unpublished Letters*, ed. Earl Leslie Griggs. London, 1932. 2 Vols.

W   ———. *The Watchman*. Bristol, 1796.

Vorlesungen   Friedrich Wilhelm Johann Schelling. *Vorlesungen über die Methode des academischen Studiums*. Tübingen, 1803.

For My Mother

Introduction

On being confronted with the common opinion that Coleridge was a great critic one's first impulse is to ask in what way he was great. The answers which have been given to this question reveal two distinct schools of thought. According to one of them he is to be admired mainly for having made penetrating observations on particular works and authors; according to the other his reputation is seen to rest instead on his successful and suggestive treatment of abstract literary problems. The two points of view are not mutually contradictory. They reflect the preference of those who hold them for either practical or theoretical criticism, and it might even be argued that it is a sign of greatness in a critic to have satisfied so many on each count. Coleridge himself would have been puzzled, however, to find how rarely it is suggested that there is any direct relationship between the quality of his practical criticism and the quality of his theoretical criticism. Even his admirers tend to use his work as a repository of unconnected critical statements from which selections may be taken at will for analysis or praise.

The most plausible excuse for this procedure is that what we have of Coleridge's criticism is fragmentary and obscure, and that we should therefore make whatever use of it we can. While there is something to be said for this policy, it is not one which commends itself to the literary historian who wants to understand Coleridge's criticism on Coleridge's terms before venturing to assess its originality or value. It is of course quite possible that there is not enough evidence for the historian to go on, but until such evidence as there is has been fully exploited we cannot justifiably consider the case closed.

Some compensation can be made for the fragmentary state of his criticism if we try to construct the context of the fragments by examining Coleridge's considerable manuscript remains as well as his published work; the editions now in progress of his letters and notebooks have already revealed a part of the rich materials that have yet to be taken into account. And if, as is occasionally suggested, Coleridge's notorious obscurity is due as much to the unfamiliarity of his terms or his inability to express himself clearly as it is to the inherent difficulty of his ideas, here again a reconstruction of the intellectual context should prove useful.

Efforts of this sort have already been made. By working from the outline of Coleridge's philosophical development which he provides for us formally in *Biographia Literaria* and more intimately in his private correspondence, it has been possible to isolate recurrent themes such as the 'reconciliation of opposites', 'reason and understanding', 'organic unity', and 'imagination and fancy', each of which has been shown to throw light on the whole body of his criticism.[1] Students of literature are usually more interested in Coleridge's criticism than in his philosophy, and it is traditional to begin by studying *Biographia Literaria* and his literary lectures and to fall back on his philosophical writings only when we cannot make sense of his criticism as it stands. This has proved in the past to be a very helpful way of clearing up difficulties. But it may be compared to the habit of looking up the unfamiliar words in a glossary when one is reading Shakespeare, and it has the same drawback—some of the words are taken for their modern counterparts, are not looked up, and, as a consequence, are misread. It has the further disadvantage of reversing the order of Coleridge's own thought. For there can be no doubt that he was a philosopher or theologian first and a critic second; our interest in his criticism and indifference to his philosophy should not prevent us from recognizing where his priorities lay. No matter how daunting or disagreeable the prospect may seem, we shall have to begin by mastering his philosophy and proceed to the criticism afterwards if we are ever to understand Coleridge on his own ground.

J. A. Appleyard's recent book, *Coleridge's Philosophy of Literature* (Cambridge, Mass., 1965), provides an admirable account of the development of Coleridge's views. The present essay is narrower in scope. It is also more polemical, exploring as it does the neglected link between Coleridge's theory of Method and his theory and practice of criticism, and arguing that his crucial distinction between Imagination and Fancy does not mean quite what it has generally been taken to mean. The emphasis throughout is upon how Coleridge thought rather than upon what he thought, upon the process rather than the conclusions of his criticism.

I

Some Biographical Circumstances

Although biographies of critics are seldom allowed to intrude much upon studies of criticism, the peculiar circumstances of Coleridge's life have an important bearing on the way in which we must approach what he has to say. Apart from his marginalia, almost all of his literary criticism was occasional, and the occasion was in each case the urgent need to make money. This point is frequently neglected, but it is worth making in some detail if we are to deal fairly with him.

Attempts to trace the beginnings of *Biographia Literaria* which record Coleridge's critical achievements and plans during the decade preceding its publication tend to give the impression that he had been feeling his way steadily towards this book and that it represented for him something of a culmination of his critical thought. In fact, the various series of literary lectures and the *Biographia* itself were improvised. Placed beside the rest of his multifarious schemes the completion of any one of them becomes recognizable for the accident it was.

Shortly after his return from Germany in 1800, Coleridge's life was complicated by poverty, marital unhappiness and ill health.[1] Besides being in debt to close friends like Thomas Poole and Charles Lamb, he was miserably aware of his obligations to his patrons, the Wedgwoods.[2] As time went on and he produced nothing of consequence, he was tempted to sustain his self-respect by pretending that he had finished works which were really fragmentary. In this unfortunate situation, he was forced back on his literary resources; we find him paralysed by his aversion to doing the necessary hack-work, and inhibited by the conviction that he was prostituting his gifts for poetry and philosophy. The twin giants 'Bread and Cheese', of whom he had complained a few years before, continued to plague him

I

until he left England for Malta in 1804. To ward off their insatiable demands Coleridge had to put his talents to use; here he was thwarted by a further complication.

As had been clear when he undertook his German trip, his own interests were moving more and more in the direction of philosophy; his ambitions had not yet become entirely philosophical, but he felt that his studies had begun to have a bad effect on his creative work. His complaint to William Sotheby, a friend and prospective publisher, describes a state of mind that was to become habitual. He complains of

> . . . metaphysical trains of Thought — which, when I trusted myself to my own Ideas, came upon me uncalled – & when I wished to write a poem, beat up Game of far other kind – instead of a Covey of poetic Partridges with whirring wings of music, or wild Ducks *shaping* their rapid flight in forms always regular . . . up came a metaphysical Bustard, urging it's slow, heavy, laborious, earth-skimming Flight, over dreary & level Wastes.[3]

This same 'metaphysical Bustard' was largely responsible for the failure of Coleridge's schemes for making money. Throughout the rest of his life he was to find that the combination of his lofty ideals and complex metaphysics was too much for his practical plans.

His particular literary assets suggested several different ways of supporting himself. Although the creative gift on which he had relied before going to Germany appeared to be failing, it might serve to turn out verses for the newspapers; in addition, he could revise earlier poems and hunt through his papers for unused metrical scraps. There was his knowledge of German, first put to use in his translation of Schiller's *Wallenstein*. As a man of intelligence who was deeply interested in politics, he could make himself useful to the newspapers by commenting on current affairs. Last, and least promising, he could apply some of the learning he had been amassing in the course of his philosophical reading.

The translation of *Wallenstein* appears to have soured Coleridge on the exploitation of his German visit, and although he had contracted to provide his publisher, Longman, with a book based on his travels, he evidently found the task too un-congenial to complete and later tried to substitute another work for it.[4] Some time later, he agreed to provide William Sotheby with a translation of Gessner's *Der erste Schiffer* and seems to have carried this project some way before abandoning it.[5] His offer to translate Voss's *Luise* was, one gathers, speculative.[6] Drawing on past composition, he contemplated publishing his play, *Osorio*, in altered form as a poem, prepared to see a new edition of his verse through the press, and announced the impending completion of *Christabel*.[7]

He is surprisingly reticent about the production of new literary works during these years, perhaps recognizing the deterioration of his ability to write fluently. He proposed a drama, and a farce, and even a comic poem which was to rival *Hudibras*.[8] But he turned most frequently to ideas for non-fiction: essays on the preternatural (to preface *Christabel*), a history of philosophy, a discussion of the Greek definite article, one book entitled, 'Concerning Tythes & Church Establishment', another called 'Concerning Poetry, & the characteristic Merits of the Poets, our Contemporaries', an edition of selections from English poetry, a history of English prose, a prefatory essay sum-marizing and purifying Hartley, a critical, historical study of Chaucer (as a puff to Godwin's forthcoming biography of the poet), and a work touchingly named, 'Consolations & Comforts'.[9] Finally there was his political journalism, the only employment which ever brought him reliable financial returns.[10] The story of Coleridge's failure to carry out any of these plans is a sad one. The plans themselves are of interest to us here because of the light they throw on the motives and methods of his writing. The various titles which he suggests reflect his interests, or more specifically, those of his interests which he thought might hold the attention of the public.

The constant pressure of having to make a living was hard on him. Coleridge always seems to have found working for hire a cramping business. His friends were tolerant, feeling, no doubt, that a man of such uncommon gifts and promise deserved more leeway than most; Mrs. Coleridge, understand-ably, found it more difficult to remain sympathetic, and towards the end of 1802 we find him reminding her of his disability in a letter: 'You know, how hateful all Money-thoughts are to

3

me! – & how idly & habitually I keep them at arm's length.'[11]
He had confided to Poole in March, 1801,

> ... I was irritated by the necessity, I was under, of inter-
> mitting most important & hitherto successful Researches, in
> order to earn a trifle of ready money by scribbling for a
> Newspaper. Having given to my own conscience proof of the
> activity & industry of my nature I seemed to myself to be
> entitled to exert those powers & that industry in the way, I
> myself approved.[12]

This sense of being set aside for important tasks is typical of
Coleridge, and his receipt of the Wedgwood annuity may well
have encouraged it.[13] His emphatic statement, '... I cannot
express to you . . . the loathing, which I once or twice felt, when
I attempted to write, merely for the Bookseller, without any
sense of the moral utility of what I was writing,' reveals the
conflict that dogged his attempts to make a living.[14] Being
naturally of a contemplative disposition, and fiercely and
vigorously absorbed in the literary, political, theological, and
philosophical issues of his time, he was exasperated beyond
measure by the irrelevant demands of practical affairs. He
considered hack-work to be utterly destructive of the impulses
that he most valued in himself, and his own sights were set too
high for him to have published much of his serious thought even
if there had been an audience for it. The book-reading public
was in fact completely unreceptive, and Coleridge was bitter.
'I am assured,' he writes to Poole in 1801, 'that such is the
depravity of the public mind that no literary man can find bread
in England except by misemploying & debasing his Talents—
that nothing of real excellence would be either felt or understood.'[15] He was compelled to attempt to please this public with
'works written purposely vile', but he had little confidence in
his ability to do so.[16]

In the meantime his plans for less perishable works were
developing. He had not altogether abandoned his hopes of
writing a major poem, but the old fluency seemed to him to
have been lost while he was engrossed in philosophical matters.
In 1801, he still feels that his callings are poetry and metaphysics, and rejects other pursuits: '... I have cheerful and

confident hopes of myself. If I can hereafter do good to my fellow creatures, as a poet, and as a metaphysician, they will know it; and any other fame than this, I consider as a serious evil. . . .'[17] But three weeks later he writes morosely to Godwin, 'The Poet is dead in me – my imagination (or rather the Some-what that had been imaginative) lies, like a Cold Snuff on the circular Rim of a Brass Candle-stick, without even a stink of Tallow to remind you that it was once cloathed & mitred with Flame.'[18] In a letter to Thomas Wedgwood, in which he is trying to make up for his failure to show any return for patron-age, he mentions brave hopes for a heroic poem. 'I have since my twentieth year,' he writes, 'meditated an heroic poem on the Siege of Jerusalem by Titus – this is the Pride, & the Stronghold of my Hope. But I never think of it except in my best moods.'[19] These moods were to become progressively less frequent.

His deepening commitment to metaphysics was more promis-ing. In the same letter to Wedgwood, Coleridge refers to 'The work, to which I dedicate the ensuing years of my Life. . . .'[20] He was still at the stage in his philosophical development which he describes in *Biographia Literaria*, struggling to overthrow the determinist associationism of Hartley and the superficiality – as it seemed to him – of empiricist thought against which his temperament rebelled.[21] He did not give up his wish to be a poet easily, and at one point even spoke of returning to poetry after 'disburthening' himself of his metaphysics;[22] but by 1801 he was absorbed in philosophical reading and had begun to feel that it would be easier for him to write a philosophical pot-boiler than the volume of German travels which he owed Longman. He wrote to Poole,

I shall propose to Longman to accept instead of these Travels a work on the originality & merits of Locke, Hobbes, & Hume which work I mean as a *Pioneer* to my greater work, and as exhibiting a proof that I have not formed opinions without an attentive Perusal of the works of my Predecessors from Aristotle to Kant.[23]

In the same letter, he makes the well-known announcement of his overthrow of '. . . the doctrine of Association, as taught by

5

Hartley, and with it all the irreligious metaphysics of modern Infidels – especially, the doctrine of Necessity'.[24] He states that he is trying to evolve the five senses from one sense, discriminating between them, and in the course of doing so, solving 'the process of Life & Consciousness'.[25] Two years later the title has changed, reflecting development in his thinking. He writes to his friend Samuel Purkis, saying that the book is to be historical rather than metaphysical:

It perhaps will merit the title of a History of Metaphysics in England from Lord Bacon to Mr. Hume, inclusive. I confine myself to facts in every part of the work, excepting that which treats of Mr. Hume: – *him* I have assuredly besprinkled copiously from the fountains of Bitterness and Contempt.[26]

To Godwin four months later he communicates details of this 'Organum verè Organum', or '*Instrument* of practical Reasoning in the business of real Life'.[27] The outline is so elaborately ambitious as to reveal another of Coleridge's weaknesses as a professional man of letters – his inability to limit his plans within practical bounds. In spite of his claim that the work is 'half-written *out*', and that the materials for the rest of it are already on paper, it is obvious that he has committed himself too deeply to compiling an immense philosophical treatise.[28] His business-like comment that 'It's profitable Sale will greatly depend on the Pushing of the Bookseller, and on it's being considered as a *practical* Book', is followed by the characteristic warning, 'I fear, that it may extend to 700 pages'.[29] When one recalls that he had already explained to Godwin that this work was to be a mere preliminary to his weightier preoccupations the heart sinks:

. . . I shall, if I live & have sufficient health, set seriously to work – in arranging what I have already written, and in pushing forward my Studies, & my Investigations relative to the omne scibile of human Nature – *what* we *are*, & *how* we *become* what we are; so as to solve the two grand Problems, how, being acted upon, we shall act; how, acting, we shall be acted upon.[30]

6

By juxtaposition with this more ambitious plan, even the 'Organum' seems believable.

It is evident that in some instances Coleridge is announcing projected works which his reading suggests to him he could write if he wanted to. Taken up with the metaphysical problems themselves, he underestimates the effort necessary for him to convert his own thoughts into communicable form; he turns a blind eye to the difference between personal notes and publishable treatises. By 1804, with the prospect of the journey to Malta before him, he was once more on the defensive, and even offered one of his correspondents a description of the way in which he proposed to divide his time each day in order to carry out a new plan, a history of English Literature.[31]

The years which preceded his departure for Malta provide evidence not only of his famous conversion, or surrender, to philosophy, but also of the growth of a most important and characteristic habit of mind. Faced with the need to make money, and driven at the same time by temperament and his deepest convictions to take on the unlimited problems of metaphysics, Coleridge still hoped to be able to furnish pleasing and improving materials for a public which he thought badly needed to be reformed. After his return from Malta, he began for the first time to carry some of these plans into effect; he succeeded in developing a technique for drawing off things that others could use. To it we owe most of what we now think is valuable in his criticism.

Coleridge returned from Malta in the autumn of 1806, ailing, and faced once again with the problem of earning his living.[32] On the sixteenth of September, he mentioned having received an application from the Royal Institution for a course of lectures, and felt inclined to accept, both, as he told his wife, for the money and for the reputation that might be gained.[33] A plan was even broached by his friend Humphry Davy by which Coleridge might have earned about £400 a year by working for the Royal and London Institutions, but this fell through.[34] Neither Wordsworth nor Southey was in favour of the lecturing scheme,[35] but as Coleridge pointed out, he needed the money, and the lectures seemed to offer the most sensible way of gaining it: 'Something,' he said, '. . . I must do, & that immediately, to get money – & this seems both the most respectable, & the least unconnected with my more serious literary plans. . . .'[36] He soon accepted the Royal Institution's offer of £120 for lectures on 'the Principles common to the Fine Arts'.[37] A year passed and debt and serious illness intervened before the series actually began.

In August, 1807, Coleridge wrote mournfully to his friend Josiah Wade: '. . . at the age of 35 I am to be penniless, resourceless, in heavy debt – my health & spirits absolutely broken down – & with scarce a friend in the world'.[38] The need to give the lectures had become more pressing, therapeutic as well as financial. Humphry Davy summed up the situation: '. . . I think he might be of material service to the public, and of benefit to his own mind, to say nothing of the benefit his purse might receive.'[39] Coleridge himself expressed some hopes of making a profit from the lectures, and was sufficiently serious about what was to be included in them to feel obliged to refuse a request from Southey to review some of Wordsworth's poems, on the grounds that by doing so he would anticipate ideas which ought to be reserved for those who paid to hear him.[40]

The actual delivery of the lectures was erratic. In the first place they were delayed by Davy's illness, and they were interrupted and eventually cut short by Coleridge's. We get mixed hints of Coleridge's way of preparing lectures during this first series from his appeals for materials and his claims to be occupied with the writing of notes. On his arrival from Malta, he had been disturbed at the possibility of losing his notebooks, without which, he maintained, he would be unable to lecture.[41] It was clearly his intention to draw upon his meditations of the past two years. On the other hand, after the course had begun, we find him asking Dr. Bell, the educational reformer, for the use of proof-sheets of his book on the Madras system, which he proposes to incorporate in his lectures.[42]

We are fortunate in having a letter which Coleridge wrote in 1819 describing how he delivered and prepared lectures. It stresses his reliance on materials he has collected over the years, and his confidence in the beneficial results of speaking spontaneously on different subjects which interested him. The letter expresses what he regarded as the ideal of his lecturing. Most important, however, is his claim that he only lectures on topics that have been part of his thought for a long time, and that his specific preparation of lectures consists in the mulling over of materials already completely thought through, so as to make them comprehensible to his audience, and not in gathering new materials or attaining new learning. The resemblance to conversation in the attempt to achieve spontaneity is clear enough; Coleridge's more unusual qualities as a lecturer are his high estimate of the years of as yet unexploited reading and his conviction that he has a duty to communicate his conclusions.

Writing in answer to a request that he undertake yet another series of lectures, he says,

> . . . I would not lecture on any subject for which I had to *acquire* the main knowledge, even though a month's or three months' previous time were allowed me; on no subject that had not employed my thoughts for a large portion of my life since earliest manhood, free of all outward and particular purpose. . . .[43]

He goes on to describe how he occupies his time while the course is in progress:

> . . . during a course of lectures, I faithfully employ *all* the intervening days in collecting and digesting the materials, whether I have or have not lectured on the same subject before, making no difference. The day of the lecture, till the hour of commencement, I devote to the consideration, what of the mass before me is best fitted to answer the purposes of a lecture. . . .[44]

He adds that on the few occasions on which he has written out lectures either because he felt too unwell to sustain the demands of speaking from rough notes, or because he hoped that copies might be 'marketable among the publishers', he has found himself unable to avoid turning away from the notes and speaking spontaneously.[45] Contemporary accounts of Coleridge's lectures bear out this description, although they record that on a few occasions he was so subdued by illness as to read spiritlessly through a prepared script.[46]

The combination of spontaneous discussion of a variety of topics and the increasingly elaborate structure of his best thought, was Coleridge's compromise between his ideals and the unremitting demands of making a living. It is not a surprising procedure for a public lecturer, but it is carried by Coleridge into his published work. The origin of his next major undertaking, *The Friend*, was similar, and he left detailed accounts of his techniques of composing it and his notions of what it would represent. He continues to cling to the apology that he is simply paving the way to more systematic works to come, and educating a public to understand them when they do. As it turned out, none of the systematic works was ever presented to the public; everything of Coleridge's that found its way into print during his lifetime or was heard in the lecture hall was part of his useful compromise.

This is not to suggest that there is no distinction between the manner of composing the lectures and the way in which *The Friend*, *The Statesman's Manual*, and *Biographia Literaria* were written. The books are less spontaneous, and they are more carefully executed both in detail and design. But there is this in common: in both cases, Coleridge is seeking to communicate seriously with the public those parts of his thought which seemed relevant to issues of the time and on which he might be considered specially qualified to speak; there is the same reliance on his long-standing preoccupations. He does not, like Southey, turn his studies to Brazilian affairs in order to write a history of Brazil; nor does he resemble Godwin, who decides that a biography of Chaucer needs to be written, sets about equipping himself for the job, and writes it. The problem which Coleridge set himself was the study of the nature of the universe, and he spent his life trying to learn something about it; this occupation was not conducive to turning out popular books. Coleridge's books, like his lectures, represent temporary diversions from the main stream of his thinking, but he relied on the main stream and selected topics relevant to it both because he could not tear himself away from it, and because he thought that it would lend force to his remarks on specific topics. It was the existence of this main stream that made him confident of having something new and important to say. He was coerced by circumstances into being satisfied with peripheral communication of his ideas, and he was no doubt comforted in this predicament by the conviction that his ideas were growing things and not yet ready to be presented formally and systematically.

Study of the stages of composition of *The Friend* supports these conclusions; the development of this book from what had been in the first place a periodical into a carefully revised and expanded 'rifacciamento', reveals Coleridge achieving as satisfactory a result as his compromise between necessity and inclination ever allowed him.

It must be borne in mind that by the time he returned to England from Malta, his reputation for having wasted his talents was becoming fixed. He was well aware that he had not yet begun to produce the work which his capacities had led others to expect of him. This fact and his own high sense of purpose helped him to persist in trying to make money by work of a serious and beneficial sort; but make money he had to. His first allusion to *The Friend* is to '. . . a plan, which secures from 12 to 20 £ a week. . . .'[47] And a year later, shortly before the periodical commenced publication, he wrote to an old acquaintance requesting his help as an advertiser; he is quite frank about the purpose of the venture:

> It's Object is – by doing as much good as I can to do some service to my Wife & children. If it succeed, (i.e. if it sell a 1000) it will put 7 or 8 hundred £, each year, in my or rather my wife's pocket . . . during it's publication. – Therefore remember old Times . . . and do me what service you can, in gaining me names.[48]

Elsewhere, justifying his appeal to his friends for publicity, he described *The Friend* as being of 'the last Importance' to him.[49] But while he expected to be a gainer by the enterprise, he had no illusions of becoming a popular author; his aims were monetary, but modestly and worthily so. He remarks to his friend Pim Nevins in a letter, 'O if money were my Object, I could procure 50 Subscribers for one, if I chose to fight the battles of any particular Party – But to convey important Truth is my main Object. . . .'[50] The statements are not incompatible, although Coleridge does tend to stress one aspect of his plans rather than another depending on the identity of his correspondent. While he needed the money, he was also hopeful of redeeming his reputation. Writing to Sir George Beaumont, a patron and friend, he declares, 'If in the goodness of Providence my Health and Spirits continue to be what they have been since my return to Grasmere, I shall not have said unmeaningly to my Friends: Decide on my moral and intellectual character from the products of the year, 1809.'[51] To Francis Jeffrey he affirms the serious and wholehearted nature of the proposed work, and refers to the impracticality of his writing up to this point: '. . . I shall . . . play off my whole Head & Heart, such as they are, in this work, as from the main pipe of the Fountain. Indeed, it is high Time.'[52] And to Poole he writes more specifically: 'I promise you on my honor, that "The Friend" shall be the main Pipe, thro' which I shall play off the whole reservoir of my collected Knowlege and of what you are pleased to believe Genius.'[53] The image is an apt one for his way of summoning his serious thought for more immediate and superficial ends. As he wrote to Daniel Stuart, contrasting himself with the author of another journal, he was bringing 'the Results of a Life of intense Study, and unremitted Meditation – of Toil, and Travel, and great & unrepayed Expence'.[54]

The Friend was to transmit the results of his best thoughts, and its audience was therefore limited. Coleridge was resigned to this state of affairs. 'I do not,' he says, 'write in this Work for the *Multitude*; but for those, who by Rank, or Fortune, or official Situation, or Talents and Habits of Reflection, are to *influence* the Multitude.'[55] At the same time, the difficulty of the underlying thought was to be lessened by simplification. Speaking of the opening essay, Coleridge informs Sir George Beaumont that the 'Thoughts will be developed *popularly*,' and goes on to define his terms – 'This is my definition of a *just popular* Style: when the Author has had his own eye fixed steadily on the *abstract*, yet permits his Readers to see only the *Concrete*.'[56]

The origins of *Biographia Literaria* in 1815 were similar. Again the need for money was pressing; again Coleridge drew on the accumulation of his thought in order to do his duty by the public; and again he qualified the project as being introductory to his greater work. The spring of 1815 was, from a financial point of view, one of the most desperate periods of his life. A pathetic letter to Joseph Cottle contains a second appeal for money:

> Incapable of any exertion in this state of mind, I have now written to Mr Hood – and have at length bowed my heart down to beg that 4 or 5 of those whom I had reason to believe interested in my welfare, would raise the sum, I mentioned, between them, should you not be able to do it – Mss Poems equal to one volume of 250 to 300 pages being sent to them immediately.[57]

The only alternative that he can think of is to dispose of all his poems and fragments for whatever a bookseller will give, and '. . . then try to get my Livelihood where I can by receiving or waiting on Day-pupils, Children or Adults – But even this I am unable to wait for without *some* assistance. . . .'[58] He concludes the catalogue of his sorrows immediate and imminent with a revealing comment on his inability to write under duress:

> . . . Composition is no voluntary business: the very necessity of doing it robs me of the power of doing it. Had I been possessed of a tolerable Competence, I should have been a voluminous Writer – but I cannot, as is feigned of the Nightingale, sing with my Breast against a Thorn.[59]

Cottle, presumably unwilling to nourish this delusion, did not reply.

A few weeks later, Coleridge appealed to Lord Byron to help him dispose of a pair of volumes of verse which '. . . my circumstances now compel me to publish. . . .'[60] To these, 'A general Preface will be pre-fixed, on the Principles of philosophic and genial criticism relatively to the Fine Arts in general; but especially to Poetry. . . .'[61] This is one of the first references to the work that was to become *Biographia Literaria.* The general preface was to grow unmanageably once Coleridge embarked upon it, until it was long enough to warrant independent publication, but its origin as part of an urgent scheme to meet his debts is apparent.

Once he had started, intending only to flesh out the volumes of poetry a little to make them more attractive bait for book-sellers, he found himself fairly launched on his favourite literary themes. He had been meaning for a long time to discuss the divergences between his theory of the imagination and Wordsworth's.[62] In a letter to R. H. Brabant, he says that he has just finished his 'Autobiographia literaria' and states:

> I have given a full account (raisonné) of the Controversy concerning Wordsworth's Poems & Theory, in which my name has been so constantly included . . . I have done my Duty to myself and to the Public, in (as I believe) compleatly subverting the Theory & in proving that the Poet himself has never acted on it except in particular Stanzas which are the Blots of his Compositions.[63]

Already the sense of high aims, of public responsibility, has swamped the original quest for gain. But even so Coleridge was unwilling or unable to restrict himself. 'One long passage,' he says

> . . . a disquisition on the powers of association with the History of the Opinions on this subject from Aristotle to Hartley, and on the generic difference between the faculties of Fancy and Imagination – I did not indeed altogether insert, but I certainly extended and elaborated, with a view to your perusal – as laying the foundation Stones of the Constructive or Dynamic Philosophy in opposition to the merely mechanic . . . .[64]

Coleridge is remaining true to form; his history of philosophy has finally been revived for use and included as preparatory to the scheme of philosophy which he now embraces. The order in which *Biographia Literaria* is described here as being planned is justifiable enough – first the specific issue of Wordsworth's poetry and theory to be discussed as relevant to Coleridge's poems,[65] then the history of philosophy and introduction to Dynamic philosophy as a necessary and explanatory addition. But there is a spontaneous reliance on his own favourite lines of thought and a willingness to follow where they lead which reminds one of the conditions and the origins of the lecture series and *The Friend*.

Together, the 1807–8 series of literary lectures, *The Friend*, and *Biographia Literaria*, reveal the motives and procedure behind Coleridge's prose works of the period from 1807 to 1819 during which all his literary criticism of consequence appeared.[66] There can be little doubt that philosophy was his central activity, and that the criticism along with other journalistic enterprises was a digression from it. It is evident that Coleridge's philosophical studies provided him with an unfailing source of material. How many of the distinctive virtues of Coleridge's criticism may be attributed to this practice is another question, the answer to which I shall attempt to offer in the remainder of this essay. But it is clear that his criticism, in common with the rest of his prose of this period, is his astonishing substitute for hack-work; that while he undertook it earnestly in the hope of doing good, he regarded it as being of a lower order than the serious treatises to which he was devoting his life. Had it not been for his need to earn a living it seems improbable that he would have felt sufficiently pressed to complete works of such limited scope. In 1801 he wrote longingly, '*O for a lodge* in a Land, where human Life was an end, to which Labor was only a Means, instead of being, as it [is] here, a mere means of carrying on Labor.'[67] No doubt he would have been a happier man in such a place, but it is likely that the criticism we admire today would have been part of the price of his contentment.

The dependent status of Coleridge's prose has important implications for our study of his criticism. If his criticism was in fact, as the evidence presented here suggests, in the nature of an inspired aside, it is obvious that the philosophy which lies behind it must be studied – no matter what its quality as philosophy may be.[68] It is essential that we should understand what Coleridge was thinking about and what he regarded as most important. The occasional nature of his criticism accounts for most of the faults for which he is sometimes blamed. Charges of obscurity, lack of organization, plagiarism, and downright intellectual charlatanism, have all been levelled from time to time; most of them derive from the subsidiary place which the criticism occupied in his attention.

It is a convenient circumstance that Coleridge's most direct published statement of his philosophy, his series of essays on Method, is contemporaneous with his criticism. The essays appeared in two forms, one authorized, the other apparently not. His *Treatise on Method* was originally intended as a preface to the new *Encyclopaedia Metropolitana*, but when the editors of the encyclopaedia decided to change the scheme of the work Coleridge severed his connection with them. He was not asked to revise the essay, and when it appeared he claimed it had been mangled.[69] He decided to publish an authorized version in *The Friend* 'rifacciamento' of 1818 – a version less specifically devoted to the development of encyclopaedic method.[70] Most of Coleridge's best criticism precedes the completion of the essays on Method, and they represent a greater sophistication of thought than one would have expected from him at the time when, for example, the 1811–12 lecture series was in progress. But the essays do throw light on the direction in which Coleridge's thought was moving even during those early years of his criticism, and they help to clarify many of the otherwise puzzling and difficult terms of *Biographia Literaria*.

Ideally one would like to set each phase of his intellectual life beside the criticism that emerged from it, and the substitute offered in this essay is, relative to such an ideal, a crude one. But in the absence of a satisfactory history of the development of Coleridge's mind, we must make the best of imperfect aids. We must put up with hints, and the essays on Method are rich in them. Like the criticism, these essays are occasional; but they are closer to the centre of his thinking, and even if they are not as exhaustive as he might have made them, or as free from faults, they benefit from their origin.

Alice D. Snyder has discussed the circumstances surrounding Coleridge's *Treatise on Method* in detail, weighing its claim to authority against the claim made by Coleridge himself for his 1818 revision.[71] Two additional points are relevant to our purpose: the years during which this essay in philosophy was planned and executed and the light in which Coleridge regarded it.

On or about the twenty-sixth of November, 1813, Coleridge wrote to Henry Crabb Robinson requesting the loan of a number of German works. Among them he mentioned

'Schelling's Methodologie': '. . . if you would add Schelling's Methodologie you would not only oblige but really serve me – for I have a plan maturing, to w[hich] that work would be serv[iceable.]'[72] The book in question was Schelling's *Vorlesungen über die Methode des academischen Studiums* of 1803, and Coleridge's request for it antedates his association with the *Encyclopaedia Metropolitana* by some three and a half years. Schelling's lectures have much in common with Coleridge's essays on Method. If we may assume that Crabb Robinson complied with Coleridge's request – and there is no reason for supposing that he did not – we may suppose that Coleridge absorbed Schelling's approach to the problem of philosophic Method about two years before he embarked on *Biographia Literaria*, and that his acquaintance with it precedes all but his earliest critical lectures. It is possible that Coleridge knew the *Vorlesungen* even earlier, and since they constitute a delicate expression in theoretical form of many of the convictions about the procedure of philosophical investigation which he had been advocating for years, they represent for him an increase in the detail of his consideration of the problem and not a change of mind. The essays on Method carry the increase farther, making fuller use of Schelling's other works (notably his *System des transcendentalen Idealismus*), but they do not suggest any change of direction. It would be fair to say that the search for a satisfactory philosophical Method is contemporaneous with the whole of Coleridge's most important criticism, and that the Schellingian exposition of it is relevant to the greater part.

The second point to be cleared up is the importance of the theory of Method to Coleridge's thought. And here again we find him describing published work as introductory to the major work to come; to some extent it is analogous to *Biographia Literaria* and *The Friend*. Writing to C. A. Tulk, Coleridge says,

Within a few months I expect to see in print an Essay of mine on Methodology, or the nature and science of Method. In this Essay you will find the ground-work or shall I rather say the general views of my Philosophy: and in as popular a form as the nature of the Subject admits.[73]

The treatise was evidently not meant simply to introduce the method of the new encyclopaedia. Coleridge, as has been mentioned, was sufficiently upset over its being maimed by the booksellers and included in a work which had not been composed according to the principles which he was advocating to try to have it withdrawn and, having failed in that, to repudiate the essay as it actually appeared and revise it for the third volume of *The Friend*.

The essay on Method, like the other published works and the lectures, was written under the pressure of making money,[74] and should not be taken as a reflection on the intended quality of the 'Opus Maximum' for which it was to prepare the way; but it is of great interest to students of Coleridge's criticism, both because it was the only public statement of his philosophical views at the time when his criticism was at its height, (and because its principal aim – to outline a method of philosophical investigation – sheds light directly on Coleridge's critical practice) and because in making his case he drew to an unprecedented extent on his metaphysics. Later he was to disparage these ideas, just as he later spoke slightingly of the philosophical sections of *Biographia Literaria*,[75] but by then he had ceased to be an active critic. The later position is interesting if we want to speculate about what sort of critic Coleridge might have become had he continued to concern himself with criticism, but it is of minor importance to a study of the literary criticism we actually have from him.

The essays on Method in *The Friend* are the authorized version of Coleridge's views, and they are less concerned with the specificities of encyclopaedic method than the preface to the *Encyclopaedia Metropolitana* had been. With auxiliary support from Coleridge's other philosophical writings, published and unpublished, they provide us with the means to an understanding of two concerns which seem to dominate Coleridge's criticism, but which have as yet received scant attention. Like his famous disposition to 'the Vast', these have their roots in his childhood in the form of temperamental leanings, and were realized gradually and hesitantly in philosophic form during the rest of his life. As will, I hope, become clear in the course of this discussion they eventually join with the Vast to form one; but for many years they appear to have enjoyed independent existence in Coleridge's own consciousness, and so far as one can ascertain they continue independent in the minds of most of his readers to this day. The two concerns are his search for principles on which to ground criticism, and his examination of the nature of creative thought.

I propose to trace these concerns up to their final statement in his essays on Method; and then to show how an awareness of them is not only necessary for us if we are to understand what he meant by his critical utterances, but was instrumental for Coleridge himself in coming to the conclusions about literature with which we are familiar.

It is unlikely that the metaphysical scheme revealed by this approach will appeal to many, but as Coleridge tries to demonstrate, it is the necessary connection between meta-physics and criticism which is important. Miss Snyder pointed out long ago, that

> ... Of even more immediate significance than ... specific philosophic tenets, is Coleridge's general method of philo-sophizing, his attitude towards speculative thought. For there is that in Coleridge's criticism which inevitably brings the investigator back, sooner or later, to a study of the man's philosophical temperament.[76]

Coleridge does not ask us to adopt his conclusions; it is one of his more original contributions to criticism that he invites us to tussle with the grounds for them instead. It is important for historical reasons at least that we should understand what he was trying to do.

Some years ago, Sir Herbert Read suggested that the method of Coleridge's criticism was the method outlined in the essays in *The Friend*.[77] It was, I believe, the first time such an observa-tion had been made in print; little use has been made of it since. Sir Herbert refrained from developing the suggestion farther, but as it stands it seems to point straight at the heart of the matter. I shall try to indicate why we should accept his suggestion, and what the acceptance will involve. In doing so I shall also be following at a respectful distance in the foot-steps of J. Shawcross, who said in his preface to *Biographia Literaria*:

Coleridge was essentially a teacher, and conscious of a message to his age; and his examination of principles was rarely directed by a purely speculative interest. The search for a criterion of poetry involved him in the wider search for a criterion of life. His theory of the imagination, upon which his whole art-philosophy hinges, was primarily the vindication of a particular attitude to life and reality.[7]

The essays on Method, combined with his other philosophical writings, published and unpublished, reveal something of that particular attitude.

2

The Search for Principles

In the course of giving a political speech in 1795, Coleridge endorsed the view that '. . . it should be infamous for a man, who had reached the years of discretion, not to have formed an opinion concerning the state of affairs in his country, and treasonable, having formed one, not to propagate it by every legal mean in his power'.[1] War with France was the occasion of his speech, but the public spirit which he was showing at this early date remained with him as he grew older. His sense of political obligation to society was gradually absorbed into one of general intellectual obligation as he came to the conclusion that many social problems could be attributed to the bad habits of thought into which his contemporaries had fallen. Their indifference to principles worried him most of all, and he took it upon himself to point out the dangers of this indifference, stressing its relevance to difficulties of the time and defining the sort of principles which he believed they should adopt.

Coleridge refers to his contribution towards national reform in a letter written to his friend Daniel Stuart in 1814:

> I dare assert, that the science of reasoning and judging concerning the productions of Literature, the characters & measures of public men, and the events of nations by a systematic Subsumption of them under PRINCIPLES deduced from the Nature of MAN . . . was as good as unknown in the Public Prints before the year, 1795–96.[2]

As Stuart was himself a newspaper editor, he was in a tolerably good position to estimate the truth of such a claim; Coleridge presumably would not have made it without believing it. In the cause of principle, he regarded himself as a leading spirit.

21

But he was a reformer without being a radical. He saw himself as the advocate of old, forgotten truths, trying to win the dazzled adherents of modern heresies back to their birthright. He was sceptical of the possibilities of developing philosophy into a science and openly contemptuous of suggestions that eighteenth-century empiricism had already achieved such a feat. He remarks in 1814, 'I revere . . . the writings of the wise men who were before us; and rejoice whenever I can derive from their authority ornament and additional support to my own convictions. I ever feel myself weakest when I suppose myself most original.'[3] Support of principles was not intended as something new; Coleridge wished, modestly enough, to revive the ideas of illustrious predecessors.

In 1795 he had maintained that the only way to change the conduct of contemporary political life for the better was to replace the bigoted claims of rival factions with coolly applied philosophical principles. He outlined his aims:

> It will . . . be our endeavour, not so much to excite the torpid, as to regulate the feelings of the ardent; and above all, to evince the necessity of *bottoming* on fixed principles, that so we may not be the unstable patriots of passion or accident, nor hurried away by names of which we have not sifted the meaning, and by tenets of which we have not examined the consequences. The times are trying; and in order to be prepared against their difficulties, we should have acquired a prompt facility of adverting in all our doubts to some grand and comprehensive truth.[4]

The assumption that 'some grand and comprehensive truth' should guide political decisions may have been based on temperament; in any case, Coleridge stuck to it. His argument in later years differed only in that he gradually developed reasoning to support his conviction and was able to point out more specifically what sort of truth, what kind of principles, he had in mind.

Years later, in *The Friend*, he repeats his analysis of the causes of human misery in similar terms:

> O that my readers would look round the world, as it now is,

and make to themselves a faithful catalogue of its many miseries! From what do these proceed, and on what do they depend for their continuance? Assuredly for the greater part on the actions of men, and those again on the want of a vital principle of action.'[5]

By this time he has come to regard faulty thinking rather than force of circumstance as the cause. He proposes two remedies: the adoption of principles in place of expedients, and the abandonment of false principles. What he objects to most is the unthinking acceptance of political aphorisms as political axioms. He declares 'I have not a deeper conviction on earth, than that the principles both of Taste, Morals, and Religion, which are taught in the commonest books of recent composition, are false, injurious, and debasing'.[6] He lashes out against the expediency of governments. 'We must content ourselves with expedient-makers,' he says, '– with fire-engines against fires, Life-boats against inundations; but no houses built fire-proof, no dams that rise above the water-mark.'[7] And he expresses his impatience at having his recommendations of reforms met by appeals to the unsupported opinions of men in authority:

Much and often have I suffered from having ventured to avow my doubts concerning the truth of certain opinions, which had been sanctified in the minds of my hearers, by the authority of some reigning great name: even though in addition to my own reasons, I had all the greatest names from the Reformation to the Revolution on my side.[8]

Coleridge believed that indifference to sound principles, support of false ones, and docile acceptance of debatable opinions, were modern phenomena, not necessary conditions of humanity. '. . . I have fully persuaded my own mind,' he writes, 'that formerly MEN WERE WORSE THAN THEIR PRINCIPLES, but that at present THE PRINCIPLES ARE WORSE THAN THE MEN.'[9] Characteristically, he casts a swift, explanatory glance over the whole sweep of modern European thought, tracing the development of late eighteenth-century political upheavals from the adoption of 'Mechanical Philosophy' at the time of the Blood-less Revolution; for, as he remarks elsewhere,

> In every state not wholly barbarous, a philosophy, good or bad, there must be. However slightingly it may be the fashion to talk of speculation and theory, as opposed (sillily and nonsensically opposed) to practice, it would not be difficult to prove, that such as is the existing spirit of specula-tion, during any given period, such will be the spirit and tone of the religion, legislation, and morals. . . .[10]

Making the point that the revolution itself was only a return to the true sense of the constitution, and that the new philosophy was dignified, not by its own worth, but by the accident of its having begun at the same time, he notes the 'Wise and neces-sitated confirmation and explanation of the law of England, erroneously entitled *The English Revolution* of 1688 – Mechanical Philosophy, hailed as a kindred revolution in philosophy, and espoused, as a common cause, by the partizans of the revolution in the state.'[11] To this new spirit of philosophy he attributed the general decline of government and social behaviour.[12]

Coleridge held that the substitution of new-fangled opinions for traditional beliefs was responsible. In 1809 he writes:

> . . . if ever there was a time, when those fundamental truths, those groundworks of thought, feeling, and action, which sermons *ought* to teach us, should mingle with our opinions, and influence our conduct relatively to political questions and public events, that time is now present! for we live in an age of trouble, anxious expectation, and fearful uncer-tainty: and now, if ever, we need that faith and those principles, which contain in themselves the power and spirit of prophecy! which are in themselves an *implicit* prudence! a moral algebra, that assures us of the final result, though the process remains undeciphered![13]

And in *The Friend* he asserts that as long as principles are dis-missed as impractical, 'state-craft' will take the place of 'state-wisdom', and the 'cleverness of an embarrassed spendthrift' will be the substitute for the 'talent of the governor'.[14] It was partly to rectify this situation that Coleridge had undertaken the publication of *The Friend* in 1809. He had communicated his intentions to John Colson:

> ... the Object of *'the Friend'* is to establish, elucidate, & recommend *Principle* instead of *mere Expedience* – & therefore *Principles*: Principles in Taste, (Poetry, Prose, Painting, Music, Dress, &c &c &c) *Principles* in private morality – Principles in general *Religion*, as distinct from Superstition, from Enthusiasm, & from atheism, & common to all who have indeed a *Religion*, in whatever sect – Principles in Legislation, and the duties of Legislators – especial[l]y Principles for Englishmen whether Electors, or elected, Governors or Governed – adapted to the present aweful Times & relative to France . . . .[15]

His aim is reform on all fronts, reform made the more urgent by the dimensions of the war with France and the consequent suppression of liberties and perversion of law at home. Coleridge's proffered remedy claims to be more than another expedient, to be instead a general solution of a philosophical kind, an ideal to be carried into practice. It is interesting to observe that he is first goaded into public advocacy of thought based on principles by political events. His theme in *The Friend* seems to be political in origin, it is philosophical in exposition, and eventually, as we shall see, of consequence to his literary criticism.

For the purposes of discussion, his support of principles can conveniently be divided into three sections: his consideration of the usefulness of principles, and the relative uselessness of unargued opinions; his views on the most effective ways of communicating the principles, in other words, his views on education; and finally his exposition of the very specific kind of thinking which he believed to be necessary to provide a sure foundation for principles. Each of these sections will be treated separately.

I

Coleridge was disturbed by the undeserved influence of

25

opinions and the widespread lack of concern for what lies behind them. His anxiety is connected with his preference for the essence rather than the accidental, the whole rather than the part, and the argument rather than the conclusion; but it comes into the open most unequivocally on the following issue. Coleridge disagrees with the common belief that an aphorism – in its ideal form a capsule expression of a sustained chain of thought, but often a deceptive substitute for it – is an important source of wisdom and a reliable guide to action. He regrets the common neglect of the prologue necessary to make an aphorism effective. He believes that this neglect leads to the acceptance of authorities on the grounds merely that they are authorities without either a corresponding investigation of their claims to authority or sufficient attention to the original context of their remarks. Coleridge regards this use of aphoristic knowledge as being typical of Oriental philosophy and French rationalism. He does not reject unsupported opinions out of hand, however, and admits their usefulness when they sum up an argument and when they are proffered by 'men of genius' as a token of the reasoning on which they are based.[15a]

In *The Friend*, Coleridge asks, 'Of what value . . . to a sane mind, are the likings or dislikings of one man, grounded on the mere assertions of another? Opinions formed from opinions – what are they, but clouds sailing under clouds, which impress shadows upon shadows?'[16] He remarks later in the same work that 'The widest maxims of *prudence* are like arms without hearts, disjoined from those feelings which flow forth from *principle* as from a fountain.'[17] And yet, as he had stated years before, opinions and not arguments were being used in the political arena by his contemporaries. He considered it impudence for a man to offer unusual or new opinions without at the same time offering the reasons for holding them. 'It is *insolent*,' he says, 'to *differ* from the public *opinion* in *opinion*, if it be only *opinion*. It is sticking up little *i by itself i* against the whole alphabet.'[18] Elsewhere he speaks of a 'mere *ipse dixi*' as 'impertinent on all occasions'.[19] He makes only one exception:

A few extraordinary minds may be allowed to pass a mere *opinion*: though in point of fact those, who alone are entitled to this privilege, are ever the last to avail themselves of it.

Add too, that even the mere opinions of such men may in general be regarded either as promissory notes, or as receipts referring to a former payment.[20]

There are obvious implications here for the writer who wishes to communicate new ideas or to controvert accepted ones. He has a duty to offer arguments. And his duty extends farther: if he wishes to inform or persuade the public, he ought to make himself well informed on his subject and to provide proof of the extent and nature of his information. Coleridge asks for the presentation of pedigrees by philosophers, pedigrees which will disclose their educational background and temperamental bias. In a key statement in *The Friend* he outlines the requirements which he thinks should be fulfilled by any person who wishes to persuade the public to turn from its opinion to his:

If the honest warmth, which results from the strength of the particular conviction, be tempered by the modesty which belongs to the sense of general fallibility; if the emotions, which accompany all vivid perceptions, are preserved distinct from the expression of personal passions, and from appeals to them in the heart of others; if the Reasoner asks no respect for the opinion, as *his* opinion, but only in proportion as it is acknowledged by that Reason, which is common to all men; and, lastly, if he supports an opinion on no subject which he has not previously examined, and furnishes proof both that he possesses the means of enquiry by his education or the nature of his own pursuits, and that he has endeavoured to avail himself of those means; then, and with these conditions, every human Being is authorized to make public the *grounds* of any opinion which he holds, and of course the opinion itself, as the object of them.[21]

The three requisites are: study of the subject sufficient to warrant comment upon it; revelation of whatever personal factors may affect one's views; and presentation of the steps of reasoning and the principles which underlie the opinions offered.

Not only is thought based on unsupported opinion unworthy

of attention, it is, in Coleridge's eyes, a throwback to pre-Classical philosophy and an invitation to inconsistency (which he identifies with weakness). He recognizes the importance of attending to opinions which have endured for a long time, especially opinions in areas not readily susceptible of examination by the senses; as he admits,

> . . . in subjects not under the cognizance of the senses wise men have always attached a high value to general and long-continued assent, as a presumption of truth. After all the subtle reasonings and fair analogies which logic and induction could supply to a mighty intellect, it is yet on this ground that the Socrates of Plato mainly rests his faith in the immortality of the soul, and the moral Government of the universe.[22]

But he considers it to have been the special contribution of the mediaeval philosophers to develop from Greek and Roman predecessors the skill of arguing from one point to the next by force of logical connection and thereby supplanting the Oriental practice of collecting wise sayings. He fears that the writers of the eighteenth century have tended to return to reliance on collected maxims, and, even more dangerous, because more seductive, pointed epigrams. Speaking of Scholastic philosophy in the course of his philosophical lectures of 1819, Coleridge affirms that

> . . . it introduced into all the languages of Europe, as far as the languages were susceptible of it, the power and force of Greek and Roman connexion. It forever precluded our falling – or at least it should seem to have promised so to do – to have precluded our falling into the mere aphoristic style of the Oriental nations, in which thought is heaped upon thought by simple aggregation of words. In truth, what our Schoolmen had so well labored to prepare, and what the great writers before our revolution had so admirably elaborated and exemplified, the writers since then have seemed to take equal pains to destroy: to remove as an offence all the marks of connexion, to make each sentence an independent

one, easily indeed understood, but still more easily forgotten.[23]

Dependence on aphorism or opinion, then, is not only impudence; it implies the rejection of one of the major advances of European thought. When this rejection is combined with the abandonment of traditional wisdom in favour of new opinions, unsupported and untried, disastrous results were in his view only to be expected.

Coleridge attempts to show that principled thought has the practical advantage of consistency, whereas its opposite has all the weaknesses of mutually warring expedients. One of his arguments for the need for consistency resembles Aristotle's reason for advocating the study of rhetoric – namely, that the weapon is in the hands of the enemy and must be opposed in kind. As Coleridge points out,

> . . . independently of right and wrong, there is a power given by principle itself to every cause, in which it is acted upon, a consistency in the plans, a harmony and combination of the means, and a steadiness in the execution, which can never be successfully resisted, except by an equal firmness and unity of principle in its opponents.[24]

This was Coleridge's diagnosis of the actions and successes of Napoleon. Speaking of him he says that

> . . . the abandonment of all principle of right enables the soul to choose and act upon a principle of wrong, and to subordinate to this one principle all the various vices of human nature. Hence too the means of accomplishing a given end are multiplied incalculably, because all means are considered as lawful.[25]

He believes that Napoleon's power '. . . subsists, for the greater part, in the consistency and systematic perfection of its possessor's vices. . . .'[26] And again,

> If . . . the power with which wickedness can invest the human being be thus tremendous, greatly does it behove us

to enquire into its source and causes. So doing we shall quickly discover that it is not vice, as vice, which is thus mighty; but *systematic* vice! . . . The abandonment of all *principle* of right enables the soul to chuse and act upon a *principle* of wrong, and to subordinate to this one principle all the various vices of human nature.[27]

Coleridge considers that perfect consistency is beyond the capacity of man, but thinks that an approach to it realizes his capacity to its fullest extent. It cannot be successfully opposed without a similar effort:

> . . . the obstacles which a consistently evil mind no longer finds in itself, it finds in its own unsuitableness to human nature. A limit is fixed to its power: but within that limit, both as to the extent and duration of its influence, there is little hope of checking its career, if giant and united vices are opposed only by mixed and scattered virtues: and those too, probably, from the want of some combining PRINCIPLE, which assigns to each its due place and rank, at civil war with themselves, or at best perplexing and counteracting each other.[28]

This internal civil war is the cause to which Coleridge attributes the failure of the armies of Charles V of Spain – 'a diversity of *principles* in the provinces themselves, an ally that fought for the tyrant in the *consciences* of the confederates!'[29]

In a letter written to Sir George Beaumont in 1808, Coleridge maintains – misleadingly – that the principal object of *The Friend* is to be to argue the need for principles and systematic opposition to Napoleon. 'What,' he asks, '. . . must be the power, when one pre-eminently wicked Man wields the whole strength and cunning of a wicked Nation? Is there any Strength adequate to resist this?' His answer is an immediate and sure affirmative:

> Yes! one and only one. Consistency, energy, and unanimity in national wickedness must be counter-balanced by consistency and undistracted Energy in national Virtue, which

fully exerted bring with them, from the recesses of their own nature, a greater consistency, a more enduring Energy.[30]

The argument for the use of principles in political affairs holds when transferred to other activities – principled thought must of necessity be more consistent, and hence more powerful, than thought which deals with problems separately and piecemeal. If 'calculating Prudence ... without high general Principles' can be responsible for 'that confluent Small-pox of Infamy, the Cintra Convention',[31] the same sorry outcome may be anticipated when it is applied to any intellectual or social problem. Principles are the key to power; lack of them the way to weakness. Two questions remain; what principles, and how can they be transmitted?

II

Coleridge's views on the way in which principles and ideas should be transmitted reflect his concepts of education and knowledge and his belief that both had fallen on evil days. The heedless acceptance of opinions, and the 'Frenchified' preference for aphoristic truths went hand in hand with a widespread assumption that learning should be an amusing and agreeable employment, and that it should be available to all.[32] In *The Friend*, Coleridge launches out on one of his bitterest diatribes against the frivolous and trivial pursuits of his contemporaries:

> ... how shall I avert the scorn of those critics who laugh at the oldness of my topics, Evil and Good, Necessity and Arbitrement, Immortality and the Ultimate Aim? By what shall I regain *their* favour? My themes must be *new*, a French constitution; a balloon; a change of ministry; a fresh batch of kings on the Continent, or of peers in our happier island. ... Or if I must be philosophical, the latest chemical discoveries, provided I do not trouble my reader with the principle which gives them their highest interest. ...[33]

As Coleridge believed that the mind, like the body, needed exercise if it was to function well, he was understandably concerned.[34] He writes to a friend in 1809,

> . . . I feel the sadning conviction, that no real information can be given, no important errors overthrown in Politics, Morals, or Literature without requiring some effort of Thought – & that the aversion from this is the mother Evil of all the other Evils, that I have to attack – consequently, I am like a Physician who prescribes exercise with the dumb bells to a Patient paralytic in both arms . . . .[35]

In his attempt to convert his audience to the adoption of just principles, Coleridge felt obliged to justify his very exposition.

He did not expect to have many readers; instead he was satisfied to direct his remarks to the 'learned class' he was later to call the 'clerisy'. He accuses the politicians who addressed a larger audience of being unrealistic, and warns them of the probable result of their error: 'Statesmen should know that a learned class is an essential element of a state – at least of a Christian state. But *you* wish for general illumination! You begin with the attempt to *popularize* learning and philosophy; but you will end in the *plebification* of knowledge.[36] Rejecting such illusions of a royal road to learning, Coleridge promises hard knocks. His notion of teaching is not to relieve the student of the necessity of working, but to help him avoid working unprofitably. As he puts it:

> The reader, who would follow a close reasoner to the summit and absolute principle of any one important subject, has chosen a Chamois-hunter for his guide. Our guide will, indeed, take us the shortest way, will save us many a wearisome and perilous wandering, and warn us of many a mock road that had formerly led himself to the brink of chasms and precipices, or at best in an idle circle to the spot from whence he started. But he cannot carry us on his shoulders: we must strain our own sinews, as he has strained his; and make firm footing on the smooth rock for ourselves, by the blood of toil from our own feet.[37]

He questions the validity of an easier approach:

> In works of reasoning, as distinguished from narration of events or statements of facts; but more particularly in works,

the object of which is to make us better acquainted with our own nature, a writer, whose meaning is everywhere comprehended as quickly as his sentences can be read, may indeed have produced an amusing composition, nay, by awakening and re-enlivening our recollections, a useful one; but most assuredly he will not have *added* either to the stock of our knowledge, or to the vigour of our intellect. For how can we gather strength, but by exercise? How can a truth, new to us, be made our own without examination and self-questioning. . . . But whatever demands effort, requires time. Ignorance seldom *vaults* into knowledge, but passes into it through an intermediate state of obscurity, even as night into day through twilight.[38]

Coleridge was not speaking theoretically; he wanted to prepare his readers for the difficulties which he himself was about to set before them.

He claims a further educative purpose: '. . . to convey not instruction merely, but fundamental instruction; not so much to shew my Reader this or that fact, as to kindle his own torch for him, and leave it to himself to chuse the particular objects, which he might wish to examine by its light.'[39] Here he comes to one of the most important aspects of his attempt to effect intellectual reforms – his effort to help his readers to think for themselves. In addition to the mental exercise which he promises, and which he thinks will make their minds more vigorous, he is anxious to leave his readers with a developed skill. Consequently, presentation of the way in which he has come to his conclusions is more important to him than advocacy of the conclusions themselves. The principles on which the conclusions are based need not be invalidated by the untruth of the conclusions.

In order that this educative aim be achieved, Coleridge advocates the presentation of thought in action. In a letter to his friend Thomas Poole written in 1810, he excuses himself for over-indulgence in parenthetical remarks:

– Of Parentheses I may be too fond – and will be on my guard in this respect –. But I am certain that no work of empassioned & eloquent reasoning ever did or could subsist without them – They are the *drama* of Reason – & present the thought growing, instead of a mere Hortus siccus. The aversion to them is one of the numberless symptoms of a feeble Frenchified Public.[40]

In support of this procedure he quotes Bacon's distinction in *The Advancement of Learning* between using a tree piecemeal and transferring it as a living thing into new soil:

> . . . if you have at heart the advancement of education, as that which proposes to itself the general discipline of the mind for its end and aim, be less anxious concerning the trunks, and let it be your care, that the roots should be extracted entire, even though a small portion of the soil should adhere to them: so that at all events you may be able, by this means, both to review your own scientific acquirements, re-measuring as it were the steps of your knowledge for your own satisfaction, and at the same time to transplant it into the minds of others, just as it grew in your own.[41]

He attributes the ulterior motive of education to Plato as well. Referring to the unsatisfactory nature of some of Plato's conclusions, he suggests that

> . . . with the clear insight that the purpose of the writer is not so much to establish any particular truth, as to remove the obstacles, the continuance of which is preclusive of all truth; the whole scheme assumes a different aspect, and justifies itself in all its dimensions. We see . . . that the EDUCATION of the intellect, by awakening the principle and *method* of self-development, was his proposed object, not any specific information that can be *conveyed into it* from without: . . . to place the [mind] in such relations of circumstance as should gradually excite the germinal power that craves no knowledge but what it can take up into itself, what it can appropriate, and re-produce in fruits of its own.[42]

Coleridge's arguments, in short, were intended to do double duty by revealing the grounds for his conclusions – the principles on which he based his opinions – and by training the reader in the way of argument so that he would be able to carry on on his own. There is humility in such an approach, assuming as it does that the arguments he is presenting are neither absolute nor ultimate.[43]

Although Coleridge expected his readers to make an effort, and indeed wanted them to, he did not mean to ask the impossible. He realized that his own 'aversion to the epigrammatic unconnected periods of the fashionable *Anglo-gallican* taste' might stand in his way when he tried to communicate with readers who were used to them.[44] His statement at the beginning of *The Friend* that he would '. . . deem it even presumptuous to aim at other or higher object than that of *amusing* a small portion of the reading public' seems disingenuous,[45] but he did not forget the weaknesses of his contemporaries. He maintains that

> . . . in respect to the *entertainingness* of moral writings, if in entertainment be included whatever delights the imagination or affects the generous passions, so far from rejecting such a mean of persuading the human soul, my very system compels me to defend not only the propriety but the absolute necessity of adopting it, if we really intend to render our fellow-creatures better or wiser.[46]

His solution to this problem turned out, in the event, to be inadequate. Rather than slacken the pace of his exposition in *The Friend*, Coleridge adopted the policy of inserting chapters of an 'excursive and miscellaneous' nature to afford relief.[47] He states that

> THE FRIEND does not indeed exclude from his plan occasional interludes; and vacations of innocent entertainment and promiscuous information, but still in the main he proposes to himself the communication of such delight as rewards the march of Truth, rather than to collect the flowers which diversify its track. . . .'[48]

These interludes were the so-called 'Landing-places'; he miscalculated when he hoped that they would keep his passengers 'in good humour with the vehicle and its driver'.[49]

35

The special influence of Schelling's thought on Coleridge seems to extend from about 1813 to 1818 – the period of Coleridge's greatest activity as a critic. During these years, Coleridge's long-standing advocacy of principle and his opposition to the futile reiteration of opinions was given new force and direction by his adoption of the Transcendentalist theories of thought which he presented slightly altered in his *Treatise on Method* and in his essays on Method in the 1818 edition of *The Friend*. His reliance on Schelling does not imply a desertion of his earlier views; rather he found in the German philosopher the detailed analysis of the problem of philosophical method that he needed in order to make his own position explicit. His argument is not simply a translation of Schelling, but the German deserves the credit for most of the original thought. Coleridge was a critical exponent, and, in fact, he rejected much of the Schellingian paraphernalia in the years after 1818 and regretted that *Biographia Literaria* had been weakened by the immaturity of his philosophical development. But despite his eventual disenchantment, his exposition of Schelling is important as a key to his literary criticism of the period. It allowed him to turn from advocacy of principles in general to the special support of a particular kind of principles.

Coleridge's theory of Method serves two purposes. It is an analysis of thought, and as such comprehends both the constructions of philosophy and the creation of art; and it also fulfils for Coleridge the function to which we have already referred in that it provides a way of communicating thought which may be useful, even if the thought in question is unacceptable, by helping us to find acceptable substitutes and put them to use. It is with Method as a prescribed intellectual procedure that we are concerned in this chapter. In the chapter that follows we shall consider the extent to which Coleridge's critical procedures are influenced by these theories.

Coleridge is fairly expansive in his description of the nature of the Method he is recommending, and in his general account hints helpfully at the direction his thought was taking. At first sight, his demand for a Method which depends on 'a principle of unity with progression' seems to be merely an obscure rendering of his earlier pleadings for principles and consistency. But it soon becomes clear that he is mounting an attack on empiricism and the popular experimental modes of thought by claiming that they are inadequate – a point which few of their advocates would have denied if pressed – and replacing them with an Idealism which would be adequate by defining the terms of its own adequacy.

If Coleridge is sceptical about the claims made for empiricism, he is also alert to the dangers of Idealism. What he is doing is adopting the now familiar opposition between Platonic and Aristotelian thought as 'synthetic' and 'analytic' respectively,[50] between the view that one should construct a theory first and then test it against reality, and the view that one should observe reality and construct an adequate theory from one's observations. In Kantian terms these two impulses are shown as predilections for *noumena* and *phenomena* respectively; Coleridge inclines to the former. It will be seen in Chapter Four that his advocacy has an elaborately argued metaphysical justification.

Coleridge outlines the scope of his theory in the opening pages of his *Treatise on Method*:

> ... it becomes us at the commencement, clearly to explain ... what we mean by ['Method']; to exhibit the Principles on which alone a correct Philosophical Method can be founded; to illustrate those principles by their application to distinct studies and to the History of the Human Mind; and lastly to apply them to the general concatenation of the several Arts and Sciences, and to the most perspicuous, elegant, and useful manner of developing each particular study.[51]

And he defines his limits in similar but less ringing terms in *The Friend*: 'Our discussion ... is confined to Method as employed in the formation of the understanding, and in the constructions of science and literature. It would indeed be superfluous to attempt a proof of its importance in the business and economy of active or domestic life.'[52] As we have seen, Coleridge believed that Method was relevant to all activity,

but science – and he uses the term in its wider sense of knowledge – and literature, and the development of the mind, had
become his immediate subjects. His theory is expressed in terms
of these specific concerns, but is intended to carry implications
for all. He reaffirms his wish to educate the reader as well as
inform him; the theory of Method was intended as a workable
technique, and he made considerable claims for it. He writes:

> . . . I can conceive no object of inquiry more appropriate,
> none which, commencing with the most familiar truths, with
> facts of hourly experience, and gradually winning its way to
> positions the most comprehensive and sublime, will more
> aptly prepare the mind for the reception of specific know-
> ledge, than the full exposition of a principle which is the
> condition of all intellectual progress, and which may be said
> even to *constitute* the science of education, alike in the
> narrowest and in the most extensive sense of the word.[53]

Coleridge describes his Method as '*a way*, or *path of Transit*',
to the attainment of knowledge, and he justifies this use of the
term by recalling the Greek roots of the word μέθοδος.[54] He
distinguishes between this sort of Method and mere classifica-
tion or arrangement of materials. 'Thus,' he tells us, 'we extol
the Elements of Euclid, or Socrates' discourse with the slave in
the Menon, as *methodical*, a term which no one who holds himself bound to think or speak correctly, would apply to the
alphabetical order or arrangement of a common dictionary.[55]
The sort of Method which Coleridge is advocating is '*a progressive transition* from one step in any course to another',[56] the
notion of building a structure of thought on the basis of accepted
axioms rather than organizing the elements of thought into a
convenient form on such an accidental principle as an alphabet.
Coleridge does not reject arrangement – indeed, he considers
it a necessary first step in any enquiry – but he wishes to avoid
having it confused with Method in his sense of the word.[57] Up
to this point he has said little not already implicit in his earlier
support of principles; the next step, however, is more difficult.
    After saying that '. . . the first idea of Method is *a progressive
transition* from one step in any course to another', Coleridge goes
on to assert that '. . . where the word Method is applied with

reference to many such transitions in continuity, it necessarily implies a Principle of UNITY WITH PROGRESSION'.[58] This statement makes two points: first that a principle *is* implied, and second, that it is *this* principle. The two points must be taken as Coleridge's assumptions; his meaning remains to be fathomed. 'Progression' seems clear enough, but what of 'Unity'? 'Unity', it appears, is achieved by the existence of a preconception which will determine the nature and direction of the progression. And here an analogy may be helpful.

If one were to attempt the reconstruction of a mosaic from a collection of its pieces in a state of complete disorder, one might begin by collecting the pieces according to their colours. The red pieces could be put in one pile, the blue in another, and so on. This would be *arrangement*, and a useful beginning.[59] The purpose of the exercise, however, would be to put the pieces together again so as to reconstitute the original picture, building it, as it were, step by step or piece by piece. This process would be progression, or progressive transition. But if one had no idea what the picture was originally of, if there were no guiding principle to determine which step should follow which, the process would be entirely haphazard and only extravagantly good luck could result in its successful completion. If, on the other hand, one were to conjecture about the picture, it would be possible to order the progression accordingly, and one could test the validity of the conjecture by its result. The conjecture would be the preconception. This is apparently what Coleridge is getting at when he says that '. . . as, without continuous transition, there can be no Method, so without a pre-conception there can be no transition with continuity'.[60]

But the reconstruction of a mosaic is a simple matter compared to the philosophical reconstruction of the universe; to think of the two procedures as being analogous involves some more assumptions – about the universe – which Coleridge makes. First, and most important, is the assumption that the universe, like the mosaic, is in fact ordered. Coleridge carries the analogy a step farther by believing that the order of the universe was imposed by God as its maker. As a consequence, just as the mosaic may be assumed to be the plan of an intellect which can be guessed at or preconceived by another intellect seeking to reconstruct it, so the universe, being the plan of intellect, may be sought after by the preconception and progression of another intellect. Again he makes an assumption: that the human intellect and the divine are similar in kind.

To pursue our analogy again, if one were to accept any pre-conception, the results would be almost as haphazard as they would have been without a pre-conception. Clearly if this theory of Method is to be a practical and not just a hypothetical affair, some limits must be placed upon the sort of pre-conceptions admitted. Referring to the principle of '*Unity with progression*', Coleridge offers the following: '... that which unites, and makes many things *one* in the Mind of Man, must be an act of the Mind itself, a manifestation of intellect, and not a spontaneous and uncertain production of circumstances.'[61] He invokes the authority of Bacon for his alternative to the chaos of haphazard preconception:

> ... Lord Bacon equally with ourselves, demands what we have ventured to call the intellectual or mental initiative, as the motive and guide of every philosophical experiment; some well-grounded purpose, some distinct impression of the probable results, some self-consistent anticipation as the ground of the '*prudens quæstio*' (the fore-thoughtful query), which he affirms to be the prior *half* of the knowledge sought, *dimidium scientiæ.*[62]

Although well disguised, the sort of preconception Coleridge is arguing for seems to be what we should nowadays less reverently call a hunch. And if he has dignified the humble origin of great discoveries, it is only because it is of such importance to him that, humble or not, it be recognized as the origin.[63] He terms it the *initiative* of Method: 'This act of the Mind, ... this leading thought, this "key note" of the harmony, this "subtile, cementing, subterraneous" power, borrowing a phrase from the nomenclature of legislation, we may not inaptly call the INITIATIVE of all Method.'[64]

Coleridge goes some way towards defining the exact nature of the initiative requisite to Method. As he points out, 'It is manifest, that the wider the sphere of transition is, the more comprehensive and commanding must be the initiative. . . .'[65]

And the original initiative may be productive of others which must follow of necessity: 'From the first, or initiative Idea, as from a seed, successive Ideas germinate. Thus, from the Idea of a triangle, necessarily follows that of equality between the sum of its three angles and two right angles.'[66] This kind of progression, followed out 'through all its ramifications',[67] clearly depends for its validity on the 'proper choice of an initiative'.[68] Here we are presented with some more assumptions. First of all, that although the initiative may be derived from observation, or may at least be stimulated by observation, it cannot be simply a generalization of observation, because some prior theory of preconception would be necessary to the selection of points of observation to be generalized.

We have seen that a previous act and conception of the mind is indispensible even to the mere semblances of Method: that neither fashion, mode, nor orderly arrangement can be produced without a prior purpose, and 'a pre-cogitation *ad intentionem ejus quod quæritur*', though this purpose may have been itself excited, and this 'pre-cogitation' itself abstracted from the perceived likenesses and differences of the objects to be arranged. But it has likewise been shown, that fashion, mode, ordonnance, are not Method, inasmuch as all Method supposes A PRINCIPLE OF UNITY WITH PROGRESSION; in other words, progressive transition without breach of continuity. But such a principle, it has been proved, can never in the sciences of experiment or in those of observation be adequately supplied by a theory built on generalization. For what shall determine the mind to abstract and generalize one common point rather than another? and within what limits, from what number of individual objects, shall the generalization be made? The theory must still require a prior theory for its own legitimate construction.[69]

Where is such a theory to be found? Coleridge's answer is an assertion: '. . . if we would discover an *universal Method*, by which every step in our progress through the whole circle of Art and Science should be directed, it is absolutely necessary that we should seek it in the very interior and central essence of the Human intellect.'[70]

While he defines the source, Coleridge accepts that there is a variety of initiatives or Ideas. He informs us that

> The Idea may exist in a clear, distinct, definite form, as that of a circle in the Mind of an accurate Geometrician; or it may be a mere *instinct*, a vague appetancy towards something which the Mind incessantly hunts for, but cannot find, like a name which has escaped our recollection, or the impulse which fills the young Poet's eye with tears, he knows not why.[71]

Which Idea may befit the solution of a particular problem depends on the nature of the problem. Obviously, if we wish to solve some problem of Euclidean geometry, the presence of accepted axioms and of terms whose existence is dependent on our definition of them, allows us to expect a leading Idea or initiative of a more specific kind than could be expected if the nature of the universe were being considered. Coleridge goes on to maintain that the objects which we consider may be related to one another in two ways: by the relation of Law, and the relation of Theory.

He distinguishes between these two ways as follows. 'Where the former alone are in question,' he says, 'the Method is one of necessary connection throughout; where the latter alone, though the connection be considered as one of cause and effect, yet the necessity is less obvious, and the connection itself less close.'[72] And again,

> One of them is the relation by which we understand that a thing *must be*: the other, that by which we merely perceive that it *is*. The one, we call the relation of LAW, using that word in its highest and original sense, namely, that of *laying down* a rule to which the subjects of the LAW must necessarily conform. The other, we call the relation of THEORY.[73]

The relation of Law is in Coleridge's view the higher form, and he declares in his essay on Method in *The Friend* that 'To prove the high value as well as the superior dignity' of it, and '... to evince, that on this alone a *perfect* Method can be grounded, and that the Methods attainable by the second are at best but approximations to the first, or tentative exercises in the hope of discovering it, form the first object of the present disquisition'.[74] He expounds the relation of Law by using analogies. The first of these is the notion of a universe created by God to which we have referred above, for Coleridge tells us that this relation, '. . . in its absolute perfection, is conceivable only of the Supreme Being, whose creative IDEA not only appoints to each thing its *position*, but in that position, and in consequence of that position, gives it its qualities, yea, gives it its very existence, as *that particular* thing'.[75] Here Coleridge is proposing an ideal to all intents and purposes unattainable, an ideal apprehension of the universe which he finds projected by Plato:

> The grand problem, the solution of which forms, according to Plato, the final object and distinctive character of philosophy, is this: *for all that exists conditionally* (i.e. the existence of which is inconceivable except under the condition of its dependency on some other as its antecedent) *to find a ground that is unconditional and absolute, and thereby to reduce the aggregate of human knowledge to a system.*[76]

Coleridge indicates how far man may hope to partake of this divine knowledge, this awareness of a series of necessary connections or relations which comprehends all knowledge, when he states that '. . . the Human Mind is capable of viewing some relations of things as necessarily existent; that is to say, as predetermined by a truth in the Mind itself, pregnant with the consequence of other truths in an indefinite progression'.[77] And he provides examples:

> . . . in whatever science the relation of the parts to each other and to the whole is predetermined by a truth originating in the *mind*, and not abstracted or generalized from observation of the parts, there we affirm the presence of a *law*, if we are speaking of the physical sciences, as of Astronomy for instance; or the presence of fundamental *ideas*, if our discourse be upon those sciences, the truths of which, as truths absolute, not merely have an independent *origin* in the mind, but continue to exist in and for the mind alone. Such,

for instance, is Geometry, and such are the ideas of a perfect circle, of asymptots, &c.[78]

The problem is to achieve the bridge between an apprehension of the relation of Law in a thing like geometry which is created by man and apprehension of the relation of Law assumed to exist in the universe created by God.

Coleridge, fully realizing the attendant difficulties, sees philosophy as the attempt to attain Law as 'the sufficient cause of the reality correspondent thereto. . . .'[79] And while he considers it 'exclusively an attribute of the Supreme Being', he adds that '. . . from the contemplation of law in this, its only perfect form, must be derived all true insight into all other grounds and principles necessary to Method, as the science common to all sciences, which in each τυγχάνει ὄν ἄλλο αὐτῆς τῆς ἐπιήμης.' He concludes that, 'Alienated from this (intuition shall we call it? or stedfast faith?) ingenious men may produce schemes, conducive to the peculiar purposes of particular sciences, but no scientific system.'[80] The relation of Law, then, is an ideal progression unified by an ideal and all-embracing initiative or Idea. Any conclusive solution of the problem of knowledge would be achieved by a Method based on the contemplation of this relation. For practical purposes one must be satisfied to attempt to find such Ideas or initiatives in one's intuition, and to extend the range of necessary connections between things observed. Method based on the relation of Law is an ideal to bear in mind, to seek to approximate by using a similar manner of thought based on less satisfactory human intuition, but not an ideal which one can really expect to achieve.[81]

Method can also be based on the relation of Theory, which depends upon one's observation.[82] That is, observation precedes and suggests the initiative which is to unify the progression, instead of following it, as is the case with relations of Law. Whereas, what Coleridge calls the Pure Sciences, geometry, for example, depend on the relation of Law, the Applied Sciences depend on the relation of Theory. According to him:

> The second relation is that of THEORY, in which the existing forms and qualities of objects, discovered by observation,

suggest a given arrangement of them to the Mind, not merely for the purposes of more easy remembrance and communication; but for those of understanding, and sometimes of controlling them. The studies to which this class of relations is subservient, are more properly called *Scientific Arts* than Sciences. Medicine, Chemistry, and Physiology are examples of a Method founded on this second sort of relation. . . .[83]

Physics falls into the same category:

> . . . in physics, that is, in all the sciences which have for their objects the things of nature, and not the *entia rationis* – more philosophically, intellectual acts and the products of those acts, existing exclusively in and for the intellect itself – the definition must follow, and not precede the reasoning. It is representative not constitutive, and is indeed little more than an abbreviature of the preceding observation, and the deductions therefrom.[84]

The drawback of this kind of Method, for Coleridge, is that observation must, in the nature of things, be incomplete.[85] He had earlier pointed out the distinction between 'an apprehension of the *whole* of a truth, even where that apprehension is dim and indistinct', and 'a *partial* perception of the same rashly *assumed*, as a perception of the whole'.[86] Coleridge manifestly prefers the 'dim and indistinct' perception of the whole as a means of seeking a solution to the problem of finding the extent to which appearance and reality are coincident. He cites Plato's rejection of Democritus, and of Zeno and the Eleatics, to the effect

> . . . that in both alike the basis is too narrow to support the superstructure; that the grounds of both are false or disputable; and that, if these were conceded, yet neither the one nor the other is adequate to the solution of the problem: viz. what is the ground of the coincidence between reason and experience? Or between the laws of matter and the ideas of the pure intellect.[87]

And he declares that

The only answer which Plato deemed the question capable of receiving, compels the reason to pass out of itself and seek the ground of this agreement in a supersensual essence, which being at once the *ideal* of the reason and the cause of the material world, is the pre-establisher of the harmony in and between both.[88]

Lest Coleridge should seem to be an impractical dreamer, it is important for us to realize the extent of his scepticism about the capacities of human knowing. Far from harbouring unrealistic hopes of perfect knowledge, he appears to have maintained an essential distrust of the intellect – early revealed in his preference at points of conflict for the heart over the head – and an especial hatred of that intellectual arrogance of his contemporaries which he came to identify with Jacobinism in his later political essays.[89] In his *Philosophical Lectures*, he states outright that 'A perfect theory . . . is possible in mathematics only, the mathematician creating his terms, that is, determining that his imagination has had such and such acts.'[90] He had abandoned the sort of idealism characterized by his youthful plans for a pantisocracy as 'extravagant'.[91] He criticizes the principles of Cartwright on the grounds that they suppose figments of the imagination rather than real people: '. . . his universal principles, as far as they are principles and universal, necessarily suppose uniform and perfect subjects, which are to be found in the *Ideas* of pure Geometry and (I trust) in the *Realities* of Heaven, but never, never, in creatures of flesh and blood.'[92] This sort of scepticism Coleridge thought characteristic of Kant, and it is this which persuades him of the necessity of assuming a form of reality beyond human reason towards which philosophical investigations should tend. He observes:

> . . . our will is to a certain degree in our power, and where it is not it is owing to some prior fault of ours; but the consequences of that will are not in our power, and hence there arises a moral interest that a Being should be assumed in whom is the only will, and the power that involves all consequences as one and the same. . . . This is Kant's scepticism. It is a modest humility with regard to the powers of the intellect.[93]

46

This is an acceptance of the spirit of Cartesian scepticism, but at the same time a rejection of the Cartesian and empiricist attempts to circumvent the unreliability of the senses. Coleridge's theory of Method is part of an attempt at a new scepticism, proposed in the hope, not that it will achieve answers to the most pressing questions of philosophy, but that it will prove a better path of investigation than the empiricist one which he deemed by definition to be founded on insufficient and unreliable grounds. Turning from confident experimental observation of phenomena towards the older preference for half-understood acts of the mind, Coleridge closes off certain areas of speculation as being beyond the human intellect.[94]

3

Principles in Literary Criticism

Coleridge's efforts to reform literary criticism follow much the same patterns. The prevalence of biting, opinionated reviews seemed to him to be another instance of the intellectual weakness of his age. His opposition to reviewing is part and parcel of his more general attempt to improve the way in which his contemporaries thought. Again we find him attacking reliance on mere opinions, advocating dependence on principles, recommending the advantages of hard thinking, and finally describing a specific Method and attempting to implement it. It is generally accepted that he did recommend criticism based on principles; some have gone so far as to hail this recommendation and his subsequent attempt to fulfil it as being his special contribution to criticism; but the exact nature of the critical Method which he was proposing and the implications of it in his critical practice have not been treated publicly at any length.

By the turn of the century Coleridge had already shown his scepticism of reviewers. Like most young authors he was interested in what they had to say about his own work, but he was scornful of their claims to be taken seriously. Youthful gratification and irony combine in a letter written to his friend J. P. Estlin in 1796 announcing the public reception of his *Poems*: 'The Reviews have been wonderful – The Monthly has *cataracted* panegyric on my poems; the Critical has *cascaded* it; and the Analytical has *dribbled* it with very tolerable civility.'[1] And he adds to a similar account in a letter to Thomas Poole, that 'as to the British Critic, they *durst not* condemn and they would not praise – so contented themselves with "commending me, as a *Poet*["] – and allowed me "tenderness of sentiment & elegance of diction". –'[2] At the same time Coleridge was himself earning some money as a reviewer, and such examples of his work as are reliably identified as his seem to have been written seriously enough.[3] His early comments on reviewing reveal a mild concern for reviews of his own poetry, the conviction that reviews in general should be written with a sense of responsibility, and the belief that readers ought not to rely on reviewers as infallible guides. His verses of 1801 on the 'candid critic' single out hostile unfairness as the main offence:

> Most candid critic, what if I,
> By way of joke, pull out your eye,
> And holding up the fragment, cry,
> 'Ha! ha! that men such fools should be!
> Behold this shapeless Dab! – and he
> Who own'd it, fancied it could *see*!'
> The joke were mighty analytic,
> But should you like it, candid critic?[4]

In the early years of the nineteenth century, a new force appeared in periodical literature. A handful of publications emanating from Edinburgh began to alter the tone of public literary discussion to such effect as to damage Coleridge's reputation both as a writer and as a man, and to induce him to crystallize his attitude to reviewing into one of outright antagonism. In 1802 the *Edinburgh Review* appeared; it was soon followed by the *Quarterly Review*, and eventually, in 1817, by *Blackwood's Magazine*. Coleridge was at first unconcerned. He writes reassuringly to Southey, whose *Thalaba* had attracted the attention of the fledgling *Edinburgh Review*: '– I heard of the Edingburgh review, & heard the name of your Reviewer – but forgot it –. Reviews may sell 50 or 100 copies in the first three months – & there their Influence ends.'[5] Southey was less sanguine, and a few months later we find Coleridge applauding his doubts:

Your prophecy concerning the Edingburgh Review did credit to your penetration. The second number is altogether despicable – the hum-drum of pert attorneys' Clerks, very pert & yet prolix & dull as a superannuated Judge. . . . the first article on Kant you may believe on my authority to be impudent & senseless Babble.[6]

By midsummer of 1803, Coleridge felt able to express a considered opinion of the new periodical and the city of its birth:

> – I have not seen the Edingburgh Review – the truth is, that Edingburgh is a place of literary Gossip – & even *I* have had my portion of Puff there – & of course, my portion of Hatred & Envy. – One man puffs me up – he has seen & talked with me – another hears him, goes & reads my poems, written when almost a boy – & candidly & logically hates me, because he does not admire my poems in the proportion in which one of his acquaintances had admired me.[7]

But he is still uncertain of the influence enjoyed by the magazine, for he concludes lamely that '– It is difficult to say whether these Reviewers do you harm or good. –'[8]

The early years of the *Edinburgh Review* were sufficiently spectacular to jolt Coleridge out of his Olympian indifference; it rapidly became popular, and its standards were, to his way of thinking, debased and vicious. One cannot tell precisely when Coleridge realized its power for doing mischief – his return from Malta after two years absence may have alerted him in 1806, and sympathy for the Wordsworths' concern over Jeffrey's hostility in 1808 may have confirmed his suspicions.[9] Whenever, and for whatever reason, Coleridge changed his mind, his comments about reviewing begin to assume the tone of a passionate crusade after 1808.

In 1808 he wrote conciliatingly to Francis Jeffrey to persuade that worthy – Coleridge had recently rebuked Southey gently for calling him 'Judge Jeffrey' –[10] to honour Thomas Clarkson's book on the slave trade with a fair hearing. The cause and the man were dear to him:

> . . . I write to you now merely to intreat – for the sake of mankind – an honorable review of Mr Clarkson's History of the Abolition of the Slave Trade. . . . It would be presumptuous in me to offer to write the Review of his Work – yet I

should be glad were I permitted to submit to you the many thoughts, which occurred to me during it's perusal.[11]

Jeffrey allowed Coleridge to write the review, but altered it slightly before publishing it. His alterations seem to have been accepted meekly enough at the time. Writing to Jeffrey himself, Coleridge is mild indeed; and he is only moderately critical when mentioning the changes in a letter to T. G. Street.[12] Yet within four months he writes in the following terms to Humphry Davy whose Bakerian Lecture had been savaged:

The Passage in question was the grossest and most disgusting KECK-UP of Envy, that has deformed even the E. R. Had the Author had the Truth before his Eyes, and purposely written in diametrical opposition, he could not have succeeded better –. It is high Time, that the spear of Ithuriel should touch this Toad at the ear of the Public.[13]

A little more than a year later, Coleridge maintained that the alterations in his review of Clarkson had merely confirmed his disapproval. '. . . Reviewing,' he writes, 'which is more profitable & abundantly more easy, I cannot engage in, as I hold it utterly immoral – and was confirmed in it by the changes, Jeffray made, in my Review of Clarkson's Hist. of Ab. in the ED. REV., the *only* case in which I thought myself warranted to make an exception.'[14] Personal grievance may have played some part in his reaction, but it does not seem to have been the decisive element.

In the years that followed, Coleridge began to argue his opposition. He objected to the assertiveness and personal rancour which he detected in contemporary reviews, and he contended that this castigation of sinners rather than sins was the more unpardonable for being anonymous. In a letter to Lady Beaumont of 1810, Coleridge had explained why he could not write reviews: '. . . I deem anonymous Criticism altogether immoral, and our *Reviews* without any exception among the most pernicious publications of the age, and as aggravating the Disease, of which they are the symptoms.'[15] It was a matter of ethics.

In 1811 he opened his course on Shakespeare and Milton

with an introductory lecture on false criticism and its causes. He divided the causes into those of an accidental and those of a permanent nature. The accidental he defines as those which arise out of differences between the circumstances in which we live and those of past writers.[16] This appeal for historical perspective, though admirable and uncommon for the time, does not concern us immediately. Among the particular circumstances he names, however, he includes 'The prevalence of reviews, magazines, newspapers, novels, &c.'[17] Reviews, he declares, are 'pernicious', for three reasons: 'because the writers determine without reference to fixed principles – because reviews are usually filled with personalities; and, above all, because they teach people rather to judge than to consider, to decide than to reflect. . . .'[18] Pursuing the indulgence in personality, an 'accidental' cause, he continues:

> The crying sin of modern criticism is that it is overloaded with personality. If an author commit an error, there is no wish to set him right for the sake of truth, but for the sake of triumph – that the reviewer may show how much wiser, or how much abler he is than the writer. . . . This is an age of personality and political gossip. . . . This style of criticism is at the present moment one of the chief pillars of the Scotch professorial court. . . .[19]

The bulk of his attack is directed at the spiteful motives and manners of the critics, their impudent assumption of superiority, and their irresponsible exploitation of the advantage of being nameless. He himself, he assures his listeners, will forgo such tactics; 'above all, whether I speak of those whom I know, or of those whom I do not know, of friends or of enemies, of the dead or of the living, my great aim will be to be strictly impartial.'[20]

In 1815, Coleridge writes to Lady Beaumont promising to wreak vengeance upon the reviewer of Wordsworth's *Excursion* in the *Edinburgh Review*. Lapsing into an incoherence unusual for him, he declares passionately: 'If ever Guilt lay on a Writer's head, and if malignity, slander, hypocrisy and self-contradicting Baseness can constitute Guilt, I dare openly, and openly (please God!) I will, impeach the Writer of that Article. . . .'[21] His first and only book of criticism was at that time in the process of being written; it gave him the opportunity of airing the question of reviewing at some length. In *Biographia Literaria*, Chapter Three and the concluding part of Chapter Ten, Chapter Twenty-one, and the Conclusion, are all devoted to this theme. Combined with Coleridge's recommendations of ideal alternatives, the remarks on contemporary reviewing comprise more than a fifth of the book.[22]

He was soon to accept a makeshift truce with his enemies,[23] but before he did so, Coleridge had publicly developed his observation of contemporary critical evils into clear diagnosis and prescriptive antidote. Like his more general suggestions for the reform of contemporary thought as a means of effecting social improvement, his analysis of critical shortcomings concentrates on the dangerous habit of offering opinions and making assertive judgements, and on the widespread indifference to the need for some canon of principles. Referring again to the decline of mental activity and the prevalence of intellectual apathy, Coleridge pleads the case for hard thought on the part of readers of criticism. Finally, putting to use the theory of Method which he was currently developing, he proposes a Method of philosophical criticism and attempts to offer an example in illustration of what he is advocating. He was openly sceptical of his attempt when he made it, and he invited improvements and argument.

I

Coleridge associated the bare assertion of opinions with the spirit of critical arrogance he deplored. Speaking in *The Friend* of 'The true marks, by which Presumption or Arrogance may be detected', he links the expression of opinion and abuse of one's opponents:

> ... as I confine my present observations to literature, I deem such criteria neither difficult to determine or to apply. The first mark, as it appears to me, is a frequent bare *assertion* of opinions not generally received, without condescending to prefix or annex the facts and reasons on which such opinions were formed; especially if this absence of logical courtesy is supplied by contemptuous or abusive

treatment of such as happen to doubt of, or oppose, the decisive *ipse dixi*.[24]

Although he does not say so in so many words, such abuse of opinion presumably lies behind Coleridge's decision to expound 'THE PRINCIPLES OF POETRY, AND THEIR *Application as Grounds of Criticism*' in his 1811–12 series of literary lectures.[25] His criticism is aimed not at the opinions themselves, but at the custom of presenting them unsupported. As he points out in the same lecture series, 'These reviewers might be compared with the Roman *praegustatores* whose business it was to tell you what was fit to be eaten, and like the *praegustatores* the reviewers gave their opinions, but carefully concealed all the reasons for such judgements.'[26] In a manuscript fragment Coleridge asks,

> To what purpose should we reason with a Critic, who without affording a single proof of his competence or perhaps in spite of the most glaring proofs to the contrary, (nay, in spite of his own consciousness that he has never made himself master even of the means of studying the question;) will yet assure the Public, that a writer's arguments are nonsense, and his inductions falsehoods?[27]

Argument, then, is one of the signs that a reviewer deserves our attention. When a reviewer merely sets his opinion against the opinion of the author he is reviewing, the author, whose claim is self-evident, is more deserving of a respectful hearing. 'I know no claim,' Coleridge writes, 'that the mere *opinion* of any individual can have to weigh down the *opinion* of the author himself; against the probability of whose parental partiality we ought to set that of his having thought longer and more deeply on the subject.'[28]

In *Biographia Literaria*, Coleridge tries to give evidence of his own competence and to show himself 'master of the means of studying the question'. The autobiographical materials introduced into the work are calculated to explain to us the bias of his taste and to reveal the steps of thought by which he arrived at the ideas which he wishes to expound.[29] A propagandist for a critical theory might have been better advised to conceal such a past, but Coleridge appears to be making a genuine effort to promote truth without at the same time believing that he enjoys a monopoly of it himself. Much of what he says about his schooldays shows us his later predilections in embryo, and no doubt he selected his material accordingly. In 1801 he had planned 'a work on the originality & merits of Locke, Hobbes, & Hume', as 'a *Pioneer* to my greater work, and as exhibiting a proof that I have not formed opinions without an attentive Perusal of the works of my Predecessors from Aristotle to Kant'.[30] We have noticed later manifestations of this early conviction that a philosopher ought to present evidence of his intellectual pedigree; in *Biographia Literaria* Coleridge is able to act upon it.

More important than the lack of such pedigree or guarantees of competence in the reviews, however, was the absence of accepted canons of criticism implied by popular reliance on tendentious opinions. Coleridge asserts that

> ... it is a truth of no difficult demonstration, that neither our literary or political Libellers could possess the influence, which it is too notorious that they now exert, but from the absence of all *principles*, and therefore of all safe and certain *rules*, of METHOD in the formation of the Reflection, the Taste, and the moral Tact as far as the great majority of English Readers are in question. . . .[31]

In *Biographia Literaria* he refers contemptuously to

> ... the substitution of assertion for argument; to the frequency of arbitrary and sometimes petulant verdicts, not seldom unsupported even by a single quotation from the work condemned, which might at least have explained the critic's meaning, if it did not prove the justice of his sentence.[32]

'Even where this is not the case,' he says, 'the extracts are too often made without reference to any general grounds or rules from which the faultiness or inadmissibility of the qualities attributed may be deduced; and without any attempt to show,

that the qualities *are* attributable to the passage extracted.'[32]
What sort of 'general grounds or rules' he has in mind by this
time appears from his statement, also in *Biographia Literaria*,
that

> . . . till reviews are conducted on far other principles, and
> with far other motives; till in the place of arbitrary dictation
> and petulant sneers, the reviewers support their decisions by
> reference to fixed canons of criticism, previously established
> and deduced from the nature of man; reflecting minds will
> pronounce it arrogance in them thus to announce themselves
> to men of letters, as the guides of their taste and judgment.[33]

Having diagnosed reliance on opinion as one of the chief
failings of contemporary criticism, and having explained that
its weaknesses are attributable to the lack of any testimony of
competence and the absence of principles, ultimately of philosophical principles, Coleridge, like a true reformer, sets about
offering examples of his alternative. As early as 1796, long
before he was concerned with combating the malign influence
of the reviews, he had announced that the reviews in *The Watchman* would be conducted according to fixed principles – this
was in accordance with his lifelong preference for this mode of
discourse.[34] In his literary lectures, some fifteen years later, he
is reported as promising something closer to the canons of
criticism he hoped for: 'the whole of the fabric he should raise
in a manner rested upon laying the foundation firmly and
distinctly. . . .'[35] But his first extensive public attempt to
provide an example is the series of essays which appeared originally in *Felix Farley's Bristol Journal* in 1814 under the title 'On
the Principles of Genial Criticism Concerning the Fine Arts'.
He had already expressed himself privately in the 'Fragment
of an Essay on Taste' written in 1810, and had posed the
question 'whether taste in any one of the fine arts has any fixed
principle or ideal. . . .'[36] Looking back over his own intellectual development, Coleridge describes how he came to seek
solutions to such problems: 'actuated . . . by my former passion
for metaphysical investigations; I labored at a solid foundation,
on which permanently to ground my opinions, in the com-
ponent faculties of the human mind itself. . . .'[37] *Biographia*

Literaria was to be the most elaborate presentation of these labours which he was ever to lay before the public.

In 1815 he wrote to Byron about the 'Biographical Sketches' he was engaged upon, and stated that his object was 'to reduce criticism to a system, by the deduction of the Causes from Principles involved in our faculties'.[38] He wrote in similar terms to Daniel Stuart of '. . . Biographical Sketches of my literary life, & opini[ons] (with the principles, on which they are grounded, & the arguments by which they were deduced) on Politics, Religion, Philosophy, and *Poetry*. . . .'[39] In the *Biographia*, Coleridge apologized for the inclusion of so much philosophical argument. He assures his readers:

> I would gladly . . . spare both myself and others this labor, if I knew how without it to present an intelligible statement of my poetic creed, not as my *opinions*, which weigh for nothing, but as deductions from established premises conveyed in such a form, as is calculated either to effect a fundamental conviction, or to receive a fundamental confutation.[40]

He introduces his critique of Wordsworth's poetry in similar terms: '. . . I have advanced no opinion either for praise or censure, other than as texts introductory to the reasons which compel me to form it.'[41] His intention of rectifying critical malpractice is apparent. In an extended statement he outlines what he takes to be the correct way of criticizing:

> . . . I should call that investigation fair and philosophical, in which the critic announces and endeavors to establish the principles, which he holds for the foundation of poetry in general, with the specification of these in their application to the different *classes* of poetry. Having thus prepared his canons of criticism for praise and condemnation, he would proceed to particularize the most striking passages to which he deems them applicable. . . . Then if his premises be rational, his deductions legitimate, and his conclusions justly applied, the reader, and possibly the poet himself, may adopt his judgement in the light of judgement and in the independence of free-agency. If he has erred, he presents his errors in

a definite place and tangible form, and holds the torch and guides the way to their detection.[42]

Coleridge felt himself bound to attempt criticism of such a 'fair and philosophical' nature with the aim of clearing up some of the misunderstandings and disagreements which were produced by opinionated criticism. He repeats his suggestion, that the grounds are more important than the opinion which is derived from them. Speaking of his disagreements with his contemporaries, he says:

> . . . where I had reason to suppose my convictions fundamentally different, it has been my habit, and I may add, the impulse of my nature, to assign the grounds of my belief, rather than the belief itself; and not to express dissent, till I could establish some points of complete sympathy, some grounds common to both sides, from which to commence its explanation.[43]

The same spirit is exhibited at the conclusion of his criticism of Wordsworth.[44]

This was to be the corrective to the bad habits of contemporary reviewing, replacing special pleading with impartiality, achieving consistency by relying on fixed principles, and advancing our knowledge of literature and skill at criticizing it in a co-operative attempt to find grounds for general agreement. Coleridge's effort to reform criticism should, as I have endeavoured to make plain, be considered as part of his wider campaign for national reform, and not as an isolated literary attitude. It springs from basic assumptions about intellectual activity and is not simply an unbiased diagnosis of critical failings. The new reviews provided him with an occasion to express these assumptions, just as unsatisfactory political developments had, and, by bringing abstract theories to grips with concrete situations, to dramatize and illustrate what he believed.

II

When he turns to consider the 'permanent causes' of false criticism in his 1811–12 lecture series, Coleridge identifies three, the first two of which constitute his third reason for describing reviews as 'pernicious'. These are: 'the great pleasure we feel in being told of the knowledge we possess, rather than of the ignorance we suffer', and 'the custom which some people have established of judging of books by books'.[45] These 'causes' recall Coleridge's views on education and the transmission of knowledge: namely that learning and knowing depend on effort, that there is no easy way to attain either, and that one of the failings of his time is the preoccupation with talismans which promise to make effort unnecessary. Coleridge had warned of this dangerous characteristic of reviews seven years earlier in a letter to Southey in which he refers to 'the necessary Evil involved in their Essence, of breeding a crumbliness of mind in the Readers. . . .'[46] In the lecture series, when he criticizes the Reviews 'above all, because they teach people rather to judge than to consider, to decide than to reflect . . . ,'[47] he refers to the consequences of this shortcoming in similar terms: 'they encourage superficiality, and induce the thoughtless and the idle to adopt sentiments conveyed under the authoritative WE, and not, by the working and subsequent clearing of their own minds, to form just original opinions.'[48] This comment is part of the broader assault which we have already seen him bent upon in the original issues of *The Friend*. Again he uses his image of the chamois-hunter:

> . . . who but a fool, if unpractised, would attempt to follow him? it is not intrepidity alone that is necessary, but he who would imitate the hunter must have gone through the same process for the acquisition of strength, skill, and knowledge: he must exert, and be capable of exerting, the same muscular energies, and display the same perseverance and courage, or all his efforts will be worse than fruitless: they will lead not only to disappointment, but to destruction.[49]

Coleridge makes the connection with criticism explicit, and he seems to be suggesting that the reviewer cannot be a surrogate thinker for the reader. He asks:

> Why has nature given limbs, if they are not to be applied to motion and action; why abilities, if they are to lie asleep,

while we avail ourselves of the eyes, ears, and understandings of others? As men often employ servants, to spare them the nuisance of rising from their seats and walking across a room, so men employ reviews in order to save themselves the trouble of exercising their own powers of judging: it is only mental slothfulness and sluggishness that induce so many to adopt, and take for granted the opinions of others.[50]

Here Coleridge has taken a major step forward by proposing not only that the methods of criticism must be changed, but that they be directed towards other purposes. To suggest that reviews should devote themselves to teaching readers to read critically, instead of relieving them of the necessity of doing so by telling them what to read and what to ignore, was reform indeed! It would not be enough to outline principles of criticism and persuade others to accept them – Coleridge is no naïve exponent of systematic panaceas. The readers' minds must be accustomed to philosophic thinking; readers must be taught not to accept canons of criticism, but to construct them for themselves. This is the implication of Coleridge's disparagement of the over-optimistic school-books of his day:

> Attempts have been made to compose and adapt systems of education; but it appears to me something like putting Greek and Latin grammars into the hands of boys, before they understand a word of Greek or Latin. These grammars contain instructions on all the minutiæ and refinements of language, but of what use are they to persons who do not comprehend the first rudiments? Why are you to furnish the means of judging, before you give the capacity to judge?[51]

Grammar and criticism are not, of course, entirely analogous, because while grammatical principles have been worked out and broadly agreed upon, critical principles are still in dispute. In criticism, if anywhere, the teacher is a student among students, offering not truth, but, for what they may be worth, his own efforts to discover truth. Coleridge is fully aware of the tentative nature of the discipline he is embarking upon, and he is willing to forgo the niceties of polished presentation in order

to rough out his preliminary efforts. As he puts it later in the
same series of lectures,

> It is true that my matter may not be so accurately arranged:
> it may not dovetail and fit at all times as nicely as could be
> wished; but you shall have my thoughts warm from my
> heart, and fresh from my understanding: you shall have the
> whole skeleton, although the bones may not be put together
> with the utmost anatomical skill.[52]

It is his critical version of the '*drama* of Reason', the presentation
of 'the thought growing, instead of a mere Hortus siccus', which
we saw him recommend in the preceding chapter. It is a modest
invitation to the co-operation of his readers.

Given Coleridge's conviction that one must labour to learn,
and his desire to teach in a fundamental way rather than simply
to inform, it is not surprising that *Biographia Literaria* should be
a forbidding book. Coleridge knew that his argument would
not be understood by many, and he gives specific instructions
to his reader in Chapter 11 when he asks that 'he will either
pass over the following chapter altogether, or read the whole
connectedly'.[53] He admits that not everyone can, or even need,
be a philosopher,[54] and launches off on his well-known comparison of the philosophical and non-philosophical ways of
knowing:

> The first range of hills, that encircles the scanty vale of human
> life, is the horizon for the majority of its inhabitants. On
> *its* ridges the common sun is born and departs. From *them*
> the stars rise, and touching *them* they vanish. By the many,
> even this range, the natural limit and bulwark of the vale,
> is but imperfectly known. . . . But in all ages there have
> been a few, who measuring and sounding the rivers of the
> vale at the feet of their furthest inaccessible falls have learnt,
> that the sources must be far higher and far inward. . . .[55]

Coleridge is for the moment more interested in the 'few', but
he is anxious lest the obstacles he is placing in their way may
be too much for even these stalwarts. He voices his anxiety
when introducing the ten theses 'for those of my readers, who

are willing to accompany me through the following Chapter.
. . .'[56] And in his much-maligned letter to himself he is able to
joke about the bewilderment which many are likely to feel.

This letter deserves more respectful attention than it usually
gets. It is true that Coleridge, by using it as an escape device,
admits that he cannot yet entirely explain the philosophy he is
expounding, and that he encourages the suspicion that he has
not yet thought the whole of it out to his own satisfaction; but
to suggest, as Hazlitt and Christopher North were the first to
do, that Coleridge was perpetrating a wordy fraud on his
readers, will not do. As I shall try to show later in this essay,
the failure to include the promised chapter does not seriously
damage what is left, and his suggestion that it be reserved for
his *announced treatises on the Logos or communicative intellect in Man
and Deity*' is far from being the bombastic insincerity it is sometimes taken for.[57] In fact, Coleridge foresees the very criticisms
which have been levelled at him ever since, and puts them so
wrily that one feels that only the extreme hostility of his age
to the kind of thought he was advocating could have denied
him the sympathetic and charitable hearing he had asked for
others.[58]

Coleridge's mysterious 'friend' mentions the unfamiliar ring
of his views and exposition:

> *your opinions and method of argument were not only so* new *to me,
> but so directly the reverse of all I had ever been accustomed to con-
> sider as truth, that even if I had comprehended your premises suffi-
> ciently to have admitted them, and had seen the necessity of your
> conclusions, . . . I should have felt as if I had been standing on my
> head.*[59]

Stepping briefly out of character, the 'friend' comments more
knowingly: '*You have been obliged to omit so many links, from the
necessity of compression, that what remains, looks . . . like the fragments of the winding steps of an old ruined tower*'.[60] As the letter
implies, and as readers have continued to point out ever since,
Coleridge's educational experiment was a failure. It was not
that he had neglected to make allowances for the frailties of
students – the interspersed autobiographical materials were
ingeniously contrived to make his position clear on various

matters on which he felt he had been misunderstood, and they serve much the same function as the 'Landing-places' so tolerantly scattered through *The Friend*, but that he failed to bridge the gap between his own thought, habituated to Transcendentalist notions and terms, and the thought of his contemporaries.[61] It was a question of underestimating the requirements of his audience, not of being indifferent to them. What matters here is that we be aware of his wish to instruct fundamentally, and of his belief that such instruction was the true role of criticism.

III

The final step in Coleridge's attempt to reform criticism is his proposal of specific philosophical principles on which it should be based. We considered in the preceding chapter Coleridge's recommendations of the way in which thought should be conducted, his outline of the process of Method. *Biographia Literaria* is Coleridge's attempt to carry his Method into practice in the particular sphere of criticism. We have learned that 'progressive transition' is the essential characteristic, and that it should be unified by being based upon a preconception derived from the 'interior of the human intellect'. It remains for us to show that *Biographia Literaria* was intended to exemplify this theory of Method, and to indicate how apt an example it is.

Coleridge says at one point in the *Biographia* that 'The ultimate end of criticism is much more to establish the principles of writing, than to furnish *rules* how to pass judgement on what has been written by others; if indeed it were possible that the two could be separated.'[62] He had noticed long before the damaging effect which the vague use of terms would have on any such enterprise,[63] and he now makes a related assertion: 'The first lesson of philosophic discipline is to wean the student's attention from the DEGREES of things, which alone form the vocabulary of common life, and to direct it to the KIND abstracted from degree.'[64] His attempt to clarify his differences with Wordsworth over the distinction between Imagination and Fancy is relevant to all three concerns – the establishment of principles of writing, the discrimination of critical terms, and the drawing of attention from degrees of things to kinds of things. And it is in his attempt to distinguish between Imagination and Fancy that Coleridge tries to put his Method into effect. In doing so he provides an example of what he meant by Method.

The first step in carrying out such a plan is, as we have learned, to settle upon a preconception, initiative or Idea. Coleridge devotes considerable space to establishing it. His opening argument in Chapter 12 is reminiscent of the terms used in his description of Method itself. 'A system,' he says, 'which aims to deduce the memory with all the other functions of intelligence, must of course place its first position from beyond the memory, and anterior to it, otherwise the principle of solution would be itself a part of the problem to be solved.[65] He calls again on the analogy of geometry: 'In geometry the primary construction is not demonstrated, but postulated.'[66] 'Geometry therefore,' he continues, 'supplies philosophy with the example of a primary intuition, from which every science that lays claim to *evidence* must take its commencement. The mathematician does not begin with a demonstrable proposition, but with an intuition, a practical idea.'[67] He recognizes the limits of his analogy by pointing out that the greater complexity of philosophy denies it the convenience of diagrammatic illustration: 'Philosophy is employed on objects of the INNER SENSE, and cannot, like geometry appropriate to every construction a correspondent *outward* intuition.'[68]

The problem is one which we have already encountered in our consideration of Coleridge's treatment of Method. He persists in spite of the inherent difficulties: 'Nevertheless philosophy, if it is to arrive at evidence, must proceed from the most original construction, and the question then is, what is the most original construction or first productive act for the INNER SENSE.'[69] In trying to answer this question Coleridge goes farther than he does in his Method essays, by discriminating between the degrees of 'inner sense' possessed by different people. Just as some are philosophers and some are not, some are capable of attaining 'to a notion of [their] notions' and some are not.[70] The absence of simplifying visual representations of 'notions' makes transmission of them to those whose 'inner sense' is undeveloped or lacking difficult or impossible. Coleridge writes that,

To an Esquimaux or New Zealander our most popular philosophy would be wholly unintelligible. The sense, the inward organ for it, is not yet born in him. So is there many a one among us, yes, and some who think themselves philosophers too, to whom the philosophic organ is entirely wanting. To such a man, philosophy is a mere play of words and notions, like a theory of music to the deaf. . . .[71]

As a prelude to a philosophical statement, such reasoning is likely to seem tendentious or unfair, disqualifying those who disagree as being philosophically deficient – indeed the tone of it may have exasperated some of Coleridge's own reviewers – but it is of a piece with his later remark in his *Philosophical Lectures*: 'There is a point which is above all intellect, and there are truths derived from that point which must be presumed, . . . and when such principles are denied you may at least candidly say, "We differ on principles", and charitably think that that man must be made a better before he can be made a wiser man.'[72] It certainly is not a matter for argument, and Coleridge, whatever he may think about its consequences, makes no attempt to pass off his statement as more than the assumption that it is.

Rather abruptly, he now declares that the postulate of philosophy is the injunction 'KNOW THYSELF'.[73] We shall consider his attempt to delve into the way in which one can know anything in the next chapter; for the time being it suffices to notice the course of Coleridge's argument. He is introducing the problem of the relationship between the perceiver and the things perceived – or to use his synonyms, between Subject and Object, Self and Nature. He is content to paraphrase Schelling when discussing the question of the precedence of Subject and Object, and by falling back on the German philosopher as a sort of shorthand he is perhaps overdoing the presentation of the 'drama of Reason'. While one can make something of this discussion in the light of his general philosophical aims and efforts, a reader denied access to such aids is likely to feel baffled by the sudden administration of a Transcendental bolus.[74] Having forearmed ourselves by our examination of the essays on Method, however, the problem and the terms used should seem less strange.

Coleridge begins by describing two ways of thinking about how we know things. He remarks that 'During the act of knowledge itself, the objective and subjective are so instantly united, that we cannot determine to which of the two the priority belongs'.[75] Having admitted so much, he goes on to suppose them separable for the purpose of examining the nature of their union, and discusses the implications first of holding that the objective precedes the subjective, and then of holding that this succession is reversed.

In reading his account, we should bear in mind the relations of Law and Theory. If the objective is taken to be the first, we have what Coleridge calls 'the problem of natural philosophy'.[76] This is what in the essays on Method he has called the relation of Theory. Having assumed that nature precedes the observing self, Coleridge maintains, the natural philosopher moves from nature to the self, or intelligence: 'The necessary tendence . . . of all natural philosophy is from nature to intelligence; and this, and no other[,] is the true ground and occasion of the instinctive striving to introduce theory into our views of natural phænomena.'[77] Moving from observation of material things, the scientist tries to achieve universal principles of laws: 'The highest perfection of natural philosophy would consist in the perfect spiritualization of all the laws of nature into laws of intuition and intellect.'[78] In *Biographia Literaria* Coleridge withholds the expression of scepticism about the likelihood of achieving satisfactory results which he was later to permit himself.[79] In the 1818 *Friend* he describes the sequence of scientific thinking uncompromisingly as 'representative not constitutive, and . . . indeed little more than an abbreviature of the preceding observation, and the deductions therefrom'.[80] In the *Biographia* he refrains from condemnation and describes the ideal end of science:

The Phænomena . . . must wholly disappear, and the laws alone . . . must remain. Thence it comes, that in nature itself the more the principle of law breaks forth, the more does the *husk* drop off, the phænomena themselves become more spiritual and at length cease altogether in our consciousness. . . . The theory of natural philosophy would . . . be completed, when all nature was demonstrated to be identical in essence with that, which in its highest known power exists in man as intelligence and self-consciousness. . . .[81]

The essays on Method have provided us with the technical meaning of the phrase 'the principle of law' for Coleridge.

'Natural Philosophy' represents the extreme of materialistic investigation for Coleridge, and he wishes to show that even in it the investigator is led unconsciously to the subjective:

> . . . even natural science, which commences with the material phænomenon as the reality and substance of things existing, does yet by the necessity of theorising unconsciously, and as it were instinctively, end in nature as an intelligence; and by this tendency the science of nature becomes finally natural philosophy, the one of the two poles of fundamental science.[82]

Ideal though this process may be for science, philosophy, according to Coleridge, demands a different one.

He now examines the consequences of supposing the opposite – that the subjective precedes the objective. As one might have anticipated, it turns out to be the supposition of 'the transcendental or intelligential philosopher', and it is analogous to the relation of Law. When thinking in this manner, one is careful 'to preclude all interpolation of the objective into the subjective principles of [one's] science. . .'.[83] This result is achieved by means of 'an absolute and scientific scepticism to which the mind voluntar[il]y determines itself for the specific purpose of future certainty'.[84] It is a constitutive philosophy which tries to deal with two widely held assumptions or positions, one of which Coleridge wishes to criticize, and the other of which, while he holds it up for view as an assumption, he feels cannot be dismissed. Coleridge tells us that the philosopher's scepticism is aimed not at 'the prejudices of education and circumstance, but those original and innate prejudices which nature herself has planted in all men, and which to all but the philosopher are the first principles of knowledge, and the final test of truth'.[85] He reduces these to 'the one fundamental presumption, THAT THERE EXIST THINGS WITHOUT US'.[86] A presumption, be it noticed, on which the scientific relation of Theory he has just described is predicated. Coleridge does not attempt to prove that the 'prejudice' is not correct, but he suggests the impossibility of demonstrating that it is:

> ... inasmuch as [the presumption] refers to something essentially different from ourselves, nay even in opposition to ourselves, [it] leaves it inconceivable how it could possibly become a part of our immediate consciousness; (in other words how that, which ex hypothesi is and continues to be extrinsic and alien to our being, should become a modification of our being). . . .[87]

The fact that the presumption is indemonstrable rules it out as a foundation stone for philosophy as far as Coleridge is concerned.

The other fundamental presumption, the sense of self-consciousness (or as Coleridge cryptically calls it, 'I Am') is also indemonstrable; however, he finds it impossible to abandon. 'It is,' he admits, 'groundless indeed; but then in the very idea it precludes all ground, and separated from the immediate consciousness loses its whole sense and import. It is groundless; but only because it is itself the ground of all other certainty.'[88] As he points out, there is a difference between the 'certainty' of this position and the position that there exist things without us, but he is heedful of the widespread acceptance of the latter and he seeks to reconcile the disparity, which 'the transcendental philosopher can solve only by the supposition, that the former is unconsciously involved in the latter; that it is not only coherent but identical, and one and the same thing with our own immediate self consciousness'.[89] He concludes that 'the office and object' of the transcendental philosophy is 'To demonstrate this identity. . . .'[90] Unfortunately Coleridge does not unravel the problem here; instead he refers us to his promised but uncompleted Logosophia. In its place he offers the ten 'theses' with the excuse that 'The science of arithmetic furnishes instances, that a rule may be useful in practical application, and for the particular purpose may be sufficiently authenticated by the result, before it has itself been fully demonstrated.'[91] We have, it seems, come to a link in Coleridge's chain of reasoning which he has not yet worked out to his satisfaction. In a sense too we have come to the end of a false start; the explication was too detailed to be kept up.

Coleridge does not abandon the chase, he simply embarks upon it anew with a statement of the results which he had hoped to arrive at, and tells us that they 'will be applied to the deduction of the imagination, and with it the principles of production and of genial criticism in the fine arts'. [92] While the theses may not be as full a discussion as we might wish, or as full as Coleridge evidently felt was desirable, they are in themselves sufficient to provide us with a general picture of the lines on which he has been thinking. This time he restricts his attention to the relation of Law.

He begins by asserting the correlation of Knowledge and Reality, [93] a necessary preliminary if one is proposing to apply metaphysical conclusions to something as relatively concrete as 'imagination'. He goes on to distinguish between 'mediate' and 'immediate' or 'original' truths, pointing out that in order to have 'mediate' truths one must first have 'immediate' ones. The immediate truths must therefore be sought first. In the third thesis, Coleridge states that 'We are to seek . . . for some absolute truth capable of communicating to other positions a certainty, which it has not itself borrowed; a truth self-grounded, unconditional and known by its own light. In short, we have to find a somewhat which *is*, simply because it *is*.' [94] Such a truth must be its own predicate, and there must be no possibility of 'requiring a cause or anticedent [*sic*] without an absurdity'. [95] The fourth thesis states that there can be only one such principle, [96] and the fifth, that it can be found 'neither in object or subject taken separately', and must, therefore, be found in that 'which is the identity of both'. [97]

Coleridge has now brought us to the point which he had previously tried to reach by a different route, this time omitting the relation of Theory. He next expands a little upon the absolute Truth which he is looking for. In Thesis VI he describes it:

This principle . . . manifests itself in the Sum or I AM, which I shall hereafter indiscriminately express by the words spirit, self, and self-consciousness. In this, and in this alone, object and subject, being and knowing, are identical, each involving and supposing the other. In other words, it is a subject which becomes a subject by the act of constructing itself objectively to itself; but which never is an object except for itself, and only so far as by the very same act it becomes a subject.[98]

This 'spirit, self, and self-consciousness', according to Thesis VII must be an act – and here Coleridge appears to be tipping the balance of the 'coinstantaneous' union of subject and object in favour of the subject –; 'the spirit (originally the identity of object and subject) must in some sense dissolve this identity, in order to be conscious of it: fit alter et idem. But this implies an act. . . .'[99] Coleridge maintains that an act necessarily presupposes a will: 'it follows therefore that intelligence or self-consciousness is impossible, except by and in a will'.[100] And here he casts off another shackle of the mechanistic philosophy which he has earlier ridiculed, by affirming that the will is free: 'The self-conscious spirit therefore is a will; and freedom must be assumed as a *ground* of philosophy, and can never be deduced from it. [101] This 'self-consciousness', being a union of subject and object, 'can be conceived neither as infinite or finite exclusively, but as the most original union of both'.[102]

In his ninth thesis, Coleridge reminds us that he is not now referring to the science which moves from object to subject, but exclusively to the kind which moves from subject to object: 'This principium commune essendi et cognoscendi, as subsisting in a WILL, or primary ACT of self-duplication, is the mediate or indirect principle of every science; but it is the immediate and direct principle of the ultimate science alone, i.e. of transcendental philosophy alone.'[103] He is not offering an exposition of being, but only of knowing, for beyond knowledge it is impossible to inquire: 'The principle of our knowing is sought within the sphere of our knowing. . . . It is asserted only, that the act of self-consciousness is for *us* the source and principle of all *our* possible knowledge.'[104]

Coleridge has now completed his attempt to establish an initial Idea, the initiative of the critical system he wishes to expound. I do not think that one can praise his organization of material, and yet, for all his irresolution, for all his circling and weaving around the point he is trying to make, his meaning is fairly clear. He is belittling thought based on the observation of phenomena (the relation of Theory, the method of natural science) and advocating thought based on scrutiny of the mind itself (the relation of Law). If we are to attain the sort of absolute knowledge which Coleridge believes is essential, we must begin with the Self and not with Nature. Coleridge declares his ultimate ambition to be 'to construct by a series of intuitions the progressive schemes . . . till I arrive at the fulness of the *human* intelligence'.[105] For the present, however, he is only concerned with arriving at an explanation of the poetic faculty of imagination; he assumes the fuller exposition of the position 'I Am' into 'the fulness of the *human* intelligence' as his principle, 'in order to deduce from it a faculty, the generation, agency, and application of which form the contents of the ensuing chapter.'[106] He is again admitting a gap in the chain, but a gap in detail; we are being asked to accept the results and implications of an argument which he promises to expound later. He is not giving up the attempt to arrive at a description of the creative act of poetry derived from first principles. Boldly he informs his readers: 'I shall now proceed to the nature and genesis of the imagination. . . .'[107]

It is at this point that commentators tend to lose patience with Coleridge.[108] Having been twice balked by lacunæ which demand considerable charity on the part of the reader, they jib at the third one which Coleridge lightheartedly ushers in with the fanfare of an expostulatory letter from his judicious 'friend'. After an opening bow in Chapter Thirteen to his eminent predecessors Descartes and Kant, Coleridge abruptly gives up. This time he offers 'results' with a vengeance: '. . . I shall content myself for the present with stating the main result of the Chapter, which I have reserved for that future publication, a detailed prospectus of which the reader will find at the close of the second volume.'[109] It was only adding insult to injury to omit even the prospectus. The 'main result' is, of course, the familiar description of 'Primary Imagination', 'Secondary Imagination', and 'Fancy'.

I shall recur to these definitions in the fifth chapter, and shall try to show the relevance which the philosophical discussion we have just traced has to them; for the moment, however, we are only concerned with the extent to which the 'deduction' of Imagination from first principles may be said to exemplify the theory of Method which Coleridge has advocated. It must be admitted, for a start, that it is likely to win few converts. The difficulty with Coleridge's procedure is that the reader is not permitted to know where he is being taken or why he is being taken there; by obscuring the end in view, the intricacies of the way are allowed to become confusing and even irritating. Indeed, unless one is thinking within a framework of ideas which is at least roughly similar to Coleridge's before beginning to read him, the whole enterprise is likely to seem unforgivably capricious. By way of palliating this indictment, it may be noted that Coleridge's discussion in earlier chapters of his track through the works of various philosophers, if followed carefully, goes a long way towards providing the necessary framework. What Coleridge has failed to do is to make the link clear.

Inadequate though it may be, there can be little doubt that Coleridge intended *Biographia Literaria* as an example of the Method we have watched him expound. It will be enough to recall its characteristics. First of all, an *initiative* upon which 'progressive transition' may be built. 'It is manifest, that the wider the sphere of transition is, the more comprehensive and commanding must be the initiative. . . .'[110] The sphere of transition could scarcely be wider than that attempted in the *Biographia* – to deduce the faculty of Imagination from first principles. The nature of the initiative depends on the nature of the relations between the objects observed. As I have suggested, the relation of Law prevails; for it an absolute and unconditional ground is necessary, 'a truth in the Mind itself, pregnant with the consequence of other truths in an indefinite progression'.[111] In just such terms, Coleridge has offered the position 'I Am' – the one original and immediate truth. Next comes the progressive transition itself, pursued 'through all its ramifications'.[112] Here, as we have seen, Coleridge has offered only a token – it is in the matter of 'progressive transition' that he falls down – but his failure is one of execution not of intent. The attempt to carry out this aspect of Method is evident enough. As we have noticed, Coleridge thought it unlikely that Method based on the relation of Law could be completely within the capacity of man; nevertheless he shared the ideal he attributes to Plato – '. . . *to find a ground that is unconditional and absolute, and thereby to reduce the aggregate of human knowledge to a system'.*[113] Like Kant, he hoped that some part of the ideal might be achieved. The definition of Imagination was the fruit of his efforts.

Hegel once remarked of Schelling that he conducted his education in public, and much the same might be said of Coleridge. It is not that his ideas are presented inconsistently, or that he keeps changing his views, but that he offers his thinking to the public before he has come to the end of it. In *Biographia Literaria* we have neither the relentless Kantian progress which he admired, nor even the indefatigable exhaustiveness of Hartley, but rather a trial run of ideas which he has conceived in their general outlines and not yet articulated in particular details. As a whole it resembles personal notes for a philosophy. Coleridge knew that he had not given a very convincing demonstration of his Method of criticism, and his reference to it as 'so immethodical a miscellany' is apter than one might have guessed at first reading.[114] Years later he was to regret the inadequacy of the philosophical passages in the *Biographia*.[115]

Why then should he have placed them before the public at all? What did he think he might achieve by doing so? The answer lies, I think, in the two motives for publication discussed in our first chapter – financial necessity and reforming zeal. The first forced him to publish something, and a book of criticism seemed possible to him; the second encouraged him to try to right contemporary wrongs and may have overridden the dissatisfaction he felt at having to offer ideas so incomplete. His references at each gap to works which he will publish in due course are, one feels, genuine enough as evidence of what he meant to do and they must have acted as a salve to his conscience. Even if we regard his publication of his critical Method before its time as ill-advised, we should pause before rejecting it as still-born.

Coleridge's contemporaries, and particularly the haughty reviewers of Edinburgh, were predisposed to condemn any philosophical work which smacked of German metaphysics. In the twentieth century, although Transcendentalism is in eclipse, there is no longer so general an impulse to be intolerant of it. It has been pointed out that one of the most interesting aspects of Coleridge's criticism is the critical method it implies. Gordon McKenzie, for example, states that 'The most important value of Coleridge for modern literary criticism lies in his attempts to formulate a method and a technique by which literature may be approached.'[116] More recently Sir Herbert Read has maintained that 'The distinction of Coleridge, which puts him head and shoulders above every other English critic, is due to his introduction of a philosophical method of criticism.'[117] It is not that the example is successful, but that it suggests how one might go about attempting a philosophic method for oneself.

It is appropriate to conclude by recalling what Coleridge had to say in the course of his *Philosophical Lectures* on the construction of philosophies:

> Every truly great mind is to be considered in two points of view, the first is that in which he may be said to exist universally, to act upon all men in all ages; and that is the grand idea which he first originates, the grand form and scheme of generalization. And the next is, when quitting the part of the architect, he himself becomes one of the labourers and one of the masons. There you will find in him the imperfections, of course, of every human individual; and while you give him every praise where he succeeds you will never permit it to detract from his merits where he fails.[118]

Coleridge the critic was architect of the work on which he became so indifferent a labourer; the essays on Method provide us with an essential part of the blue-print of his intentions.

4

The Communicative Intelligence

As J. Shawcross pointed out half a century ago, one of the most
important differences between Coleridge's argument and the
one which he borrowed from Schelling in *Biographia Literaria* is
his insistence on the necessary inclusion of God in any interpretation of the nature of the universe.[1] This difference is not
merely a sign of disenchantment with Schelling's thought; it is
central to any consideration of Coleridge's account of knowledge, and it precedes his acquaintance with the German
philosopher.

A passage in the well-known autobiographical letter to
Thomas Poole records early evidence of a way of thinking that
remained characteristic of Coleridge. It runs: '. . . from my
early reading of Faery Tales, & Genii &c &c – my mind had
been habituated *to the Vast* – & I never regarded *my senses* in
any way as the criteria of my belief. I regulated all my creeds
by my conceptions not by my *sight*. . . .'[2] Awareness of 'the
Vast' and the wish to accommodate it in his metaphysical
speculations combine with distrust of the senses and a preference
for 'conceptions', to provide us with something more than a
caricature of Coleridge's intellectual life. On some occasions
we find him estimating the truth of various philosophies by
their appeal to the heart, by a sub- or supra-rational criterion;
on others, trying to develop a philosophy himself which will
rely more on the resources of the philosopher's mind than on
his observations of his surroundings.

The two impulses are not necessarily incompatible, but unless
we keep them firmly in mind they are liable to appear in his
writings as inconsistency.[3] In all Coleridge's investigations a
limit is assumed; within that limit he is willing to conduct free
enquiry. If we imagine the limit as a circle identified as God,

and the centre as man, Coleridge's philosophical pursuits may be thought of as a series of attempts, using whatever philosophies come to hand, to bridge the gap with an argued radius. Although he is convinced that he can prove that the attempts of some previous philosophers have been unsuccessful, he is never satisfied with his own results.

In 'Conciones ad Populum' (1795), he refers to the desirability that in times of trouble, '. . . we should have acquired a prompt facility of adverting in all our doubts to some grand and comprehensive truth'.[4] This is both a statement of faith and an expression of scepticism – faith in God, and scepticism of man. Coleridge describes some of the stages of his thinking on this matter in *Biographia Literaria*. To begin with, he tells us, he verged upon complete scepticism of philosophy:

> After I had successively studied in the schools of Locke, Berkeley, Leibnitz, and Hartley, and could find in neither of them an abiding place for my reason, I began to ask myself; is a system of philosophy, as different from mere history and historic classification possible? If possible, what are its necessary conditions? I was for a while disposed to answer the first question in the negative, and to admit that the sole practicable employment for the human mind was to observe, to collect, and to classify.[5]

But this pessimism did not satisfy him. '. . . I soon felt,' he says, 'that human nature itself fought up against this wilful resignation of intellect; and as soon did I find, that the scheme taken with all its consequences and cleared of all inconsistencies was not less impracticable, than contra-natural'.[6]

At the same time, Coleridge found himself helped by the writings of the mystics to rise above passive dissatisfaction with philosophies, and to discern that an adequate one must involve more than intellect alone could provide.

> They contributed to keep alive the *heart* in the *head*; gave me an indistinct, yet stirring and working presentment, that all the products of the mere *reflective* faculty partook of DEATH, and were as the rattling twigs and sprays in winter, into which a sap was yet to be propelled, from some root to which

I had not penetrated, if they were to afford my soul either food or shelter.[7]

The root was God, and given that root Coleridge found himself able to choose at will from different philosophies, deeming them all, faulty though they might be, fragments of the comprehensive truth he was looking for. He quotes Leibniz approvingly on the 'criterion of a true philosophy':

> . . . it would at once explain and collect the fragments of truth scattered through systems apparently the most incongruous. The truth . . . is diffused more widely than is commonly believed; but it is often painted, yet oftener masked, and is sometimes mutilated and sometimes, alas! in close alliance with mischievous errors. The deeper, however, we penetrate into the ground of things, the more truth we discover in the doctrines of the greater number of the philosophical sects.[8]

Faith in a comprehensive truth and willingness to learn from any attempts to discover it typify Coleridge's thought.

His investigations centred on the study of perception, or more specifically, on the study of the relationship between our thoughts and ourselves, and the relationship between our thoughts and our surroundings. This choice, of course, had been made for Coleridge by his predecessors in the eighteenth century; but his early disposition to trust his conceptions and not his senses seems to have determined the direction of his thinking. In his *Philosophical Lectures* (1818–19), he defines the 'fundamental notions of ancient materialism':

> . . . mind is but a species of sensation, and all the processes of perception and of reflexion purely passive, and all the acts (or more accurately all the phenomena or appearances of life, just as the seeming acts of a dream) are wholly mechanical or produced by necessitating antecedents.[9]

Such ideas did not ring true to him, and it was to this strain of speculation in writers like Locke and Hartley that he objected. At first he was satisfied to point out the two ways of approaching the problem of perception. In a letter written to Josiah Wedgwood in 1801 he had referred to the similarity between the opinions of Descartes and Locke on 'the original sources of our Ideas' (he is questioning Locke's reputation for originality):

> They both taught . . . that the Objects of human Knowledge are either Ideas imprinted on the Senses, or else such as are perceived by attending to the passions and operations of the mind, or lastly Ideas formed by Help of Memory and Imagination, either compounding, dividing, or barely representing those originally perceived in the aforesaid Ways.[10]

During his illness in the spring of 1801, this question of the relative roles of ideas and impressions had absorbed his attention. He writes to Humphry Davy: 'I have been *thinking* vigorously during my illness. . . . The subject of my meditations ha[s] been the Relations of Thoughts to Things, in the language of Hume, of Ideas to Impressions. . . .'[11] He cites the experience of Descartes, who was satisfied that it was necessary to believe in a God:

> . . . he found in himself certain Ideas of *Relation*, certain Ideas, or rather modes of contemplating Ideas, of which he had acquired the knowlege by attending to the operations of his own Thoughts, and which did not depend in any degree on his Will. In these he recognized the fountains of Truth, and of Truth immutable, because it did not depend upon the existence of any Archetypes. These Truths in his early works he called Innate Ideas. . . . By these, according to him, we may acquire the knowlege, that there is a God, and from the Veracity implied in the Idea of an absolutely perfect Being deduce a complete Assurance, that all these Things are real to the belief of the Reality of which our Reason doth truly & irresistably compel us.[12]

And again,

> . . . he found himself compelled to turn his view inward upon his own frame and faculties in order to determine what share they had in the making up both of his Ideas and of his

Judgements on them. He now saw clearly, that the objects, which he had hitherto supposed to have been intromitted into his mind by his senses, must be the joint production of his Mind, his Senses, and an unknown Tertium Aliquid all which might possibly be developements of his own Nature, in a way unknown to him.[13]

Coleridge himself proposed to follow a similar path, analysing the components of nature and thinking about the way in which they were observed in order to understand the totality he felt. In *Biographia Literaria* he describes the procedure as being the true function of philosophy:

> The office of philosophical *disquisition* consists in just *distinction*; while it is the priviledge of the philosopher to preserve himself constantly aware, that distinction is not division. In order to obtain adequate notions of any truth, we must intellectually separate its distinguishable parts; and this is the technical *process* of philosophy. But having so done, we must then restore them in our conceptions to the unity, in which they actually co-exist; and this is the *result* of philosophy.[14]

The conclusion (to revert to our earlier image, the circumference of the circle) is foreseen; the purpose of philosophy is to provide the argument towards it.

What is perhaps Coleridge's earliest reference to a work on logic occurs in a letter to William Godwin in 1803.[15] He mentions it quite often over the years, but describes it in considerable detail during the crucial period from 1814 to 1816. The 'Logosophia', as he usually styles it, was never finished, although lengthy sections of it survive in manuscript; but even the plans provide us with useful hints of the sort of philosophy he was striving after. The most interesting aspect of it for our present purpose is the recurrence of variations of the phrase, 'the Logos human & Divine',[16] called in a letter written in 1814, more explicitly, 'the Logos, or communicative Intelligence, Natural, Human, and Divine'.[17] The two constants in the descriptions are the assumptions that there is more than one way of attaining knowledge and that man's knowledge is bound to be incomplete. As Coleridge's thinking on the subject is detailed and occasionally serpentine, it seems worthwhile to identify pervasive Coleridgean themes before discussing the results of them, and to have in mind the direction in which he was moving before we investigate the paths he chose to take on the way. If the assumptions which he sometimes neglects to emphasize in his published works are ignored, the arguments which follow on them are likely to seem perverse.

It is difficult to work out a satisfactory chronology for the development of Coleridge's metaphysics, partly because so much of the evidence is in manuscript form and still awaits editing, and partly because Coleridge himself appears to advance by fits and starts, circling round and round, recalling fragments of discarded theory and jettisoning thoughts more recently adopted. This chapter is an attempt to reconstruct the state of his thinking during the period from about 1808 to 1819, and it is drawn principally from his published works of these years with some additional help from unpublished manu-scripts.[18]

I

Coleridge regarded God's consciousness as absolute knowledge. The concept was not a new one; as A. O. Lovejoy has pointed out, Kant himself had been anticipated in this kind of reasoning by the English neo-Platonists. The mind of God was hypo-thesized by analogy with the mind of man:

> ... since ... the world of experience as a coherent system of rationally interrelated objects is possible for me only in so far as its content subsists and is categorized within the unity of *my* mind – which provides the synthetizing system of spatial, temporal, and other relations but is itself something more than a term of those relations – so the whole of reality, including all finite minds, can be conceived only as subsisting within the unity of a single, all-comprehending, self-determining, and completely rational Eternal Mind or Absolute Experience.[19]

When, therefore, Coleridge recommended the relation of Law

as deserving 'the first place in the science of Method', he gave an example of it and suggested how hard it would be to attain, by saying that '. . . we contemplate it as exclusively an attribute of the Supreme Being, inseparable from the idea of God. . . .'[20] Human knowledge must depend on imperfect attempts to achieve something of divine knowledge: '. . . from the contemplation of law in this, its only perfect form, must be derived all true insight into all other grounds and principles necessary to Method. . . .'[21] This relationship between man and God is another way of putting the circumference–radius analogy, the circumference representing absolute knowledge and the radius the human attempt to attain it. It is fundamental to Coleridge's treatment of the nature of creative thought.

In his manuscript 'Treatise on Logic', Coleridge remarks that 'By the Supreme mind doubtless every object is contemplated with the same insight to their necessity as the properties of [a] circle or the functions of an Algebraic term are by the human Mathematician'.[22] The geometrical illustration had also been used by Coleridge to explain the kind of 'adamantine chain' which he wished to have follow upon an initiative or Idea of Method. In geometry the argument could be perfect because the geometer could define his own terms and by limiting them and requiring of them only an ideal existence could be said to have absolute knowledge. This procedure, Coleridge argued, was preferable to Method based on the relation of Theory, in which hypotheses are erected on the basis of observation. Because observation must necessarily be selective and incomplete, one can never be sure that the relevant elements have been exhausted. God's knowledge of the universe, by what appears at first to be a paradox, may be thought of as based either on the relations of Law or on the relations of Theory; the two are reconciled in Him. As the Creator of the universe, He enjoys the privilege of the geometer – understanding the necessary connection of every part. And as Creator of the universe, He is also capable of considering it in its entirety. As Coleridge contends in a letter written to Thomas Clarkson in 1806,

. . . all *our* Thoughts are in the language of the old Logicians *inadequate*; i.e. no *thought*, which I have, of any *thing* comprizes the whole of that Thing. I have a distinct Thought of a Rose-Tree; but what countless properties and goings-on of that plant are there, not included in my *Thought* of it?

By contrast,

> ... the Thoughts of God ... are all IDEAS, archetypal, and anterior to all but himself alone: therefore consummately *adequate*: and therefore according to our common habits of conception and expression, incomparably more *real* than all things besides, & which do all depend on and proceed from them in some sort perhaps as our Thoughts from those *Things*. . . .[23]

This is the ideal of knowledge for Coleridge, and it should always be borne in mind when one is reading philosophical passages in his criticism.

Coleridge has called the Logos 'the communicative intelligence'. Communication of the ideal knowledge is one of his basic assumptions. Man in his system is not a solitary creature seeking to know in an indifferent universe. God offers him glimpses of His absolute knowledge. Each person has some share, but the shares are not all equal. In the letter to Clarkson quoted above, Coleridge outlines a hierarchy reminiscent of the Chain of Being: '. . . to the highest consciousness short of Deity there must subsist infinite orderly degrees. . . .'[24] He expands this thought in a letter to Cottle eight years later:

> Mind . . . may be regarded as a distinct genus, in the scale ascending above brutes, and including the whole of intellectual existences; advancing from *thought*, (that mysterious thing!) in its lowest form, through all the gradations of sentient and rational beings, till it arrives at a Bacon, a Newton, and then, when unincumbered by matter, extending its illimitable sway through Seraph and Archangel, till we are lost in the GREAT INFINITE!'[25]

The same notion appears again in the *Treatise on Method*, but this time it is expressed in terms of initiatives or Ideas which imply the absolute. There is, he says, '. . . a gradation of Ideas, as of ranks in a well-ordered State, or of commands in a well-regulated army; and thus above all partial forms, there is one universal form of GOOD and FAIR, the καλοκἀγαθον of the Platonic Philosophy'.[26] In 1819 Coleridge had touched on this sense of degree when speaking of Kant's contribution to philosophy:

> ... he determined the nature of religious truth and its connexion with the understanding and made it felt to the full that the reason itself, considered as merely intellectual, was but a subordinate part of our nature; that there was a higher part, the will and the conscience; and that if the intellect of man was the cherub that flew with wings it flew after the flaming seraph and but followed its track. . . .[27]

Coleridge recognized a variety of ways of following in the track of 'the flaming seraph' towards the knowledge possible only for God, but he thought that some were better than others. He believed that knowledge could best be achieved by scrutiny of one's own mind; this was the track in which he chose to follow, and his choice has bearing on most of his most famous critical distinctions, terms, and judgements.

II

In *The Friend*, Coleridge describes his 'metaphysics' as '. . . merely the referring of the mind to its own consciousness for truths indispensable to its own happiness!'[28] In a political essay published at about the same time he mentions the dangers of rejecting this source of truth by referring the reader to the second chapter of the 'Wisdom of Solomon':

> ... there he will find THE CALCULATOR'S PROGRESS from self-confiding philosophy (or rather *psilosophy*) which refuses the aid of all moral instincts, and laughs at 'the voice within' as a superstitition – his progress, first to sensuality, that infallible heart-hardener; and thence to oppression and remorseless cruelty.[29]

The dramatic consequences detailed here are less important than the rejection which leads to them. The 'voice within' is the source of truth; it ought not to be denied.

Given that the interior of the mind is the source, there remains the problem of drawing upon it. Coleridge considers

this question in *Biographia Literaria*: 'It is demanded ...
whether there be found any means in philosophy to determine
the direction of the INNER SENSE, as in mathematics it is deter-
minable by its specific image or outward picture.'[30] He also
refers to the futility of trying to probe farther than our first act
of consciousness. 'The transcendental philosopher,' he says,
'does not enquire, what ultimate ground of our knowledge
there may lie out of our knowing, but what is the last in our
knowing itself, beyond which *we* cannot pass.'[31] While he does
not, however, think it practicable to press a philosophical discussion beyond this point, he makes an interesting suggestion
about what may lie beyond it:

> That the self-consciousness is the fixt point, to which for *us*
> all is morticed and annexed, needs no further proof. But that
> the self-consciousness may be the modification of a higher
> form of being, perhaps of a higher consciousness, and this
> again of a yet higher, and so on in an infinite regressus; in
> short, that self-consciousness may be itself something explic-
> able into something, which must lie beyond the possibility
> of our knowledge, ... does not at all concern us as trans-
> cendental philosophers.[32]

The notion of a hierarchy of consciousness, even if some of the
degrees of it are inaccessible to us, may usefully be compared
with the hierarchy of ideas from man to God, and to the
conclusions which Coleridge had found in Descartes in 1801:
'. . . that the objects, which he had hitherto supposed to have
been intromitted into his mind by his senses, must be the joint
production of his Mind, his Senses, and an unknown Tertium
Aliquid all which might possibly be developements of his own
Nature, in a way unknown to him.[33] Concentration on the act
of self-consciousness in Coleridge's system results from his own
explicit disavowal, in *Biographia Literaria*, of concern for anything prior to it: but the disavowal seems to be merely a
temporary expedient and should not be regarded as typical of
his thought. The existence of the unconscious is relevant to
Coleridge's critical argument, and it is central to his estimate
of the kinds and degrees of the poetic faculties.[33a] We may
suppose that Coleridge shirked discussion of it in *Biographia*

Literaria because he felt that he had not yet worked out an adequate account of it – in fact his first evident attempt to do so occurs a few years later in his 'Treatise on Logic' – but it is relevant as a foreseen conclusion, even if the proof or demonstration follows after a respectful interval.

Reference to a 'Tertium Aliquid' and a 'higher consciousness' suggests that Coleridge had been thinking about the obscure powers of the mind by the time he wrote *Biographia Literaria*. The discussion of the occurrence of Ideas in the essays on Method also suggests the assumption of an unconscious source. Describing Plato's educational aims, Coleridge mentions that he tried to place the 'Human Soul' '. . . in such relations of circumstance as should gradually excite its vegetating and germinating powers to produce new fruits of Thought, new Conceptions, and Imaginations, and Ideas'.[34] In the 'Treatise on Logic' he confronts the possibilities of this process directly and describes the sense we have of uncontrolled or half controlled mental activity:

> There will be many . . . I doubt not unwilling to confess that they have been sometimes in that state of mind which they could perhaps describe by no other term than that of thinking and yet if questioned of what they were thinking about must answer nothing. Nay this is a state which not seldom takes place when the mind is preparing itself for the highest efforts of thought and even during such efforts the energy continuing during the momentary occultations of the part objects of the consciousness, as we continue the act of gazing in the brief intervals of the flashes at night in a storm of thunder and lightning.[35]

Later in the 'Treatise on Logic', Coleridge comes to the problem which he had attempted to formulate in *Biographia Literaria* in his account of the priorities of Subjective and Objective in the act of knowledge and again in the ten theses. In seeking once more to arrive at the position I Am, but this time forgoing simple assertion, he notes the implications of his attempt:

> If the enquiry were confined to the principium sciendi, the

quomodo scimus nos scire? the answer must doubtless be self consciousness inasmuch as the terms are identical. But we have enquired for something more and higher than this self consciousness, which supposes reflection and reflection an act antecedent thereto.[36]

He describes what this 'something more and higher' is like. 'Without the primary act or unity of apperception,' he says, 'we could have nothing to be conscious of. Without the repetition or re-presentation of this act in the understanding completes the consciousness we should be conscious of nothing.'[37] Then in a key passage which commits him for the moment to the open advocacy of the priority of the subjective which he avoids in *Biographia Literaria*, Coleridge characterizes the activity of the unconscious mind as being synthetic – as opposed to analytic – 'Experience has shewn us that numerous acts of Perception or to use our own Logical terms, that the function of synthetic unity has been long at work and the products multiplied previously to the dawning of a distinct consciousness or reflection on the same.'[38]

In a letter written to Thomas Poole in 1801, Coleridge had edged tentatively towards identifying philosophy and religion. 'My opinion,' he writes, 'is this – that deep Thinking is attainable only by a man of deep Feeling, and that all Truth is a species of Revelation.'[39] A few years later, when he came to ponder on the existence and nature of the unconscious, Coleridge often observed that it has a peculiar and important connection with God. It becomes evident that he regards the unconscious as being in a special sense the gift of God, the raw stuff of the divine knowledge which God offers to those who strive to understand Him. In a letter written to Humphry Davy in 1809, Coleridge congratulates his scientific friend on having

... furnished to my Understanding & Conscience proofs more convincing, than the dim Analogies of natural organization to human Mechanism, both of the Supreme Reason as superessential to the World of the Senses; of an analogous Mind in Man not resulting from it's perishable Machine, nor even from the general Spirit of Life, it's inclosed steam or perfluent water-force; and of the moral connection between the finite and infinite Reason, and the aweful majesty of the former as both the Revelation and the exponent Voice of the Latter, immortal Time-piece [of] an eternal Sun.[40]

And in *Biographia Literaria* he mentions Plato's belief that 'ideas' are 'mysterious powers, living, seminal, formative, and exempt from time'.[41] He recognizes the mysterious quality of the unconscious himself, and supposes that it is significant. Describing man, for example, he terms him '. . . a being endowed with reason, with the moral sense, and with the strong yearnings, which, like all other powerful effects in nature, prophesy some future effect'.[42] Crabb Robinson reports him as speculating on the nature of these 'strong yearnings' or 'obscure ideas':

> . . . he digressed *à l'Allemagne* – on the distinction between obscure ideas and clear notions. Our notions resemble the index and hand of the dial; our feelings are the hidden springs which impel the machine, with this difference, that notions and feelings react on each other reciprocally. The veneration for the Supreme Being, sense of mysterious existence, not to be profaned by the intrusion of clear notions.[43]

The unconscious, then, was for Coleridge a region of the mind, half-sensed, half-understood, for which he had profound respect as a repository of fundamental if largely inaccessible power. He identified it with Revelation and the infinite mind of God.

He was not satisfied just to admit the existence of the unconscious; with him, to recognize a source of power was to investigate the possibilities of tapping it. Coleridge believed that some at least of the power was made available to man – that it was one of the modes of Revelation used by God. He writes to Cottle in 1814:

> The supreme Governor of the world, and the Father of our spirits, has seen fit to disclose to us much of his will, and the whole of his natural and moral perfections. In some instances he has given his *word* only, and demanded our *faith*; while

87

on other momentous subjects, instead of bestowing a full revelation, like the *Via Lactea*, he has furnished a glimpse only, through either the medium of inspiration, or by the exercise of those rational faculties with which he has endowed us.[44]

In this account not only the 'medium of inspiration' but also 'the exercise of . . . rational faculties' depends on the unconscious; as Coleridge wrote to Clarkson in 1806, 'Reason is . . . most eminently the Revelation of an immortal soul, and it's best Synonime – it is the forma formans, which contains in itself the law of it's own conceptions.'[45]

It was the reliance on the immortal soul, or the unconscious which is its manifestation, which, in 1819, Coleridge praised in the work of Sir Joshua Reynolds as a healthy reaction against the mechanism of the eighteenth century. He writes:

> . . . I am happy to see and feel that men are craving for a better diet than the wretched trash they have been fed with for the last century; that they will be taught that what is sound must come out of themselves, and that they cannot find good with their eyes or with their ears or with their hands, that they will not discover them in the crucible or bring them out of a machine, but must look into the living soul which God has made His image, in order to learn, even in fragments, what that power is by which we are to execute the delegated power entrusted to us by Him.[46]

This is the presupposition which underlies Coleridge's insistence on the precedence of the 'interior of the mind' as a hunting-ground for philosophy. 'Know thyself' has taken on the additional meaning 'Know God in thyself'. His early predisposition to guide his beliefs by his ideas and not by his senses emerges in the new dignity of a religious context.

III

Once the special role of the unconscious in the attainment of knowledge is understood as part of the human attempt to know God, it is easier to see what Coleridge meant by dividing 'the Logos, or communicative Intelligence' into the three modes, the 'Natural, Human, and Divine'.[47] Revelation may be thought of in Coleridge's scheme as Revelation of God in nature, as Revelation through the unconscious, or in its traditional sense as Revelation recorded in the New Testament. Coleridge's published writings qualify and derogate the first of these, and they urge and expound the third: but it is with the second, Revelation through the unconscious, that he seems to have been most deeply concerned during the period which we are considering.

The Statesman's Manual (1816) was Coleridge's first extended study of the traditional Revelation. Despite its abstruse appendices, it was intended as a practical rather than a theoretical book; Coleridge meant to study the matter in more abstract terms. In a letter written to Daniel Stuart in 1814, he promised to consider it in his '. . . ὁ Λόγος ὁ θεάνθρωπος (the divine Logos incarnate) a full Commentary on the Gospel of St. John. . . .'[48] This commentary was never completed; it would, one feels, have demanded a more sustained exhibition of learning than Coleridge was ever able to display. One can only gather hints of the direction of his thoughts about the problem.

Coleridge accepts the Gospels as being inspired by God. He was enough of a Biblical scholar to have opinions about the authenticity, provenance, and relative importance of different parts of the New Testament,[49] but the bulk of his attention is devoted to the implications of Scripture and it is on implications that one supposes his commentary on St. John would have concentrated. He makes, for example, an interesting distinction between two sorts of Christian Revelation:

> . . . the distinction between the objective and general revelation, by which the whole Church is walled around and kept together (*principium totalitatis et cohæsionis*), and the subjective revelation, the light from the life (*John* i. 4.), by which the individual believers, each according to the grace given, grow in faith. For the former, the Apostles' Creed, in its present form, is more than enough; for the latter, it might be truly said in the words of the fourth Gospel, that all the books which the world could contain, would not suffice to set forth explicitly that mystery in which all treasures of knowledge are hidden, *reconduntur*.[50]

He considers the Bible as contributing to both kinds of Revelation, providing source material for the 'subjective revelation'. A rhapsodic passage in *The Statesman's Manual* connects this notion with a term by now familiar to us, 'O what a mine of undiscovered treasures,' he writes, 'what a new world of Power and Truth would the Bible promise to our future meditation, if in some gracious moment one solitary text of all its inspired contents should but dawn upon us in the pure untroubled brightness of an IDEA. . . .'[51]

It is apparent that it is the Gospel as a preserve of inspired implications which appeals most to Coleridge, although he admits the validity of it as a record of what we must believe even if we do not fully understand. But the Bible as implication does not seem to be the most powerful source for Coleridge personally. As Professor Coburn has noticed, '. . . Coleridge's return to orthodox Christianity is through the Logos, not the Gospels, a metaphysical rather than a historical approach.'[52] To rephrase the same judgement, Coleridge's return is through a Logos other than 'the divine Logos incarnate'. Coleridge's most pressing concern is to affirm the superiority of the Human mode of the Communicative Intelligence, or of the unconscious, over the Natural mode; and it is the relative claims of these two forms of Revelation which bear ultimately on his critical theory.

In the early nineteenth century, Revelation in the traditional sense was still recognized as the authoritative witness of the mind of God, and hence, to the devout, the best source of knowledge. Coleridge observed that the mechanistic philosophers of the eighteenth century whose views had, he believed, gained an alarming currency, were in effect trying to supplement this course of knowledge by the systematic scrutiny of nature.[53] This practice is the context of Coleridge's discussion.

The basis of Coleridge's attack on the Natural as a form of the Communicative Intelligence is similar to the ground of his rejection of the relation of Theory – observation, he maintains, is too incomplete, the terms of nature are for all practical purposes inexhaustible. As he mentions in a letter to Sir George Beaumont in 1808, some had gone so far as to test the teachings of traditional religion against their own limited study of nature. He refers to '. . . prudential understanding, which employing it's mole Eyes in an impossible calculation of Consequences perverts and mutilates its own Being, untenanting the function which it is incapable of occupying'. He adds:

> This is Infidelity, essential Infidelity, however goodly it's Garb, however seemly it's name – and this I have long deemed the Disease, nay, let me speak out – the *Guilt* of the Age – therefore, and not *chiefly* because it has produced a spirit of enquiry into the external evidences of instituted Religion, it is an Infidel age.[54]

Coleridge makes the same charge in the *Treatise on Method*:

> The world has suffered much, in modern times, from a sub-version of the natural and necessary order of Science: from elevating the terrestrial, as it has been called, above the celestial; and from summoning Reason and Faith to the bar of that limited Physical experience, to which, by the true laws of Method, they owe no obedience.[55]

Physical laws – of memory, of vision, of vegetation, of crystal-lization (to use Coleridge's own examples)[56] – depend for their validity on the accuracy of the observation of nature on which they are based. These Ideas of 'natural existence' differ from Ideas of 'essential property', 'Physical Ideas' differ from 'Metaphysical Ideas', and because of the difference cannot be accepted as evidence of them.

The limitation of the Natural mode does not make it useless. Coleridge recognizes that it plays a part in helping us to understand the Revelations of God; what he refuses to con-template (presumably because we are imperfect observers) is the suggestion that our observation of nature is in any way a criterion of the truth of Revelation. This refusal is the ground of his objection to Hooker's suggestion that certainty based on sense impressions is greater than certainty based on 'the word of God'. Coleridge counters in a marginal note: '. . . God refers to our sensible experience to aid our will by the vividness of sensible impressions, and also to aid our understanding of the truths revealed – not to increase the conviction of their certainty where they have been understood.'[57] Elsewhere

Coleridge declares that '. . . all revelation is and must be *ab intra*; the external *phœnomena* can only awake, recal [*sic*] evidence, but never reveal.'[58] Given the assumption that Revelation is true, nature can be an aid in our efforts to understand what the Revelation means, how it is true.

The Natural mode is subsidiary but not non-existent in Coleridge's account of the Communicative Intelligence. He dwells on the limitations because he thinks that they are being forgotten by his contemporaries. His criticism of reliance on sense impressions of nature as a basis for either philosophy or theology is not the retreat into woolly obscurantism or mysticism that it is sometimes taken for; rather it is the scepticism of a thinker who believed that his mechanistic predecessors had been over-optimistic, and who was convinced that the way to knowledge was more difficult than they had suspected.

The theories advanced in Coleridge's essays on Method about the way in which the Communicative Intelligence can operate fall into the category he has called 'Human'. Revelation in the traditional sense, the Divine mode, may be set aside for the moment as being knowledge of God which we already have even if we do not understand it completely. With it we may place the opinions which have lasted through many generations, which, although they are of a lower order, deserve careful study if not uncritical acceptance as being the fruits of the Human kind of Communicative Intelligence stored up in the past. The Natural mode too may be set aside, not because of its essential inadequacy, but because of our inability to comprehend or indeed contemplate it fully – it would, as we have seen, be adequate for God.[59] The essays on Method are an attempt to describe and analyse the Human mode which he was putting forward as the best hope for substantial advance in our knowledge; and it is, I think, this part of his philosophy which we must understand if we are to fix the relationship of Coleridge's philosophy and literary criticism more exactly.

The Human mode of the Communicative Intelligence may be thought of as a series of links which together connect God and man, or absolute knowledge with mortal attempts to construct a philosophy. The first link is the unconscious, the repository of divine knowledge in the mind of man. In his *Aids to Reflection* (1825), Coleridge says that he has undertaken to defend the position that '. . . the CHRISTIAN FAITH (*in which I include every article of belief and doctrine professed by the first Reformers in common*) IS THE PERFECTION OF HUMAN INTELLIGENCE'.[60] We have already seen that Method based on the relation of Law is Coleridge's notion of 'the perfection of human intelligence', and that this Method depends on Ideas drawn from the interior of the intellect. Coleridge links the inward powers with redemption:

> O! may these precious words be written on my heart! 1. That we all need to be redeemed, and that therefore we are all in captivity to an evil: – 2. That there is a Redeemer: – 3. That the redemption relatively to each individual captive is, if not effected under certain conditions, yet manifestable as far as is fitting for the soul by certain signs and consequents: – and 4. That these signs are in myself; that the conditions under which the redemption offered to all men is promised to the individual, are fulfilled in myself. . . .[61]

Of *John*, iii. 8, 'The wind bloweth where it listeth,' he asks, 'Now if this does not express a visitation of the mind by a somewhat not in the own power or fore-thought of the mind itself, what are words meant for?'[62] He refers again to his favourite Gospel when defining 'Faith' (*John*, i. 9):

> Faith, that is, fidelity – the fealty of the finite will and understanding to the reason, *the light that lighteth every man that cometh into the world*, as one with, and representative of, the absolute will, and to the ideas or truths of the pure reason, the supersensuous truths, which in relation to the finite will, and as meant to determine the will, are moral laws, the voice and dictates of the conscience. . . .[63]

These are some of the implications of the unconscious in Coleridge's theology, and it is through them that his philosophy and theology are united. It is evident that he has identified not only absolute knowledge with God's knowledge, but also our efforts to attain something of absolute knowledge with Revelation.

In his *Philosophical Lectures*, Coleridge describes the mind of man:

> . . . we find him gifted, as it were, with a threefold mind: the one belonging to him specifically, arising I mean, necessarily, out of the peculiar mechanism of his nature and by WHICH he beholds all things perspectively from his relative position as man; the second, in which these views are again modified – too often disturbed and falsified – by his particular constitution and position, as this or that particular individual; and the third, which exists in all men *potentially* and in its germ, though it requires both effort from within and auspicious circumstances from without to evolve it into effect – by this third and higher power he places himself on the same point as Nature, and contemplates all objects, himself included, in their permanent and universal being and relations.[64]

And he mentions this valuable but elusive third in *Biographia Literaria*, when he refers to '. . . a *philosophic* . . . *consciousness*, which lies beneath or (as it were) *behind* the spontaneous consciousness natural to all reflecting beings. . . '.[65] For the philosopher, and, as we shall see, for the poet, it was essential that a means be found to make use of such latent power.

IV

Having recognized the special validity of the unconscious as a source of knowledge, Coleridge is faced with the question of finding out how such knowledge might best be put to use. In the *Treatise on Method*, he remarks upon a tendency evident in the thoughts of children: 'In the infancy of the Human Mind all our ideas are instincts; and Language is happily contrived to lead us from the vague to the distinct, from the imperfect to the full and finished form. . . .'[66] He is anxious to understand and refine upon this process. He is reported on the same theme in a lecture given in 1811 as having said:

> . . . nature had gifted us with a large portion of knowledge which might be called the rude stock which we were to work

upon; and our intellectual life was passed not so much in acquiring new facts, as in acquiring a distinct consciousness, – in making a mere gift of nature, as it were, our own, so that it was no longer a something which we now had and now was lost, but continuing with our thoughts, a regular series of cause and effect, it becomes, in the truest sense, our own – the possession of the present, and the dowry of our future nature.[67]

This acquisition of a 'distinct consciousness' was the aim of the philosophy expounded in *Biographia Literaria*. Coleridge speaks there of 'A system, the first principle of which it is to render the mind intuitive of the *spiritual* in man (i.e. of that which lies *on the other side* of our natural consciousness). . . .'[68] And he goes on to assert that, 'On the IMMEDIATE, which dwells in every man, and on the original intuition, or absolute affirmation of it, (which is likewise in every man, but does not in every man rise into consciousness) all the *certainty* of our knowledge depends. . . .'[69] We have noticed that Coleridge regarded the unconscious as a medium of divine Revelation, and that he believed that philosophy should be founded on the Inner Sense it provides. In *The Statesman's Manual*, he differentiates relevantly between Religion and Reason, calling the former, '. . . the EXECUTIVE of our nature, and on this account the name of highest dignity, and the symbol of sovereignty', and the latter, 'the LEGISLATIVE'.[70] Coleridge's account of Method asserts the executive function of the unconscious and attempts to determine the principles of legislating. Having considered the theological implications of the unconscious we are in a better position to appreciate the force of his assertion.

Reason and Religion are linked in Coleridge's discussion in a way that Understanding and Religion are not; and Reason as we have learnt underlies Method based on the relations of Law, while Understanding is the foundation of the less satisfactory Method based on the relations of Theory. The universality of the one is implied by the analogy of the unconscious with the mind of God; the limitation of the other is prescribed by the impossibility of achieving an observation of nature which is complete. 'Reason and Religion,' Coleridge maintains, '. . . differ only as a two-fold application of the same power.'[71]

95

Hence it is that he is bent on achieving the kind of philosophy he describes as being based on the relation of Law and seizes on the position 'I Am', the expression of self-consciousness, as the only possible ground for an absolute chain of argument.

Only by the acquisition of a distinct consciousness can man make fit use of the faculties he has received from God. 'Man alone,' says Coleridge, in the course of his 1811–12 series of lectures on Shakespeare and Milton, 'has been privileged to clothe himself, and to do all things so as to make him, as it were, a secondary creator of himself, and of his own happiness or misery: in this, as in all, the image of the Deity is impressed upon him.'[72] The appropriate exploitation of the God-given powers of the unconscious is the avenue of communication between God and the few men sufficiently 'cultivated' to benefit from them. As he remarks in the same lecture series:

> Man, in a secondary sense, may be looked upon in part as his own creator, for by the improvement of the faculties bestowed upon him by God, he not only enlarges them, but may be said to bring new ones into existence. The Almighty has thus condescended to communicate to man, in a high state of moral cultivation, a portion of his own great attributes.[73]

Coleridge makes it clear that not all people can expect to have access to the unconscious in so controlled a manner and with such profit. In *Biographia Literaria* he states that

> The best part of human language, properly so called, is derived from reflection on the acts of the mind itself. It is formed by a voluntary appropriation of fixed symbols to internal acts, to processes and results of imagination, the greater part of which have no place in the consciousness of uneducated man. . . .[74]

It is the duty of the philosopher, then, to appropriate fixed symbols to internal acts; the philosophical discussion of the relative priorities of Subjective and Objective thought, the ten theses in *Biographia Literaria,* and the essays on Method, are Coleridge's efforts to fulfil this duty. His absolute philosophy is to be founded on an act of faith, on a mysterious truth which can be felt to be indisputable, but which is beyond proof. This is the conviction which he expresses in *The Friend*, albeit with a sidelong glance at the authority of Aristotle:

> . . . we prefaced our inquiry into the *Science* of Method with a principle deeper than science, more certain than demonstration. For that the *very* ground, saith Aristotle, is groundless or self-grounded, is an identical proposition. From the indemonstrable flows the sap, that circulates through every branch and spray of the demonstration. To this principle we referred the choice of the final object, the control over time – or, to comprize all in one, the METHOD of the will. From this we started (or rather seemed to start: for it still moved before us as an invisible guardian and guide), and it is this whose re-appearance announces the conclusion of our circuit, and welcomes us at our goal.[75]

It is the snake with its tail in its mouth which Coleridge liked to imagine. As we shall see in the following chapter, there is a poetical counterpart to his account of philosophy.

5

The Method of Poetry – Theory

Coleridge's claim that there were principles involved in poetic composition was orthodox enough. But if the particular principles he advanced as the foundations of his philosophy seemed strange to his English contemporaries, the same applied to the fine arts must have struck them as little short of astonishing. Critical theory usually lags behind philosophy; Coleridge resolutely combined the two.

Henry Crabb Robinson describes one of the lectures which Coleridge gave in 1808. 'I came in late one day,' he writes, 'and found him in the midst of a deduction of the origin of the fine arts from the necessities of our being, which a friend who accompanied me could make neither head nor tail of, because he had not studied German metaphysics.'[1] Nine years later, Christopher North indignantly voiced the frustration he had felt on reading *Biographia Literaria* by accusing Coleridge of being unnecessarily difficult. According to his complaint, '. . . while [Coleridge] darkens what was dark before into tenfold obscurity, he so treats the most ordinary commonplaces as to give them the air of mysteries. . . .'[2] Coleridge made claims for originality, and it must be admitted that he used unfamiliar terms and offered explanations that were not sufficiently complete to make his meaning clear. It is not surprising that his contemporaries were puzzled and sceptical. We are more fortunate in having access to the fuller explanations which they were denied. By taking Crabb Robinson's hint, we are in a better position to understand what Coleridge was trying to say.

Not enough attention has been devoted to Coleridge's argument that poetry, like philosophy, is a way of trying to plumb the depths of the Communicative Intelligence. The old assertion that a poet is a prophet and that he is possessed of the

98

'divine fire' has, of course, been noticed as a popular tenet of the Romantic period. The regret for the loss of childlike innocence, the 'Fallings from us, vanishings', is sufficiently familiar.[3] But such thinking is given an individual and specific twist by Coleridge which deserves special consideration. In isolation his statements look like the verbally impressive commonplaces Christopher North took them for; combined with the philosophical speculations they reveal a more interesting and precise meaning.

Coleridge asserted in *The Watchman* in 1796 that 'imagination' was provided by 'Providence' as a means to human betterment. '. . . Providence,' he wrote, 'which has distinguished Man from the lower orders of Being by the progressiveness of his nature, forbids him to be contented. It has given us the restless faculty of *Imagination*.'[4] The same thought is elaborated later in a fragment on the education of children:

In the imagination of man exist the seeds of all moral and scientific improvement; chemistry was first alchemy, and out of astrology sprang astronomy. In the childhood of those sciences the imagination opened a way, and furnished materials, on which the ratiocinative powers in a maturer state operated with success. The imagination is the distinguishing characteristic of man as a progressive being; and I repeat that it ought to be carefully guided and strengthened as the indispensable means and instrument of continued amelioration and refinement.[5]

Imagination in this comprehensive sense seems to include the faculty of arriving at the initiatives of philosophic Method as well as the faculty normally associated with Poetry. As I have already suggested, philosophy and poetry are ultimately united in Coleridge's thinking, and it is interesting to see here his transference of a term which he was later to popularize in a more limited sense.

Coleridge carries over the idea of Imagination as a means of human improvement into his discussion of poetry. Poetry, it turns out, is for him a means of attaining to possibilities inherent in the notion of a Communicative Intelligence. In one of his lectures on Shakespeare, he compares it to religion. 'The grandest point of resemblance between them,' he says, 'is, that both have for their object . . . the perfecting, and the pointing out to us the indefinite improvement of our nature, and fixing our attention upon that. They bid us, while we are sitting in the dark at our little fire, look at the mountain-tops. . . .'[6] The similarity of this statement to the passage in the *Biographia* about 'the first range of hills' scarcely needs to be pointed out. Referring again to the religious properties and ultimate objectives of poetry, Coleridge draws the analogy of the astronomer:

> I have heard it said that an undevout astronomer is mad. In the strict sense of the word, every being capable of understanding must be mad, who remains, as it were, fixed in the ground on which he treads – who, gifted with the divine faculties of indefinite hope and fear, born with them, yet settles his faith upon that, in which neither hope nor fear has any proper field for display. Much more truly, however, might it be said that, an undevout poet is mad. . . .[7]

The poet resembles the astronomer evidently in having the grounds of faith available to him. For the poet to ignore them would be even more culpable than for the astronomer to do so, because whereas the astronomer's grounds are external, the poet's are inward, possessions of the mind.

Coleridge had lamented that Method based on the relation of Law was limited in its accounts of things by the lack of the diagrammatic means of communication available to geometry. Poetry, he finds, provides a substitute of sorts – an indirect expression of the instinct which is expressed in philosophy by Ideas. Speaking of the combination of dissimilitude and similitude which makes up imitation, he writes:

> We take the purest parts and combine them with our own minds, with our own hopes, with our own inward yearnings after perfection, and, being frail and imperfect, we wish to have a shadow, a sort of prophetic existence present to us, which tells us what we are not, but yet, blending in us much that we are, promises great things of what we may be.[8]

More explicitly Coleridge makes the same point in a letter written in 1815:

> Doubtless, to *his* eye, which alone comprehends all Past and all Future in one eternal Present, what to our short sight appears strait is but a part of the great Cycle – just as the calm Sea to us *appears* level, tho' it be indeed only a part of a *globe*. Now what the Globe is in Geography, *miniaturing* in order to *manifest* the Truth, such is a Poem to that Image of God, which we were created into, and which still seeks that Unity, or Revelation of the *One* in and by the *Many*. . . .[9]

In some way poetry is capable of transmitting and dramatizing something of the Communicative Intelligence. Its ultimate object is similar to the ultimate object of philosophy, but its means are different. Writing to Sotheby in 1802, Coleridge had hinted at the difference when he asserted that '. . . a great Poet must be, implicitè if not explicitè, a profound Metaphysician. He may not have it in logical coherence, in his Brain & Tongue; but he must have it by *Tact*. . . .'[10] Coleridge, then, claims for poetry the high office we have seen him claim for philosophy – that of seeking to convey Revelation. He devotes a large part of his literary criticism to describing the mental processes involved and to distinguishing them on the one hand from those based on the relation of Law, and on the other from those based on the relation of Theory.

I

In the course of his study of Method, Coleridge considers the Method of the Fine Arts at some length. He had, he informs us, been brought up on the idea that poetry had a logic of its own.[11] He maintains in the *Treatise on Method*, that 'Those who tread the enchanted ground of POETRY, oftentimes do not even suspect that there is such a thing as *Method* to guide their steps.'[12] Coleridge claims that poetic Method is similar in kind to the Methods we have already seen him expound: '. . . we under-take to show,' he says, 'that it not only has a necessary existence, but the strictest Philosophical application; and that it is founded on the very Philosophy which has furnished us with the Principles already laid down.'[13] At the conclusion of a brief discussion of Shakespeare he puts the case even more uncompromisingly:

> Let it not after this be said that Poetry – and under the word Poetry we will now take leave to include all the Works of the higher Imagination, whether operating by measured sound, or by the harmonies of form and colour, or by words, the more immediate and universal representatives of Thought – is not strictly Methodical; nay, does not owe its whole charm, and all its beauty, and all its power, to the Philosophical Principles of Method.[14]

Now that we have studied the theological thinking that lies behind the Coleridgean presentation of Method, and have noticed the parallel usefulness of philosophy and poetry in Coleridge's estimation as a means of getting at the Communicative Intelligence, this claim will seem less odd than it might otherwise have done.[15]

Coleridge enlarges on this theme. We have already considered his definition of the Methods, based on the relations of Law and Theory. 'Between these two,' he tells us, 'lies the Method of the FINE ARTS. . . .'[16] At this point it will be helpful to recall the definitions given earlier of these two forms of Method. Method based on the relations of Law is a progression of necessary consequents unified by an initiative derived from the interior of the intellect. Method based on relations of Theory is, by contrast, a progression unified by an initiative drawn from the observation of nature. In the mind of God, according to Coleridge, the two are reconciled; similarly, if to a lesser degree, the two are reconciled in the activity of the poet. The reconciliation is a ticklish point, for although the poet's Method partakes of both the relation of Law and the relation of Theory, the role played by each determines the kind and validity of the poetry.

The fine arts are evidently dependent on the observation of nature in a way that the philosophy derived from contemplation of the relation of Law is not: '. . . Method in the FINE ARTS . . . belongs . . . to this second or external relation, because the effect and position of the parts is always more or less influenced by the knowledge and experience of their previous qualities. . . .'[17] Yet at the same time poetry is dependent on initiatives derived from within the poet, and while it uses the materials provided by observation it is not ultimately determined by them. Coleridge goes on to say that the necessary reliance on nature constitutes '. . . a link connecting the second form of relation with the first. For in all, that truly merits the name of *Poetry* in its most comprehensive sense, there is a necessary predominance of the Ideas (i.e. of that which originates in the artist himself) and a comparative indifference of the materials.'[18]

He seems to be introducing a criterion of poetry when he argues for the 'necessary predominance of the Ideas', the dominance of the relation of Law, in poetry considered in 'its most comprehensive sense'. The source of the initiative is the deciding factor. In true poetry, the source of the initiative distinguishes the Method of the Fine Arts from the Method based on the relation of Theory: '. . . it has escaped some Critics, that in the Fine Arts the Mental initiative must necessarily proceed from within'.[19] Although in other respects the material of poetry resembles that of the applied sciences (the environment we observe around us), the Ideas must come from within the poet. According to Coleridge:

> . . . the Fine Arts belong to the outward world, for they all operate by the images of sight and sound, and other sensible impressions; and without a delicate tact for these, no man ever was, or could be, either a Musician or a Poet; nor could he attain to excellence in any one of these Arts; but as certainly he must always be a poor and unsuccessful cultivator of the Arts if he is not impelled first by a mighty, inward power, a feeling *quod nequeo monstrare, et sentio tantum*; nor can he make great advances in his Art, if, in the course of his progress, the obscure impulse does not gradually become a bright, and clear, and living Idea![20]

On so difficult a question it is not surprising that Coleridge should find words inadequate to express his meaning. But although he is imprecise, he has carried his discussion far enough in terms of the more clearly drawn Methods of Law and Theory for us to understand his general drift.

Having expressed scepticism about the human capacity for constructing a philosophy based on the relation of Law (and hence of the practicableness of the relation of Law), Coleridge wants to show the practical possibilities of poetry. That he considers it to possess a higher dignity than applied science, or the observation of nature, is plain. At the same time he recognizes that observation of nature provides poetry with the materials necessary for communication. Poetry is not, however, identical with Method based on the relation of Law, for although its initiatives are similarly derived (from the interior of the mind, or from the unconscious), it does not exhibit the same chain of reasoning based on an initiative. The effect of this elusive combination of the two kinds of philosophic Method is the nearest approach we can manage to the reconciliation of them we postulate in God. In *Biographia Literaria*, Coleridge invokes the analogy of geometry with poetry:

> Paradoxical as it may sound, one of the essential properties of Geometry is not less essential to dramatic excellence; and Aristotle has accordingly required of the poet an involution of the universal in the individual. The chief differences are, that in Geometry it is the universal truth, which is uppermost in the consciousness; in poetry the individual form, in which the truth is clothed.[21]

The essential property in question is that the initiative come from within; the difference consists in the two ways of treating the initiative.

Coleridge gives us a better glimpse of what he is getting at in the course of one of his lectures on Shakespeare: '. . . throughout his plays,' he says, 'but especially in those of the highest order, it is plain that the personages were drawn rather from meditation than from observation, or to speak correctly, more from observation, the child of meditation'.[22] The observation he is referring to is the observation of those hints of the unconscious which constitute Ideas. He goes on to differentiate between the two kinds of observation:

It is comparatively easy for a man to go about the world, as if with a pocket-book in his hand, carefully noting down what he sees and hears: by practice he acquires considerable facility in representing what he has observed, himself frequently unconscious of its worth, or its bearings. This is entirely different from the observation of a mind, which, having formed a theory and a system upon its own nature, remarks all things that are examples of its truth, confirming it in that truth, and, above all, enabling it to convey the truths of philosophy, as mere effects derived from, what we may call, the outward watchings of life.[23]

Nature is to be used in art to confirm Ideas, not to generate them.

There is an evident similarity here to the contrast between the Human and Natural modes of attaining to something of the Communicative Intelligence which we considered in the last chapter. For poetry, as for philosophy, the human unconscious and not nature is put forward as the true source of knowledge. The same objection to observation of nature (that it is too fragmentary to be supposed true) may be assumed to hold. The Ideas of the unconscious are confirmed by nature; like Revelation of God, they may be made more adequately comprehensible by observation, but they cannot be replaced by it. To quote again Coleridge's comment on Hooker: '. . . God refers to our sensible experience to aid our will by the vividness of sensible impressions, and also to aid our understanding of the truths revealed – not to increase the conviction of their certainty where they have been understood.'[24] The same may be said of Coleridge's poet.[25]

II

While it is useful for Coleridge to place poetry in his hierarchy of Methods and to characterize in this general way the combination of Methods which he takes to be requisite to the best kind of poetry, it will clearly be more interesting to find out the specific characteristics of the poetic process. It is here that Coleridge's strength as a critic is generally said to lie. But just as his well-known advocacy of criticism based on principles is predicated on abstract theories about philosophical Method which must be understood if we are to appreciate the principled criticism adequately, so his account of the poetic process benefits from being placed within the context of the philosophical speculations which we have been considering.

In his discussion of the Method appropriate to philosophy, as we have noticed, Coleridge spends some time in trying to describe the mental process involved in getting at the Ideas necessary to philosophy which lie below the consciousness. In *Biographia Literaria*, there is mention of 'A system, the first principle of which it is to render the mind intuitive of the *spiritual* in man (i.e. of that which lies *on the other side* of our natural consciousness). . . .'[26] Coleridge sets himself the task of trying to describe how the mind works in that creative phase of its activity which produced the Ideas he thought essential to the progression of poetry. He tries to impose some degree of conscious order on what he regarded as a semi-conscious activity.

In the *Treatise on Method*, Coleridge describes the state of mind conducive to the progression of philosophical Method. It holds, he maintains, '. . . a due mean between a passiveness under external impression, and an excessive activity of mere reflection; and the progress itself follows the path of the Idea from which it sets out; requiring, however, a constant wakefulness of Mind, to keep it within the due limits of its course.'[27] In his account of the Method of poetry, he goes farther and considers the state of mind involved in acquiring the Idea needed to unify such progressions; '. . . in many instances,' he affirms, 'the predominance of some mighty Passion takes the place of the guiding Thought, and the result presents the method of Nature, rather than the habit of the Individual.'[28] This is an important statement, combining as it does the Romantic notion of the excitement of the poetic mind with the philosophical account of thinking which he has been expounding.

Coleridge had long held that the poetic process involved an unusual state of mind – probably because he found that it did in his own case. In a letter written to Sotheby in 1802, for example, he had adopted this explanation: 'In my opinion every phrase, every metaphor, every personification, should have it's justifying cause in some *passion* either of the Poet's mind, or of the Characters described by the poet – But *metre itself* implies a *passion*, i.e. a state of excitement . . . in the Poet's mind. . . .'[29] By the time of his 1811–12 lecture series, the emphasis of Coleridge's account has shifted slightly to the control of a series of thoughts by this unusual state of mind, and to the assertion that it is a state of mind that cannot be acquired by discipline alone. He refers to

> That gift of true Imagination, that capability of reducing a multitude into unity of effect, or by strong passion to modify series of thoughts into one predominant thought or feeling – those were faculties which might be cultivated and improved, but could not be acquired. Only such a man as possessed them deserved the title of *poeta* who *nascitur non fit* – he was that child of Nature, and not the creature of his own efforts.[30]

In the same lecture series Coleridge remarks that 'In poetry it is the blending of passion with order that constitutes perfection. . . .'[31] By the time he came to write *Biographia Literaria*, the development of his ideas about Method had made it indispensable for him to emphasize the uncontrolled aspect of the mind in a state of passion. He contrasts it with the state productive of the 'rhetorical caprices' he finds in Cowley's Pindaric Odes, which, he feels, imply '. . . a leisure and self-possession both of thought and of feeling, incompatible with the steady fervour of a mind possessed and filled with the grandeur of its subject'.[32] Yet while he regards this activity of mind as being only semi-conscious, he believes it to be an activity consciously cultivated by the poet. In a familiar passage on 'The poet, described in *ideal* perfection,' he refers to 'This power, first put in action by the will and understanding, and retained under their irremissive, though gentle and unnoticed, controul (*laxis effertur habenis*). . . .'[33] He does not explain what this state of mind is like, although he may have said enough about it to enable anyone who has experienced it to understand what he means. It appears to be an important facet of the Human mode of transmission of the Communicative Intelligence. If it could be adequately explained, poetry would cease to be necessary to Coleridge's scheme of things. But it cannot be, and it remains a mysterious gift of God providing us with a means to Revelation, something to be used but not fully understood.

Coleridge's attempt to describe the elements which are unified by the poet's passion, and to assess the results of the union, is more satisfactory, dealing as it does with the faculties of the mind as far as his philosophy had carried their analysis and with poems themselves. It will, however, be immediately apparent that he runs a risk in trying to give an account both of causes and effects, because while in terms of early nineteenth-century philosophy his division of mental faculties may be accepted as definitions (arguable of course, but nevertheless the terms of the discussion), his statements about the relative values of the poems which he believes are the result of one faculty rather than another, and which he offers merely as as illustrations, depend very largely on his own individual preference. Coleridge is aware of the danger, and the account given in *Biographia Literaria* of the formation of his taste is intended at least partly as a remedy. But he does not always qualify his evaluations when he makes them; indeed he often seems to assume a universality for them which many readers will be unwilling to accept. It is important therefore that we should bear in mind that his illustrations are only illustrations. The fact that they sometimes illustrate something for us which differs from what they illustrate for Coleridge should lead us to seek illustrations which might suit both him and us, and not to reject the analysis of poetic faculties being illustrated. It is, I think, an invitation to misunderstanding to dwell, for example, on his recurring distinction between the verse of Milton and Cowley as representative of Imagination and Fancy respectively, and then to distinguish between the two poets ourselves in order to find out what Coleridge meant by Imagination and Fancy. Coleridge's principal aim was to analyse the poetic process, not to provide a convenient cata-logue of writers as representatives of one kind of poetry or another. If his examples are to be useful it will be necessary for us to exercise forbearance and to display a modicum of historical sympathy when faced with judgements which strike us as being wrongheaded.

Coleridge distinguishes between Primary and Secondary Imagination and Fancy, and the terms of the distinctions are those of the metaphysical formulations which we have discussed in earlier chapters. The existence of the mind of God is again taken for granted, as is the reconciliation, characteristic of that mind, of the relation of Law and the relation of Theory. Assumed too is the belief that God's is a Communicative Intelligence, and that this Intelligence may be thought of as being revealed by the Divine, Human or Natural modes. We have seen that of the two last, Coleridge believes that only the Human is reliable and in any way adequate, and that he thinks it resides in the exercise of the unconscious; the Natural mode can at best clarify the Ideas furnished by the Human. To ignore scriptural Revelation for the moment (and when Coleridge is discussing poetry he is content to lay this mode aside) one might describe the relationship of man to God as a triangle of which God is the apex, with a base extending between two of his creations, Man (or the Subject) and Nature (or the Object). The mind of God is inherent in both the Subject and the Object, but Coleridge is denying the possibility that interplay between them can be productive of Revelation. We have noticed, however, that the Method of the Fine Arts is in fact an interplay between Subject and Object which is capable of dramatizing the Revelation of the Subject. The distinction between Imagination and Fancy is a partial analysis of his interplay, and it expands Coleridge's assertion that while the Method of the Fine Arts is dependent on the relation of theory, its initiative must come from within.[34]

III

Coleridge's distinction between Imagination and Fancy in the thirteenth chapter of *Biographia Literaria* is his most detailed attempt to define the problem of probing the unconscious for the initiatives necessary to the Method of poetry. It is constantly quoted in a casual way in critical discussions, and it is the most exhaustively studied passage in all Coleridge's criticism. The distinction is phrased metaphorically, and it has long appeared to invite explication. The fact that analyses continue to be made, in spite of the attention lavished on it, is evidence of a sort that the results have not yet been entirely satisfactory. Some have suggested that the fault lies with the distinction itself; one is inclined to suggest that we do not yet understand the underlying philosophy well enough to be sure. Now that we have made an attempt to display the kind of thinking with which Coleridge was preoccupied, it may be possible to carry our interpretation of his terms a step farther. One of the most interesting effects will be, I believe, to restore Fancy to the dignity and power with which Coleridge originally endowed it – to present it once again as an integral part of great poetry, and to reject the too common misconception of it as a faculty appropriate to inferior verse only.

It will be helpful to have the distinction between Imagination and Fancy before us:

> The IMAGINATION ... I consider either as primary, or secondary. The primary IMAGINATION I hold to be the living Power and prime Agent of all human Perception, and as a repetition in the finite mind of the eternal act of creation in the infinite I AM. The secondary I consider as an echo of the former, co-existing with the conscious will, yet still as identical with the primary in the *kind* of its agency, and differing only in *degree*, and in the *mode* of its operation. It dissolves, diffuses, dissipates, in order to re-create; or where this process is rendered impossible yet still at all events it struggles to idealize and to unify. It is essentially *vital*, even as all objects (*as* objects) are essentially fixed and dead.
>
> FANCY, on the contrary, has no other counters to play with, but fixities and definites. The Fancy is indeed no other than a mode of Memory emancipated from the order of time and space; and blended with, and modified by that empirical phenomenon of the will, which we express by the word CHOICE. But equally with the ordinary memory it must receive all its materials ready made from the law of association.[35]

The prevailing explanation of these terms is the account given by Shawcross in the introduction of his edition of *Biographia Literaria*. Shawcross uses Schelling's *Transcendentalen Idealismus* as the key to Coleridge's discussion,[36] exaggerating, in my estimation, the extent to which Coleridge was passively reliant on the German philosopher when the *Biographia* was composed. He concludes from his comparison that the Primary Imagination is '. . . the imagination as universally active in consciousness (creative in that it externalizes the world of objects by opposing it to the self)', and that Secondary Imagination is '. . . the same faculty in a heightened power as creative in a poetic sense'.[37] According to this view, Primary Imagination is the consciousness shared by all men, while Secondary Imagination is limited to poets who can project the unity they discern in their consciousness upon the particulars of their environment. Fancy, for Shawcross, is '. . . the faculty of mere images or impressions, as imagination is the faculty of intuitions'.[38] He states that Coleridge sees in the opposition of Imagination and Fancy '. . . an emblem of the wider contrast between the mechanical philosophy and the dynamic, the false and the true'.[39]

Shawcross's interpretation marked a significant advance in the study of Coleridge's criticism; there can be no doubt that it was the most profound and exhaustive analysis that had been made. But Shawcross knew his subject much too well to feel entirely satisfied with his explanation. He observes that the distinction between imagination and Fancy understood in these terms hardly measures up to the ' "deduction" of the imagination' that Coleridge had promised.[40] He proposes, therefore, noting that Coleridge was not altogether committed to Schelling's theory, that the abrupt interruption of the argument in Chapter XIII, and the 'unsatisfactory vagueness of the final summary', may be attributed to the position's being Schelling's and not Coleridge's.[41]

Subsequent students have tended to accept the broad outlines of Shawcross's account and have devoted their attention to elaborating it or to developing its implications. I. A. Richards, for example, has made a courageous and remarkably successful effort to construct a viable critical instrument out of it.[42] Others, feeling that the distinction, understood as Shawcross presents it, is inadequate, have argued that it was not the distinction of kind which Coleridge had thought it, but rather one of degree.[43] T. S. Eliot has ventured the opinion that '. . . the difference between imagination and fancy amounts in practice to no more than the difference between good and bad poetry. . . .'[44] There has been little fundamental opposition to Shawcross.

The first, and so far as I am aware, the only basic disagreement is voiced in Walter Jackson Bate's essay 'Coleridge on the Function of Art'.[45] Passing by the apparent similarities to Schelling he concentrates on the terms of the distinction themselves, and maintains that Shawcross's rendering of them is not consistent with Coleridge's known attitudes. He expresses dissatisfaction with the idea that Coleridge could have meant the poetic imagination to be nothing more than an 'echo' of our consciousness of our surroundings (Shawcross's definition of Primary Imagination), and says that Secondary Imagination is '. . . rather the highest exertion of the imagination that the "finite mind" has to offer; and in its scope . . . necessarily includes universals which lie beyond the restricted field of the "secondary" imagination'.[46] Bate, then, is arguing that Primary Imagination is something more than the consciousness common to us all. This, as I shall try to show, is a very workable objection. He goes on to suggest that Primary Imagination may be connected to 'direct awareness of reason', and that the term may refer to '. . . that aspect of the creative capacity which draws down the rational insight of the universal into an individualized form of response, thus repeating "the eternal act of creation" . . .'[47]

Bate's dissatisfaction with Shawcross's interpretation of Primary Imagination focuses upon a most unfortunate and confusing ambiguity in Coleridge's definition. The account begins: 'The primary IMAGINATION I hold to be the living Power and prime Agent of all human Perception. . . .' By 'Perception' reasonably enough, Coleridge has been taken to mean sense perception. Bate, as we have seen, suggests that he means instead 'direct awareness of reason'.[48] This is, even for Coleridge, an unusual usage,[49] but it does occur in 1825 in *Aids to Reflection* with reference to perception of the unconscious. He remarks there that '. . . the lowest depth that the light of our Consciousness can visit even with a doubtful Glimmering, is still at an unknown distance from the Ground. . . . Conception is consequent on Perception. What we cannot *imagine*, we cannot, in the proper sense of the word, conceive.'[50] It seems possible at least that Coleridge is using the term 'perception' in this sense in his definition of Primary Imagination. It is worth adding that Coleridge does not in fact identify Primary

Imagination with perception; it is rather 'the living Power and prime Agent of all human Perception' – that is to say, it is in some way a condition on which the act of perception depends.[51]

Having gone so far with the orthodox interpretation of the distinction, and having noticed an important criticism of it, it is time to step back for a moment in order to get a longer view. Chapter XIII, entitled 'On the imagination, or esemplastic power', was apparently conceived of as a lengthy philosophical treatise. In the interposed letter it is said to be so long that it '... *cannot, when it is printed, amount to so little as an hundred pages....*'[52] It is not surprising that the 'main result' of such a chapter, presented without its preamble, should prove obscure. Shawcross, as we have noticed, called in the aid of Schelling; another useful approach is to enlist the help of Coleridge himself, by drawing on his metaphysics as we have reconstructed them.

A very helpful gloss, which encourages this approach, appears written in Coleridge's hand on the endpapers of a volume of Tennemann's *Geschichte der Philosophie*. It suggests an interpretation of Imagination markedly different from the ones we have been examining. The note runs as follows:

The simplest yet practically sufficient order of the mental Powers is, beginning from the

lowest	highest
Sense	Reason
Fancy	Imagination
Understanding	Understanding

Understanding	Understanding
Imagination	Fancy
Reason	Sense

Fancy and Imagination are Oscillations, *this* connecting R and U; *that* connecting Sense and Understanding.[53]

Here we have a chart of the correct disposition of Imagination between Subject and Object, Man and Nature, or, as they are termed in this instance, Reason and Sense. Imagination, it will be noted, is far removed from Sense. But in this list, Imagination is not distinguished into Primary Imagination and Secondary

Imagination, and one is faced with the question of where they could be fitted if the distinction were made. If one accepts Shawcross's explanation, or Bate's, it is an awkward problem – to be circumvented, perhaps, by the suggestion that Coleridge was not thinking in the same terms when he drew up the chart. Before rejecting the chart, however, we are well advised to ponder the meaning of the three new terms which it introduces – Reason, Understanding, and Sense – and to see whether they are relevant to the definitions of Chapter XIII.

Coleridge discusses Reason and Understanding and their relation to Sense in *The Statesman's Manual* and in the fifth essay of the third volume of the 1818 *Friend*. His treatment of Reason is difficult to follow, because he generalizes the term so as to include two similar and yet different faculties. 'I should have no objection,' he says, 'to define Reason with Jacobi, and with his friend Hemsterhuis, as an organ bearing the same relation to spiritual objects, the Universal, the Eternal, and the Necessary, as the eye bears to material and contingent phænomena.'[54] That is to say, Reason is the organ (or faculty) through whose agency we are permitted to perceive 'the Universal'. Coleridge immediately qualifies this statement: 'But then it must be added, that it is an organ identical with its appropriate objects. Thus, God, the Soul, eternal Truth, &c. are the objects of Reason; but they are themselves *reason*. We name God the Supreme Reason; and Milton says, "Whence the Soul *Reason* receives, and Reason is her Being".'[55] Reason, then, means both the Absolute and the faculty which permits us to look at the Absolute. It is in the latter sense that Coleridge is using the term when he concludes that 'Whatever is conscious *Self*-knowledge is Reason. . . .'[56] He adds, '. . . in this sense it may be safely defined the organ of the Supersensuous. . . .'[57] The same distinction is made in *The Statesman's Manual*, where Coleridge speaks of:

> The REASON, (not the abstract reason, not the reason as the mere *organ* of science, or as the faculty of scientific principles and schemes a priori; but reason) as the integral *spirit* of the regenerated man, reason substantiated and vital, '. . . the breath of the power of God, and a pure influence from the glory of the Almighty. . . .'[58]

We have, then, Reason itself, and the same word to mean the organ of Reason – another regrettable ambiguity.

In Chapter XIII, as in the manuscript chart, Coleridge is, I believe, referring to both senses of the word 'Reason' and giving them different names. In *Biographia Literaria*, Primary Imagination is Reason itself, while Secondary Imagination is the organ of Reason; in the chart, Reason is Reason itself, while Imagination is the organ of Reason. This interpretation of Coleridge's definition of Imagination varies sharply from the interpretations offered by Shawcross and Bate; it will, therefore, be necessary to display at some length the grounds for accepting it. What I am suggesting, to revert to the diagrammatic aid of the chart, may be represented as follows:

lowest	highest
Sense	Reason (Primary Imagination)
Fancy	organ of Reason (Secondary Imagination)
Understanding	Understanding

Understanding	Understanding
organ of Reason (Secondary Imagination)	Fancy
Reason (Primary Imagination)	Sense

Such an interpretation does not affect our general understanding of Coleridge's thought in any radical way, but it does alter the meaning of the distinction between Imagination and Fancy very considerably. It hinges essentially on a different account of the relation of Primary and Secondary Imagination to the unconscious and to physical phenomena.

We have already mentioned the sense in which Reason is taken by Coleridge to mean '. . . God, the Soul, eternal Truth, &c. . . .'[59] So understood it is identical with the unconscious repository of divine knowledge, or Revelation, which we have shown to be the medium for the Human mode of the Communicative Intelligence. Coleridge calls Primary Imagination, '. . . a repetition in the finite mind of the eternal act of creation in the infinite I AM'.[60] The description recalls a similar one in a letter written to Humphry Davy in 1809, in which Coleridge mentions '. . . the moral connection between the finite and infinite Reason, and the aweful majesty of the former as both the Revelation and the exponent Voice of the Latter, immortal Time-piece [of] an eternal Sun'.[61] Here we have a triple division: infinite Reason (God); and finite Reason, both as Reason itself (in man) and as the organ of Reason. In his definition of Primary Imagination, Coleridge makes no allusion to the transmission of the 'repetition in the finite mind', nor does he say that Primary Imagination is conscious. It is, in fact, 'the IMMEDIATE, which dwells in every man . . . ,' and '. . . the original intuition, or absolute affirmation of it (which is likewise in every man, but does not in every man rise into consciousness) . . .'[62] Primary Imagination may be taken as the literary term for the unconscious, and for an unconscious which has the characteristic traces of the Communicative Intelligence which Coleridge has ascribed to it.[63]

In *Biographia Literaria* Coleridge forgoes discussion of the unconscious as '. . . something, which must lie beyond the possibility of our knowledge . . .' and as of no concern to us as 'transcendental philosophers'.[64] In his 'Treatise on Logic', however, he speculates about it, and supposes it to be the result of a 'primary mental act' with the property of 'synthetic unity'.[65] He then considers the relationship between this primary act and consciousness. He begins by asserting that 'Without the primary act or unity of apperception we could have nothing to be conscious of.' He adds that 'Without the repetition or representation of this act in the understanding completes the consciousness we should be conscious of nothing.' Here the will evidently plays a part. Coleridge concludes by saying that

It will appear . . . on a moment[']s self-examination that a mere repetition of this act, a mere representation of the product of the act, could in no respect differ from the former in kind[,] at least more than the second echo from the former or a secondary Rainbow, from the principal arch; something more must take place in order to constitute it a repetition by the Understanding and this something, is the act of reflection.[66]

The 'mere repetition of this act, a mere representation of the product of the act' is very much like the definition of Secondary Imagination: 'The secondary I consider as an echo of the former, co-existing with the conscious will, yet still as identical with the primary in the *kind* of its agency. . . .'[67] Secondary Imagination is somewhere between Understanding in its full sense and the unconscious; it is not completely under the control of the mind, but it does 'co-exist' with 'the conscious will'. It is the power referred to simply as 'imagination' in Chapter XIV of the *Biographia*, as being '. . . first put in action by the will and understanding, and retained under their irremissive, though gentle and unnoticed, controul (*laxis effertur habenis*). . . .'[68]

Secondary Imagination is the faculty of mind involved in the difficult and mysterious activity of attaining the Ideas necessary to the Method of the Fine Arts; its activity is Passion. Elsewhere Coleridge calls it 'imagination' merely, and his differentiation between it and Primary Imagination in Chapter XIII seems calculated to make its kinship with the Communicative Intelligence, its source in the unconscious, explicit. The most important point about the definition is that it excludes the possibility that the material world can contribute to the Secondary Imagination – except, perhaps, in so far as it may affect the unconscious.[69] Coleridge's assertion that 'It dissolves, diffuses, dissipates, in order to recreate; or where this process is rendered impossible, yet still, at all events, it struggles to idealize and to unify,' refers to the process of deriving the 'Mental initiative' which in the Fine Arts '. . . must necessarily proceed from within . . . ,'[70] the process by which 'the obscure impulse' becomes 'a bright, and clear, and living Idea!'[71] Secondary Imagination is the faculty used to exploit the God-given resources hidden in the unconscious interior of the human mind.

In terms of Coleridge's chart, beginning with 'the highest', we have now moved from Reason (Primary Imagination) through Imagination (Secondary Imagination). The next term to be considered is Understanding. Understanding is variously described by Coleridge, but he always seems to use it in the sense of the conscious regulation of knowledge – it is a means of control rather than a source of knowledge. As we have noticed, there are in Coleridge's view two kinds of knowledge – one derived from the unconscious, and the other from material phenomena. Understanding is the faculty which controls and regulates both kinds. That is probably why it appears twice on the chart, and the line drawn between its two appearances emphasizes the dichotomy of the sources of knowledge. Used consciously and intentionally, Understanding is the element of control necessary if the Secondary Imagination is to be put to good use.[72] It corresponds to the faculty involved in the progression of Method based on the relation of Law.

We have followed and explained the progress of the chart from Reason to Understanding. The line which Coleridge now draws to separate his terms into two halves implies a bar to our moving any farther in the same direction. Instead we must start again, this time at 'the lowest', and work our way up from Sense, through Fancy, to Understanding.

By Sense, Coleridge means the faculty which allows us to perceive our environment, and which makes us aware of material things. He is fully conscious, as we have observed in our preliminary discussion of his treatment of Method in the Fine Arts, of the important role played by the evidence of the senses in poetry. He has admitted that the Fine Arts '. . . all operate by the images of sight and sound, and other sensible impressions; and [that] without a delicate tact for these, no man ever was, or could be, either a Musician or a Poet; nor could he attain to excellence in any one of these Arts. . . .'[73] Coleridge's only restriction on the powers of Sense is that, unlike the powers of Reason, they cannot rightly be thought of as hints of the mind of God, and hence they are an unsatisfactory source of the initiatives of Method in the Fine Arts. They are the source material for Method based on the relation of Theory; they are the subject-matter of the Applied Sciences.

Sense cannot be converted into Fancy, the next term on the chart, by a completely controlled act of the mind, any more than Reason can be converted in a wholly conscious manner into Secondary Imagination. Fancy is a poetic faculty, only less promising than Imagination because it does not transmit Revelation.[74] 'Fancy,' Coleridge maintains, '. . . has no other counters to play with, but fixities and definites.' That is to say, it is derived from the objects which we observe around us. It is not, however, derived from them directly. Coleridge goes on to say that '. . . equally with the ordinary memory it must receive all its materials ready made from the law of association'. The law of association is discussed at considerable length in the *Biographia,* and Coleridge's treatment of it is a much more adequate preface to his description of Fancy than his abortive preamble to the definition of Imagination is for his description of that faculty. The burden of Coleridge's account is to question the theory, put forward by Hartley, that contemporaneity is the sole determinant of what is essentially an unconscious process.[75] Were there no limiting power, were the association entirely mechanical, Coleridge argues, the result would resemble delirium.[76]

In a telling section of Chapter VII, Coleridge demonstrates convincingly that the law of association is more complicated and devious in its operation than Hartley's account of it would allow. He offers his own 'true practical general law of association':

> . . . whatever makes certain parts of a total impression more vivid or distinct than the rest, will determine the mind to recall these in preference to others equally linked together by the common condition of contemporaneity, or (what I deem a more appropriate and philosophical term) of *continuity.* But the will itself by confining and intensifying the attention may arbitrarily give vividness or distinctness to any object whatsoever. . . .[77]

Fancy is the result of this kind of association. It is, Coleridge tells us, '. . . a mode of Memory emancipated from the order of time and space. . . .'[78] An important emancipation if we recall the words of Coleridge's original announcement of his overthrow of determinist philosophy in his letter to Poole of March 16th, 1801: '. . . I have . . . completely extricated the notions of Time, and Space; . . . [I] have overthrown the doctrine of Association, as taught by Hartley, and with it all the irreligious metaphysics of modern Infidels – especially, the doctrine of Necessity.'[79] Association is also, according to Coleridge, '. . . blended with, and modified by that empirical phænomenon of the will which we express by the word CHOICE'.

Fancy is based on a semi-conscious process of association, which in turn is predicated on the 'fixities and definites' of nature that are perceived by Sense; Fancy is 'modified', but not quite determined, by the will.[80]

The poet attains the images he needs from nature by means of Fancy; as a result he can convey the Ideas he has from God. This is the 'observation' of true poetry, and it is dependent on the indirect, half-understood, half-conscious, mental activity that is Association. If Method in the Fine Arts is the reconciliation of the Method based on the relation of Law and the Method based on the relation of Theory, with the former calling the tune, Fancy is the poetic faculty which transmits the relation of Theory. Such an interpretation not only fits the general pattern which we have found in Coleridge's thought, it also makes sense of Coleridge's characterization of a writer such as Spenser – whose work he admired – as fanciful.[81]

The final item on the chart is once more Understanding – this time the completely conscious control of the products of Fancy. It is that other manifestation of Understanding which Coleridge had described in 1806 in a letter to Clarkson as

> . . . that Faculty of the Soul which apprehends and retains the mere notices of Experience, as for instance that such an object has a triangular figure, that it is of such or such a magnitude, and of such and such a color, and consistency, with the anticipation of meeting the same under the same circumstances, in other words, all the mere φαινόμενα of our nature. . . .[82]

He describes it in similar terms in *The Statesman's Manual*, calling it '. . . the science of phænomena, and their subsumption under distinct kinds and sorts. . . . Its functions supply the rules and constitute the possibility of EXPERIENCE; but remain mere logical *forms*, except as far as *materials* are given by the senses or sensations.'[83]

The two Understandings are, of course, really only one faculty – 'wakefulness of mind'. Coleridge divides it in order to show that it may be applied to two quite different sorts of perception – the perception of the interior intellect, and the perception of external nature. Both kinds play a part in the poetic process, and they can be combined in the same poem. Given such an interpretation it is difficult to see how one could disagree with Coleridge's conviction that Imagination and Fancy are '. . . two distinct and widely different faculties, instead of being . . . either two names with one meaning, or at furthest, the lower and higher degree of one and the same power'.[84] The Method of poetry is the due reconciliation of the two, in which the Imagination must predominate. The concluding sentence of Chapter XIV of the *Biographia* seems to be a much more carefully weighed statement than one had realized: 'Finally, GOOD SENSE [Understanding] is the BODY of poetic genius, FANCY its DRAPERY, . . . and IMAGINATION the SOUL that is everywhere, and in each; and forms all into one graceful and intelligent whole'.[85]

6

The Method of Poetry – Practice

There is still debate about the extent to which Coleridge's critical practice reflects or depends upon his critical theories. It would be beyond the declared scope of this essay to enter into any comprehensive discussion of the problem, but one aspect of it is relevant and may shed some light on the rest by implication. As we have seen, Secondary Imagination is the central and dominant poetic faculty in Coleridge's theory of Method in the Fine Arts, and it is behind it that he marshals his metaphysics.[1] His views on the Secondary Imagination are reflected in his practical criticism of Shakespeare and Wordsworth, and in his study of the mental activity of audiences in theatres.

Shakespeare and Wordsworth represent for Coleridge respectively the ideal poet and the nearest contemporary approach to one. More of his criticism is devoted to these two writers than to all others put together, and the fact that he presents them as ideals suggests how far his theories about the nature of the ideal poetic process are pertinent. He made, of course, numerous passing comments on their works, as he did on the works of lesser men; but his prolonged discussions of them involve the full weight of his metaphysical speculations, and probably played some part in determining the direction of his abstract thought. Coleridge did not begin by postulating an ideal of poetry and then look around him for examples; his taste for Shakespeare and Wordsworth preceded his analysis. It might be argued that the ideals he proposes are really philosophical justifications of the conviction that theirs was the highest kind of art – a criticism that philosophical Idealism seems to invite. I do not propose to investigate the question of precedence here, however; it seems more useful to demonstrate how far the critiques of Shakespeare and Wordsworth, which are generally accepted as Coleridge's most successful ventures in the field of practical criticism, imply and depend upon the theoretical preoccupations which we have been considering. By doing so it is possible to reinterpret within the abstract context of Coleridge's metaphysics what seems at first merely to smack of a bardolatry born of a highly developed sense of psychological truth.

I

In discussing Coleridge's criticism of Shakespeare, I shall not try to consider its place in the history of Shakespearean criticism. The question of Coleridge's debts to some and anticipations of others has already been well aired, if not settled. For Coleridge to have maintained that Shakespeare, contrary to the opinion of some eighteenth-century commentators, did not lack art, does not, as has been pointed out, distinguish him from a number of his contemporaries – or from a few of his predecessors. And while we may approve the taste of a critic who so evidently admired Shakespeare's skill as much as we do ourselves, it would be presumptuous to argue that this coincidence of attitude of itself attests to the quality of his criticism. It seems better to see whether or not we can find out any more about what Coleridge meant by calling Shakespeare '. . . the greatest genius, that perhaps human nature has yet produced. . . .'[2] In the attempt, it will, I think, become apparent that Coleridge's criticism of Shakespeare is more directly related to his philosophy than has been noticed hitherto.[3]

Coleridge was particularly impressed by the characters of Shakespeare's plays. They appeared to him to convey an extraordinary sense of universality and truth, without at the same time revealing much of the personality of the dramatist himself. '. . . in Shakespeare,' he says, '. . . every form is true, everything has reality for its foundation; we can all recognize the truth. . . .'[4] And again, he exclaims: 'The wonder is how Shakespeare can thus disguise himself, and possess such miraculous powers of conveying what he means without betraying the poet, and without even producing the consciousness of him.'[5] Yet in spite of the truth of the characters he brings on to the stage and the pellucid anonymity of his creation, Shakespeare does not, according to Coleridge, rely upon observation of nature. His characters are in fact 'ideal realities',[6] and Coleridge goes so far as to assert that 'Shakspeare . . . studied mankind in the *Idea* of the human race; and [that] he followed out that Idea into all its varieties, by a *Method* which never failed to guide his steps aright.'[7]

In the *Treatise on Method*, Coleridge uses Shakespeare as his example when he is expounding Method in the Fine Arts. He was, of course, aware of the dramatic effect of employing an illustration so seemingly perverse,[8] but Shakespeare's procedure as he understands it turns out to be a very apt choice. It is apropos of Shakespeare that Coleridge makes the assertion quoted in the last chapter that poetry is 'strictly Methodical', and that it owes '. . . its whole charm, and all its beauty, and all its power, to the Philosophical Principles of Method'.[9] It is in Shakespeare that he finds his best example of a Poet who practises a Method between the Methods based on the relation of Law and the relation of Theory, deriving Ideas from the Primary Imagination by means of the Secondary, and using them as initiatives for the progression of phenomena.

Coleridge lays particular emphasis on the way in which Shakespeare relies on the interior of the intellect. He maintains that '. . . throughout his plays, but especially in those of the highest order, it is plain that the personages were drawn rather from meditation than from observation. . . .'[10] Method is again implied in the statement that Shakespeare '. . . worked in the spirit of nature, by evolving the germ within by the imaginative power according to an idea. . . .'[11] The terms, 'germ within' and 'imaginative power' are those of the Primary Imagination (or Reason) and Secondary Imagination. Secondary Imagination seems to be characteristic of Shakespeare's early plays. Coleridge argues that it, and not observation, provides material for the young playwright. He asks,

What was the *Love's Labour['s] Lost?* Was it the production of a person accustomed to stroll as a vagabond about the streets, or to hold horses at a playhouse door, and who had contented himself with making observations on human nature? No such thing! There is scarcely a trace of any observation of nature in Shakespeare's earliest works.[12]

Coleridge believes that the dominance of Imagination can lead to excess in a poet who has not learned to control the expression of his Ideas. He permits himself to censure mildly this lack of control in the young Shakespeare:

> In the earlier works of Shakespeare we have a profusion of double epithets, and sometimes even the coarsest terms are employed, if they convey a more vivid image; but by degrees the associations are connected with the image they are designed to impress, and the poet descends from the ideal into the real world so far as to conjoin both – to give a sphere of active operations to the ideal, and to elevate and refine the real.[13]

Evidently the Secondary Imagination alone will not make a poet, even if it is indispensable to a great one; the restraint of the Understanding is necessary too.

Coleridge suggests that the discipline of writing for the stage, with its demand for easy comprehensibility, was instrumental in compelling Shakespeare to control his imaginative gift. As he puts it, '. . . his images followed upon each other and if his genius had not guided him to the stage, Shakespeare would by them have been rendered a writer rather to be wondered at than admired.'[14] While Coleridge recognizes the potential vulnerability of Shakespeare's mind, he has no doubt that Shakespeare triumphs over it, and that he triumphs consciously. He considers him to have been a philosopher as well as a poet, a man of learning as well as a man of inspiration. 'His education,' he declared, 'was the combination of the poet and the philosopher – a rapid mind, impatient that the means of communication were so few and defective compared with what he possessed to be communicated,'[15] Again, '. . . like a great man, he first studied deeply, read and thoroughly understood every part of human nature, which he joined with his poetical feeling, till at length it gave him that wonderful power in which he had no equal. . . .'[16] The reconciliation of the poetical and philosophical impulses which Coleridge felt had not been completely achieved in the poems, he finds in the plays: 'In Shakspeare's *poems*, the creative power, and the intellectual energy wrestle as in a war embrace. Each in its excess of strength seems to threaten the extinction of the other. At length, in the DRAMA they were reconciled, and fought each with its shield before the breast of the other.'[17]

Although Ideas or initiatives from within, are, as we have learned, necessary and decisive in the Method of the Fine Arts, the material phenomena of nature are also required. As Coleridge had admitted, '. . . without a delicate tact for these, no man ever was, or could be, either a Musician or a Poet. . . .'[18] A means of combining the products of Reason with those of the Sense was essential to the success of even Shakespeare's genius. The warring Ideas of philosophic meditation and the poetic Imagination are reconciled by Shakespeare through the medium of nature. Coleridge describes him together with Plato; the 'necessary predominance of Ideas' does not make them 'regardless of the actual existences around them'.[19] He remarks in his essay 'On Poesy or Art' that '. . . art itself might be defined as of a middle quality between a thought and a thing, or . . . the union and reconciliation of that which is nature with that which is exclusively human. It is the figured language of thought. . . .'[20] Shakespeare's art is of just such a kind, providing him with a means of expressing the Ideas of his Imagination.

For Coleridge, this expression is manifested in the characters of the plays. He considers them as the embodiments of the Ideas, '. . . the individual form, in which the truth is clothed'.[21] Coleridge's evidence for this explanation is his conviction that although they speak and act differently from any particular real people with whom we may be familiar, Shakespeare's characters always convey a sense of appropriateness. Referring to one of Othello's speeches, he asks, '. . . where was Shakespeare to observe such language as this? If he did observe it, it was with the inward eye of meditation upon his own nature. . . .'[22] His famous criticism of the Nurse's character in *Romeo and Juliet* is devoted to showing that the sense of realism could not be the result of mere observation of an actual person:

The Nurse in 'Romeo and Juliet' has sometimes been compared to a portrait by Gerard Dow, in which every hair was so exquisitely painted, that it would bear the test of the microscope. Now, I appeal confidently to my hearers whether the closest observation of the manners of one or two old nurses would have enabled Shakespeare to draw this character of admirable generalisation? Surely not.[23]

Despite the interior source, Coleridge cannot find 'a single incongruous point'.[24] The truth of the characters must depend on the truth of Shakespeare's ideas and the skill which permits him to communicate them without distortion. We have here Coleridge's ideal example of a poet who conveys the products of his Primary Imagination through the medium of his Secondary Imagination and finally expresses them under the gentle control of the Understanding.

Coleridge is reported as saying of Shakespeare:

He was a child of nature, but it was of human nature and of the most important of human nature. In the meanest characters, it was still Shakespeare; it was not the mere Nurse in *Romeo and Juliet,* or the Dogberry in *Much Ado about Nothing,* or the blundering Constable in *Measure for Measure,* but it was this great and mighty being changing himself into the Nurse or the blundering Constable, that gave delight. . . . He [Coleridge] might compare it to Proteus, who now flowed, a river; now raged, a fire; now roared, a lion – he assumed all changes, but still in the stream, in the fire, in the beast, it was not only the resemblance, but it was the divinity that appeared in it, and assumed the character.[25]

The Protean aspect of Shakespeare's art had impressed Coleridge early on. In a letter to Sotheby in 1802 he had written:

It is easy to cloathe Imaginary Beings with our own Thoughts & Feelings; but to send ourselves out of ourselves, to *think* ourselves in to the Thoughts and Feelings of Beings in circumstances wholly & strangely different from our own/hoc labor, hoc opus/ and who has achieved it? Perhaps only Shakespere.[26]

To say that a poet can shrug off himself as an individual in his work, that it is a difficult thing to do, and that Shakespeare succeeds eminently, is only the beginning for Coleridge. His interest is caught by the need to examine what is involved in a creative process of this kind, and by the question of its peculiar effectiveness.

In a note, probably an early one, in his copy of Hartley's *Observations on Man*, Coleridge had speculated that '– Ideas may become as vivid & distinct if the feelings accompanying them is [*sic*] vivid, as original impressions – And this may finally make a man independent of his Senses – One use of poetry.'[27] The idea of poetry making one independent of the senses combines with the description of Shakespeare the chameleon poet as part of Coleridge's temperamental rejection of the accidental and the particular as determinants of art. As we noticed in the preceding chapter, this attitude is expressed in a more analytic form by the metaphysical structure with which Coleridge's aesthetic is so inextricably involved.

The statement that Shakespeare '. . . was a child of nature, but . . . of human nature and of the most important of human nature. In the meanest characters, it was still Shakespeare . . . ,'[28] has an air of wilful obscurantism about it. It can usefully be placed beside another:

> . . . a vast number of personages by the simple force of meditation: he had only to imitate certain parts of his own character, or to exaggerate such as existed in possibility, and they were at once true to nature, and fragments of the divine mind that drew them. Men who see the great luminary of our system through various optical instruments declare that it seems either square, triangular, or round, when in truth it is still the sun, unchanged in shape and proportion. So with the characters of our great poet: some may think them of one form, and some of another; but they are still nature, still Shakespeare, and the creatures of his meditation.[29]

Shakespeare is apparently able to derive characters from meditation on himself, and this meditation may also be said to be on nature. Such a view, equating Shakespeare with nature and yet not with nature, can make little sense outside the context of the God-Man-Nature triangle.

As we have noticed, Coleridge believed that nature was too multiform for us to be able to comprehend it adequately, and as a consequence not a source for us of 'truths of nature'. Hence the rejection of observation as an explanation of the 'true' characters in Shakespeare's plays. Only God was capable of comprehending the nature which he had created. But God, the Communicative Intelligence according to Coleridge, has allowed us the opportunity of glimpsing his mind by making the unconscious, or Primary Imagination, its repository. Some people, among whom Shakespeare may be taken as an ideal example, are enabled by the high development of their Secondary Imagination to take advantage of this source of wisdom. The characters of Shakespeare's plays thus display a truth higher than truth to life, as it is usually understood, because Shakespeare has been able to reject the appearances with which many artists are satisfied and to enjoy a direct, if imperfect, apprehension of the reality of God.[30]

In so far as Shakespeare conveys the absolute truths of the Primary Imagination by way of the 'ideal realities' of the characters in his plays, he may, in Coleridge's view, be thought of as a vehicle for the Communicative Intelligence. This way of thinking about the matter makes more specific sense of the following statement about the dramatist:

Self-sustained, deriving his genius immediately from heaven, independent of all earthly or national influence. That such a mind involved itself in a human form is a problem indeed which my feeble powers may witness with admiration, but cannot explain. . . . Least of all poets, antient or modern, does Shakespear appear to be coloured or affected by the age in which he lived – he was of all times and countries.[31]

Coleridge is arguing that Shakespeare had access to knowledge to a degree unusual for human beings; the truths derived from that knowledge may more properly be thought of as the knowledge of the Primary Imagination latent in all men than as his own:

Shakespeare shaped his characters out of the nature within; but we cannot so safely say, out of *his own* nature, as an *individual person*. No! this latter is itself but a *natura naturata*, an effect, a product, not a *power*. It was Shakespeare's prerogative to have the *universal* which is potentially in each *particular*, opened out to him in the *homo generalis*, not as an abstraction of observation from a variety of men, but as the substance capable of endless modifications, of which his own personal existence was but one, and to use *this one* as the eye that beheld the other, and as the tongue that could convey the discovery.[32]

The source lends a special validity to the products of the Secondary Imagination. As Coleridge puts it, 'If Shakespeare be the wonder of the ignorant, he is, and ought to be, much more the wonder of the learned: not only from profundity of thought, but from his astonishing and intuitive knowledge of what man must be at all times, and under all circumstances, he is rather to be looked upon as a prophet than as a poet.'[33]

Coleridge notices that Shakespeare's characters not only seem to be true, but that they give the impression of being necessary. That is to say, we feel that such characters in such situations must have acted in the way he describes. Coleridge says of Dogberry that 'He is not the creature of the day, to disappear with the day, but the representative and abstract of truth which must ever be true, and of humour which must ever be humorous.'[34] His explanation of this phenomenon may be summed up in the assertion: 'There is not one of the plays of Shakespeare that is built upon anything but the best and surest foundation; the characters must be permanent – permanent while men continue men – because they stand upon what is absolutely necessary to our existence.'[35] Only the divinely inspired Primary Imagination could provide such a foundation; only the Secondary Imagination could attain it. This is why the Secondary Imagination is for him the mark of genius, without which poetry may be good, but never great.

II

Our discussion of the part played in poetry by the Secondary

Imagination has been carried out so far in terms of the poet and his relationship to the Communicative Intelligence. Coleridge was also interested in the question of the relation of the audience to the Communicative Intelligence. In an obvious sense, of course, the audience could be thought of as the recipients of the truths attained by poets, and indirectly, therefore, of the truths of God. But this sequence of transmission placed a greater barrier between the audience and the original source of truth than Coleridge was always able to allow. As a reader and playgoer, he noticed through introspection that even the recipient was capable of taking a more direct and active part. It appears that the action he considered appropriate to the minds of the audience has something in common with the acts of the Secondary Imagination usually thought of as being the domain of the artist alone.

In 'Satyrane's Letters', for example, Coleridge praises the classical tragedies of France for their effect on audiences:

> . . . they excite the minds of the spectators to active thought, to a striving after ideal excellence. The soul is not stupefied into mere sensations by a worthless sympathy with our own ordinary sufferings, or an empty curiosity for the surprising, undignified by the language or the situations which awe and delight the imagination.[36]

And he says of tragedians that 'Their tragic scenes were meant to affect us indeed, but within the bounds of pleasure, and in union with the activity both of our understanding and imagination.'[37] Supposing this to be the true aim of drama, Coleridge is naturally impatient with attempts to divert the audience's attention to the irrelevant claims of scenery. When he comes to consider Shakespeare's plays, he devotes much of his discussion to the difference between Elizabethan and contemporary demands on the minds of the audience; he is always firmly of the Elizabethan persuasion.[38]

At one point in his criticism of Shakespeare, Coleridge looks back with nostalgia to the active minds of the Elizabethans and comments on the fortunate circumstance that the 'absence of artificial extraneous inducements' from the sixteenth-century stage forced dramatists to rely on the imaginations of their audiences: '. . . all that was to excite the senses in a high degree was wanting. Shakespeare himself said, "We appeal to your imaginations; by your imagination you can conceive this round O to be a mighty field of monarchs. . . ." '[39] Instead of seeing deceiving representations of action, the Elizabethan spectators were offered only a token and invited to supply what was wanting by the activity of their own minds: '. . . description and narration supplied the place of visual exhibition. . . .'[40] Coleridge leaves no doubt that he considers the appeal to the faculties of the audience to be a higher form of art than the attempt to trick and beguile their senses. He may have over-estimated the difference between Shakespeare's audience and the audience of his own day, but his preference for the former serves at least to show what sort of audience he thought better. The following passage in a lecture given in 1811 suggests the reason for his preference:

> The great of that day, instead of surrounding themselves by the *chevaux de frise* of what is now called high breeding, endeavoured to distinguish themselves by attainments, by energy of thought, and consequent powers of mind. The stage, indeed, had nothing but curtains for its scenes, but this fact compelled the actor, as well as the author, to appeal to the imaginations, and not to the senses of the audience: thus was obtained a power over space and time. . . .[41]

It was a power which both the playwright and his audience conspired to produce.

Later in the same lecture Coleridge maintains that 'The power of poetry is, by a single word perhaps, to instil that energy into the mind, which compels the imagination to produce the picture.'[42] He enlarges on this explanation when he is considering Milton's description of Death in Book II of *Paradise Lost*:

> The grandest efforts of poetry are where the imagination is called forth, not to produce a distinct form, but a strong working of the mind, still offering what is still repelled, and again creating what is again rejected; the result being what

the poet wishes to impress, namely the substitution of a sublime feeling of the unimaginable for a mere image.[43]

Coleridge stresses both the presence of energy and the absence of a completely comprehensible resolution of it, and he speaks of '. . . a middle state of mind more strictly appropriate to the imagination than any other, when it is, as it were, hovering between images'. He adds that 'As soon as it is fixed on one image, it becomes understanding; but while it is unfixed and wavering between them, attaching itself permanently to none, it is imagination.'[44]

The dream state seems to have had special significance for Coleridge. In *The Friend* he makes the comment that '. . . in certain sorts of dreams the dullest Wight becomes a Shakespeare. . . .'[45] And while the dream which he describes as being analogous to the audience's state of mind during a play may be of a different sort, it suggests the possibilities inherent in semi-consciousness. Coleridge seems to have valued it for the freedom which it allows the Imagination. Plays which satisfied the senses only could not be expected to stimulate in the spectators the Ideas and Passions characteristic of the highest poetry; even the Imagination of the poet if transmitted under too restricting a control of the Understanding would, one gathers, have fallen short of the ideal stimulus of the audience. Clearly the art which demanded most from those who enjoyed it was highest in Coleridge's estimation.

All persons, he observed, were aware of the difference between our moral feelings, faculties, etc., being called forth and gratified when a soft piece of music by Cimarosa or Handel, or a fine picture by Raphael or Michael Angelo, are contemplated. In both instances the faculties are called forth, but, in one also a painful effort, unless the prospect of what we are to gain interfered and still urged us on. That which excites us to all the activity of which our nature is capable and yet demands no painful effort, and occasions no sense of effort – this is the state of mind . . . which admits the production of a highly favourable whole. . . .[46]

In a letter written to Daniel Stuart in 1816, Coleridge makes the interesting remark: 'The truth is, that Images and Thoughts possess a power in and of themselves, independent of that act of the Judgement or Understanding by which we affirm or deny the existence of a reality correspondent to them. Such is the ordinary state of the mind in Dreams.'[47] He embarks on one of his clearest descriptions of the nature of dramatic illusion. Pointing out that in dreams the power of comparison is lacking, he argues: 'It is not strictly accurate to say, that we believe our dreams to be actual while we are dreaming. We neither believe it or disbelieve it – with the will the comparing power is suspended, and without the comparing power any act of Judgement, whether affirmation or denial, is impossible.'[48] He mentions the connection between the dream condition and the condition which is dramatic illusion: 'Add to this a voluntary Lending of the Will to this suspension of one of it's own operations (i.e. that of comparison & consequent decision concerning the reality of any sensuous Impression) and you have the true Theory of Stage Illusion. . . .'[49] It is well known that Coleridge explained the nature of dramatic illusion in this way, but there has been little notice taken of the 'power in and of themselves' which he attributes to Images and Thoughts.

The terms in which Coleridge is speaking are so similar to those which he uses in his discussions of Imagination that it is only natural to wonder whether his conception of the mind of the audience is in fact analogous to his conception of the mind of the poet. Both activities evidently take place between the realm of Ideas, or the unconscious, and the realm of the Understanding. In each, the Understanding is used inasmuch as a decision is taken to suspend its operation. The 'willing suspension of disbelief' is analogous to part only of the poetic process, for while the poet relies for what is best in his poetry on the operation of the Secondary Imagination, he cannot transmit the results of that operation directly. Understanding is necessary to him, good sense, to enable him to transmit the results in such a way as to stimulate a similar state in the mind of a co-operating audience. When such a stimulus is successful, one can say, as Coleridge does with reference to Shakespeare's Sonnet XXXIII: 'You feel him to be a poet, inasmuch as, for a time, he has made you one – an active creative being.'[50]

That an audience will benefit from having its Imagination

stimulated can be gathered from Coleridge's discussion of the value of Imagination in the education of children; ultimately a moral value is involved. 'In the education of children,' according to Coleridge, 'love is first to be instilled, and out of love obedience is to be educed. Then impulse and power should be given to the intellect, and the ends of a moral being be exhibited.'[51] He goes on, using the sort of vocabulary which we have become used to, and emphasizing the permissive play of the mind:

For this object thus much is effected by works of imagination; – that they carry the mind out of self, and show the possible of the good and the great in the human character. The height, whatever it may be, of the imaginative standard will do no harm; we are commanded to imitate one who is inimitable. We should address ourselves to those faculties in a child's mind, which are first awakened by nature, and consequently first admit of cultivation, that is to say, the memory and the imagination. The comparing power, the judgment, is not at that age active, and ought not to be forcibly excited. . . .[52]

This plan for education seems to be precisely what Coleridge is recommending for audiences and readers as 'the willing suspension of disbelief'. Literature which does not stimulate the mind in this way is, in Coleridge's view, lacking in the most important potentiality of art.

In Coleridge's theory, the states of mind of poets, dreamers, children, and audiences, are similar in their highest moments; poets and audiences differ from dreamers and children in that they dream voluntarily.[53] In addition, this state of mind provides one with a special sort of access to truth. It will, perhaps, suffice to close by quoting Coleridge's comment on the text, 'Whosoever shall not receive the Kingdom of God as a little child, shall not enter therein.' He writes: 'Is it not evident that Christ here converted negatives into positives? As a babe is without malice negatively, so you must be positively and by actuation, that is, full of love and meekness; as the babe is unresisting, so must you be docile, and so on.'[54] Such is the conduct appropriate for the poet, and such the conduct he should induce in his audience.

III

It is not to be wondered at that Wordsworth was unenthusiastic about having his poetry publicly analysed by Coleridge. His reservations may have stemmed as much from the feeling that he was being embarrassingly singled out and compared to Shakespeare in an age when carefully weighed critiques tended to avoid discussion of contemporary authors, as from disagreement with Coleridge's views. It must have been a daunting prospect, even for an author as self-confident as Wordsworth, to know what sort of metaphysical apparatus and learning would inevitably be called into play. Coleridge seems to have been unaware of the diffidence which Wordsworth might have felt, and he was apparently incapable of making a shrewd estimate of the probable public reception of such a book. He seems to have been too preoccupied with the worth and justice of his cause, to say nothing of more material worries, to think much about such things.

Coleridge wished to convince the public that Wordsworth was not only a great poet, but a great poet in a particular sense. At the beginning of *Biographia Literaria* he declares his intentions:

> . . . of the objects, which I proposed to myself, it was not the least important to effect, as far as possible, a settlement of the long continued controversy concerning the true nature of poetic diction: and at the same time to define with the utmost impartiality the real *poetic* character of the poet by whose writings this controversy was first kindled, and has been since fuelled and fanned.[55]

The perceptiveness of the criticism of Wordsworth which appears in the *Biographia* was acknowledged from the first, and it is interesting to see how far the lines of Coleridge's discussion correspond to those of the sort of thinking we have been considering. There seems to be no doubt that Wordsworth, like Shakespeare, is for Coleridge a worthy exemplar of the Method

136

of the Fine Arts. Such adverse comment as he permits himself is calculated to undermine what Coleridge regards as Wordsworth's mistaken and potentially crippling poetic theories, and at the same time to direct the attention of readers away from the effects of these and towards his undeniable and more Methodical virtues. Once again, Secondary Imagination is the key presupposition of the discussion.

The nature of Coleridge's admiration of Wordsworth's poetry is displayed in a letter written to Richard Sharp in 1804. Coleridge writes that Wordsworth is

> . . . the only man who has effected a compleat and constant synthesis of Thought & Feeling and combined them with Poetic Forms, with the music of pleasurable passion and with Imagination or the *modifying* Power in that highest sense of the word in which I have ventured to oppose it to Fancy, or the *aggregating* power – in that sense in which it [Imagination] is a dim Analogue of Creation, not all that we can *believe* but all that we can *conceive* of creation.[56]

The terms used have not taken on the precision which they later gain, but Coleridge is clearly crediting Wordsworth with the faculty which he was later to call Secondary Imagination. In the *Biographia*, the evaluation is reiterated: '. . . I challenge for this poet,' he writes, 'the gift of IMAGINATION in the highest and strictest sense of the word.'[57] Coleridge goes on to say: '. . . if I should ever be fortunate enough to render my analysis of imagination, its origin and characters[,] thoroughly intelligible to the reader, he will scarcely open on a page of this poet's works without recognizing, more or less, the presence and the influences of this faculty.'[58]

There is a further similarity between Coleridges' Shakespeare and his Wordsworth – the intellectual depth which he regards as essential to great poetry. He hoped that Wordsworth might realize his great gifts in a unique literary achievement of a sort which must have been very close to his own heart. 'What Mr. Wordsworth *will* produce,' he says, 'it is not for me to prophecy; but I could pronounce with the liveliest convictions what he is capable of producing. It is the FIRST GENUINE PHILOSOPHIC POEM.'[59] With so much at stake, it is not surprising that

Coleridge should have been anxious to set Wordsworth straight on what seemed to him to be fundamental and damaging theoretical misconceptions – inappropriate though this public medium seems for advice.

Chapter XVI of *Biographia Literaria* substantiates the claim made in Wordsworth's preface to *Lyrical Ballads* that there was a need to reform an outmoded and by now artificial poetic diction. Coleridge's reservations stem from the nature of the reform proposed by Wordsworth, and he argues not only that it is based on a mistaken theory of poetry, but that it is belied by Wordsworth's own practice as a poet. He summarizes his objections:

> My own differences from certain supposed parts of Mr. Wordsworth's theory ground themselves on the assumption, that his words had been rightly interpreted, as purporting that the proper diction for poetry in general consists altogether in a language taken, with due exceptions, from the mouths of men in real life, a language which actually constitutes the natural conversation of men under the influence of natural feelings.[60]

He has an additional objection to the grounds for Wordsworth's choice of 'low and rustic life':

> *He* chose low and rustic life, 'because in that condition the essential passions of the heart find a better soil, in which they can attain their maturity, are less under restraint, and speak a plainer and more emphatic language; because in that condition of life our elementary feelings co-exist in a state of greater simplicity, and consequently may be more accurately contemplated, and more forcibly communicated; because the manners of rural life germinate from those elementary feelings; and from the necessary character of rural occupations are more easily comprehended, and are more durable; and lastly, because in that condition the passions of men are incorporated with the beautiful and permanent forms of nature.'[61]

Given Coleridge's philosophical presuppositions one could, I think, predict that he would find such a position unacceptable. And, in fact, the line of his attack, for all its appearance of growing common-sensically out of the points of disagreement themselves, seems to be predicated on his metaphysics and determined by them. To prove this would be to add another dimension to the relationship between the theoretical and practical sections of *Biographia Literaria*.

Coleridge's argument assumes the two positions which we have considered in connection with his discussion of Shakespeare and the mind of the audience. The first is that the poetic genius depends on Ideas and not on the facts of observation, however important it may be for a poet to observe nature well in order to trick out his ideas convincingly, or indeed to convey them at all. The second is that there is a special state of mind appropriate to the composition of poetry and to its adequate appreciation which can be induced but not commanded. When he turns to Wordsworth's poetry, Coleridge concentrates on the first position, and tries to show how on some occasions the poet falls beneath his usual imaginative level by allowing the facts of observation a dominant role.

It is irrelevant, from Coleridge's point of view, what the environment of a speaker may be. Aristocrat or peasant, city-dweller or countryman, no one has either the worth of his thought, nor, with some qualification, the dignity of his language enhanced by material conditions. Coleridge suggests that Wordsworth gets around his theoretical adoption of rustics by disguising characters of distinction as rustics even though their distinction cannot properly be attributed to rusticity. As he says,

> . . . the persons introduced are by no means taken *from low or rustic life* in the common acceptation of those words; and it is not less clear, that the sentiments and language, as far as they can be conceived to have been really transferred from the minds and conversation of such persons, are attributable to causes and circumstances not necessarily connected with 'their occupations and abode'.[62]

He adduces a number of instances of agrarian insensibility to prove the irrelevance of splendid rural surroundings. 'Education,' he maintains, 'or original sensibility, or both, must pre-exist, if the changes, forms, and incidents of nature are to prove a sufficient stimulant.'[63] To Wordsworth's claim that rustics '. . . hourly communicate with the best objects from which the best part of language is originally derived . . . ,' Coleridge replies:

> . . . a rustic's language, purified from all provincialism and grossness, and so far re-constructed as to be made consistent with the rules of grammar . . . will not differ from the language of any other man of common-sense, however learned or refined he may be, except as far as the notions, which the rustic has to convey, are fewer and more indiscriminate.[64]

He then adds, in terms which would seem perfectly in place in the *Treatise on Method*:

> . . . the rustic, from the more imperfect developement of his faculties, and from the lower state of their cultivation, aims almost solely to convey *insulated facts*, either those of his scanty experience or his traditional belief; while the educated man chiefly seeks to discover and express those *connections* of things, or those relative *bearings* of fact to fact, from which some more or less general law is deducible. For *facts* are valuable to a wise man, chiefly as they lead to the discovery of the indwelling *law*, which is the true *being* of things, the sole solution of their modes of existence, and in the knowledge of which consists our dignity and our power.[65]

The facts of observation, at best, can only achieve the Method of the Applied Sciences, based on the relation of Theory; and even then, it is not the facts themselves, but the acts of the mind upon them, which are to be esteemed.

The sort of language which Wordsworth is talking about is derived quite differently, according to Coleridge. 'The best part of human language, properly so called,' he says, 'is derived from reflection on the acts of the mind itself.'[66] And he describes their derivation in the familiar terminology of Method in the Fine Arts:

It is formed by a voluntary appropriation of fixed symbols to internal acts, to processes and results of imagination, the greater part of which have no place in the consciousness of uneducated man; though in civilized society, by imitation and passive remembrance of what they hear from their religious instructors and other superiors, the most uneducated share in the harvest which they neither sowed or reaped.[67]

We have here the notion of nature as the material used to clothe the Ideas of the mind. The state of mind of the rustic or un-cultivated man is portrayed by Coleridge in his *Treatise on Method*, when he describes the characterization of Mistress Quickly (except that Mistress Quickly is herself an idealization of what such a person *must* be, drawn from Shakespeare's mind and not from his observation).[68] It is described, again in terms of Method, at the opening of Chapter XVIII of the *Biographia*:

> . . . [the] order, in the intercourse of uneducated men, is distinguished from the diction of their superiors in know-ledge and power, by the greater *disjunction* and *separation* in the component parts of that, whatever it be, which they wish to communicate. There is a want of that prospectiveness of mind, that *surview*, which enables a man to foresee the whole of what he is to convey, appertaining to any one point; and by this means so to subordinate and arrange the different parts according to their relative importance, as to convey it at once, and as an organized whole.[69]

Coleridge is understandably disinclined to consider the diction of such rustics suitable for poetry, and he is convinced that Wordsworth is mistaken in supposing that he has really used it in his poems. He remarks: '. . . I reflect with delight, how little a mere theory, though of his own workmanship, interferes with the processes of genuine imagination in a man of true poetic genius, who possesses, as Mr. Wordsworth, if ever man did, most assuredly does possess, "THE VISION AND THE FACULTY DIVINE".'[70]

The second point with which Coleridge feels obliged to take issue is Wordsworth's contention that '*There neither is or can be any essential difference between the language of prose and metrical composition.*'[71] His opposition is based on his ideas about the state of mind which exists in the poet during composition and the state which should be induced in the reader or audience. Just as this state of mind differs from a normal state of mind, so the language appropriate to it will differ.

Coleridge begins by stating what he believes to have been the origin of metre:

> This I would trace to the balance in the mind effected by that spontaneous effort which strives to hold in check the workings of passion. It might be easily explained likewise in what manner this salutary antagonism is assisted by the very state, which it counteracts; and how this balance of antagonists became organized into *metre* (in the usual acceptation of that term) by a supervening act of the will and judgement, consciously and for the foreseen purpose of pleasure.[72]

This combination of the spontaneous and the voluntary closely resembles the activity of the faculties of Secondary Imagination and Understanding to which Coleridge attributes the greatest poetry. He describes each separately, calling them the 'two legitimate conditions, which the critic is entitled to expect in every metrical work'.[73] 'First,' he says, '. . . as the *elements* of metre owe their existence to a state of increased excitement, so the metre itself should be accompanied by the natural language of excitement.'[74] He is speaking of the excitement of the activity of the Secondary Imagination. 'Secondly,' he continues, '. . . as these elements are formed into metre *artificially*, by a *voluntary* act, with the design and for the purpose of blending *delight* with emotion, so the traces of present *volition* should throughout the metrical language be proportionally discernible.'[75] Here he is referring to the wholly conscious ordering of the faculty of the Understanding. The two must act together: '. . . these two conditions must be reconciled and co-present. There must be not only a partnership, but a union; an interpenetration of passion and of will, of *spontaneous* impulse and of *voluntary* purpose.'[76] As we have seen, these are the conditions of the Human mode of plumbing the Communicative Intelligence.

Coleridge has already urged that the state of mind in which

poetry is composed should be stimulated in the audience as well. He regards metre as one of the means of accomplishing this end. The effect is, he thinks, not wholly conscious. His description of this phenomenon concentrates on the stimulation of excitement in the audience, on the aspect of the mental activity of the audience which is related to the Secondary Imagination in the mind of the poet:

> As far as metre acts in and for itself, it tends to increase the vivacity and susceptibility both of the general feelings and of the attention. This effect it produces by the continued excitement of surprize, and by the quick reciprocations of curiosity still gratified and still re-excited, which are too slight indeed to be at any one moment objects of distinct consciousness, yet become considerable in their aggregate influence. As a medicated atmosphere, or as wine during animated conversation; they act powerfully, though themselves unnoticed.[77]

From the point of view of its effect, 'Metre . . . is simply a stimulant of the attention. . . .'[78]

Coleridge's final objection to Wordsworth's theory of metre is an extension of his argument that metre expresses something not wholly in the command of the consciousness; and he combines with it his objection to Wordsworth's theory of diction. He cites Wordsworth's comment that 'The distinction of rhyme and metre is voluntary and uniform, and not like that produced by (what is called) poetic diction, arbitrary and subject to infinite caprices, upon which no calculation whatever can be made.'[79] Coleridge finds a position between the exclusive alternatives of mental anarchy and tyranny. It is, he says, through the 'power of imagination' and through 'meditation' that

> . . . the poet [will] distinguish the degree and kind of the excitement produced by the very act of poetic composition. As intuitively will he know, what differences of style it at once inspires and justifies; what intermixture of conscious volition is natural to that state; and in what instances such figures and colors of speech degenerate into mere creatures of

an arbitrary purpose. . . . Could a rule be given from *without*, poetry would cease to be poetry, and sink into a mechanical art.[80]

Although Coleridge is willing to allow that Wordsworth's verse rises triumphantly above the limitations of his theory, he fears that the poet has not escaped totally unscathed. The adverse criticism in which he indulges turns on the difference of attitude implied by Wordsworth's occasional failure to trust the products of his own mind, and on his weakness for permitting phenomena to dominate Ideas instead of the reverse. Coleridge says, 'If his mistaken theory have at all influenced his poetic compositions, let the effects be pointed out, and the instances given.'[81] What he wants to ensure is that Wordsworth's merits, or even his main characteristics as a poet, are not taken to lie in those poems in which he exemplifies his mistaken theories:

> . . . it is high time to announce decisively and aloud, that the *supposed* characteristics of Mr. Wordsworth's poetry, whether admired or reprobated; whether they are simplicity or simpleness; faithful adherence to essential nature, or wilful selections from human nature of its meanest forms and under the least attractive associations; are as little the *real* characteristics of his poetry at large, as of his genius and the constitution of his mind.[82]

The last could scarcely be characteristics of the poet whom Coleridge hails as possessing 'THE VISION AND THE FACULTY DIVINE'.[83]

The two characteristic defects which Coleridge finds are an occasional incongruity of style and a quality which he apologetically calls 'matter-of-factness'. He does not dwell on the incongruity, doubtless feeling that his meaning will be clear enough to readers who have followed his treatment of Wordsworth's theory of poetic diction. He offers some examples from Wordsworth's poetry in which he finds that language 'which is only proper in prose' is unhappily juxtaposed with 'exquisite stanzas'.[84] Matter-of-factness however, he has only dealt with indirectly hitherto. He defines it:

144

This may be divided into, *first*, a laborious minuteness and fidelity in the representation of objects, and their positions, as they appeared to the poet himself; *secondly*, the insertion of accidental circumstances, in order to the full explanation of his living characters, their dispositions and actions. . . .[85]

These are two aspects of an over-emphasis on phenomena. The first is derived from the state of mind of the poet, and the second is derived from his misconception of the best state of mind of the audience.

Wordsworth's minute attention to natural description is classed by Coleridge as an excessive reliance on Fancy. Citing lines 50–73 of Book III of the *Excursion*, Coleridge maintains that 'Such descriptions too often occasion in the mind of a reader, who is determined to understand his author, a feeling of labor, not very dissimilar to that, with which he would construct a diagram, line by line, for a long geometrical proposition.'[86] He specifies the poetic faculties involved:

It seems to be like taking the pieces of a dissected map out of its box. We first look at one part, and then at another, then join and dove-tail them; and when the successive acts of attention have been completed, there is a retrogressive effort of mind to behold it as a whole. The Poet should paint to the imagination, not to the fancy; and I know no happier case to exemplify the distinction between these two faculties.[87]

It is not so much the diversity or unlikeness of objects that Coleridge is concerned about, although their diversity and unlikeness are consequents to be expected, but rather the fact that they are objects at all, and that they are allowed to predominate. Coleridge quotes from *Paradise Lost* to illustrate what he means by the painting to the imagination he prefers, and calls it '. . . *creation* rather than *painting*, or if painting, yet such, and with such co-presence of the whole picture flash'd at once upon the eye, as the sun paints in a camera obscura.'[88] The Imagination must, he insists, evidence a sense of the Ideal: '. . . the poet must . . . understand and command what Bacon calls the *vestigia communia* of the senses, the latency of all in each. . . .'[89] The awareness of essence, the unifying Idea from the interior of intellect, is more important than the manifold phenomena of any particular landscape.

Coleridge's objection to matter-of-factness in Wordsworth's choice of characters and incidents is similar. Whereas the poet should be guided by the Idea of his characters, and the characters should, by necessity, act in the way implied by the Idea, Wordsworth, in his anxiety to reform popular notions about particular classes of society, causes characters drawn from them to act in an unexpected way, and tries to justify their eccentricity by contriving explanatory circumstances. Quite apart from the fact that Coleridge regards Wordsworth's reforming purpose here to be alien to the first object of poetry – namely pleasure rather than truth – he objects to it on the grounds that it will disturb the 'willing suspension of disbelief' in the audience. When unusual characterizations are placed beside factually true description, Coleridge asserts:

> That *illusion*, contradistinguished from *delusion*, that *negative* faith, which simply permits the images presented to work by their own force, without either denial or affirmation of their real existence by the judgment, is rendered impossible by their immediate neighbourhood to words and facts of known and absolute truth.[90]

The collapse of illusion was fatal to the operation of the powers of Imagination so important to Coleridge's conception of the best mental activity of an audience.

Coleridge's careful criticism is the more poignant when one remembers how much he relied on his brother poet to achieve the sort of poem – a 'philosophic' poem – which he had felt incapable of himself. His sense of involvement in Wordsworth's enterprise is tellingly exhibited by a notebook entry of 1804: 'Mem. To write to the Recluse that he may insert something concerning *Ego*/its metaphysical Sublimity – & intimate Synthesis with the principle of Co-adunation – without *it* every where all things were a waste – nothing, &c –.'[91] The implications of the suggestion will by now be evident. It is with the same sense of personal concern that Coleridge's letter to Wordsworth expresses his disappointment with the *Excursion*.

He had hoped not only for an exemplification, but for an analysis as well, of his own philosophy:

> I supposed you first to have meditated the faculties of Man in the abstract, in their correspondence with his Sphere of action, and first, in the Feeling, Touch, and Taste, then in the Eye, & last in the Ear, to have laid a solid and immove- able foundation for the Edifice by removing the sandy Sophisms of Locke, and the Mechanic Dogmatists, and demonstrating that the Senses were living growths and developments of the Mind & Spirit in a much juster as well as higher sense, than the mind can be said to be formed by the Senses. . . .

He concludes with a summary of his expectations:

> In short, Facts elevated into Theory – Theory into Laws – & Laws into living & intelligent Powers – true Idealism necessarily perfecting itself in Realism, & Realism refining itself into Idealism.[92]

The two men had grown far apart since the days of the incep- tion of *Lyrical Ballads*.

Coleridge's discussion of Wordsworth's poetic theory, is more than the disagreement of one poet with another. There had, to be sure, been the characteristic division of labour in the composition of poems for *Lyrical Ballads*;[93] but the theory with which Coleridge took issue in *Biographia Literaria* was in part at least of his own making. In a letter to Southey of 1802, he gave the first notice of his reservations about it, but admitted that 'Wordsworth's Preface is half a child of my own Brain/& so arose out of Conversations, so frequent, that with few exceptions we could scarcely either of us perhaps positively say, which first started any particular Thought. . . .'[94] Years later, Wordsworth, by this time with a justifiable sense of impatience, confirmed Coleridge's claim, in a pencilled comment in Barron Field's manuscript biography of him, in which he says: 'I will mention that I never cared a straw about the theory – & the Preface was written at the request of Mr Coleridge out of sheer good nature.'[95]

It seems that under the pretence of correcting Wordsworth, Coleridge, doubtless unintentionally, was really attacking his own former views. The changes wrought by the intervening years did not involve a complete change of outlook or an escape from discarded opinion. Like the philosophers he admired, Coleridge had matured by coming to understand better the real meaning of the position from which he had originally started.

7

From Criticism to Theology

When Coleridge leaves the consideration of authors, audiences
and literary concepts for the study of the works themselves,
the influence of his philosophical thinking on his practical
criticism is just as marked. One is reminded once more of the
extent to which an awareness of the underlying intellectual
constructs alters his conclusions and adds to their meaning.
Perhaps the most telling proof of the real bias of Coleridge's
mind, however, is that he appears in the end almost to reverse
his priorities and to discuss literature largely as a means to
understanding and expounding philosophical and theological
problems.

It may have been as early as 1823 that he wrote the following
marginal note in his copy of Milton's *Poems on Several Occasions*:

> Of criticism we may perhaps say, that those divine poets,
> Homer, Eschylus, and the two compeers, Dante, Shake-
> speare, Spenser, Milton, who deserve to have Critics, κριταί,
> are placed above criticism in the vulgar sense, and move in
> the sphere of religion, while those who are not such scarcely
> deserve criticism in any sense.[1]

This is more than the presentation of an established canon of
great authors. It is the logical outcome of Coleridge's conviction
that literature is the vehicle of the Communicative Intelligence,
and a necessary consequence of his belief that poetry at its
best is the symbolic expression of Ideas. He became increasingly
committed to this point of view, and as he did so he drew
farther apart from contemporary English critics than ever. It
seems inevitable that his theological bent should finally have
led him to think of poetry as the handmaiden of religion; it was

149

less predictable that some of his best known critical exposition should be a by-product of the development of this attitude. A brief examination of Coleridge's progress from his character analysis of Hamlet and his interpretation of *Paradise Lost* to his study of Aeschylus's *Prometheus* suggests the direction in which his thought was moving and helps us to appreciate better the spirit in which he wrote literary criticism.

I

Coleridge set great store by his criticism of *Hamlet*. He was jealous of his claims to originality partly because he realized that he owed much of his critical reputation to his analysis of this character, and partly because it coincided so remarkably with his analysis of himself. He mentions the effect he felt his criticism of the play had had in gaining him his early reputation. '*Hamlet*,' he says, 'was the play, or rather Hamlet himself was the character in the intuition and exposition of which I first made my turn for philosophical criticism, and especially for insight into the genius of Shakespeare, *noticed*. . . .'[2] One has only to add his famous remark, 'I have a smack of Hamlet myself, if I may say so,'[3] to understand why he was so quick to resent charges of plagiarism or even of fortuitous anticipation.[4]

The analogy which he draws between himself and Hamlet extends well beyond their common irresolution and inactivity. If the prince emerges as a man with great weaknesses he is also allowed to have great though unrealized strengths; and Coleridge, however conscious he was of his own infirmities, was not above describing them in such a way as to suggest that they too were partly counterbalanced by related merits. Henry Crabb Robinson makes a shrewd comment on Coleridge's treatment of Hamlet's failings: 'I doubt whether he did not design that an application should be made to himself, and whether he is not well content to meet the censure his own remarks convey, for the sake of the reputation of those talents apparently depreciated. . . .'[5] The issues at stake were more than the mere pleasure of being acknowledged as an originator; Coleridge's Hamlet was so much a creature of his own brain that he could not bear to share the credit for him with even a German critic.

His identification of himself with Hamlet, then, delicately combines humility and pride. The phrase 'an archangel a little damaged', applied to him after his death by Lamb, would have pleased Coleridge as a description both of Hamlet and himself; he was steadily aware of the extent of the damage and felt obliged to reassure himself of the original archangel from time to time in his own notes. By identifying himself with Hamlet, however, he is able to identify himself with Shakespeare at one remove. In discussing the protean Elizabethan, Coleridge had had occasion to refer to his '. . . mode of conceiving characters out of his own intellectual and moral faculties, by conceiving any one intellectual or moral faculty in morbid excess and then placing himself, thus mutilated and diseased, under given circumstances'.[6] This was the technique he discerned in Hamlet; Hamlet was Shakespeare *manqué*. Accustomed as he was to the prospect of his own failure, Coleridge was willing to bear the brunt of the criticism implied by Hamlet's in order to claim kinship with his genius.

In the course of his discussion of the play Coleridge displays some of his basic assumptions about the aims of the author. True to his theory that Shakespeare was a combination of poet and philosopher, he ascribes to him the wish to embody thoughts in art, the wish to use his plays as a way of expressing a philosophical position. Hence it is that he opens his remarks in the twelfth lecture of his 1811–12 series by saying: 'The first question we should ask ourselves is – What did Shakespeare mean when he drew the character of Hamlet? He never wrote any thing without design, and what was his design when he sat down to produce this tragedy?'[7] He explains his premise by elaborating on this suggestion: 'My belief is, that he always regarded his story, before he began to write, much in the same light as a painter regards his canvas, before he begins to paint – as a mere vehicle for his thoughts – as the ground upon which he was to work.'[8] This account of Shakespeare's art as didactic is entirely in keeping with Coleridge's treatment of poetry as a medium for the Communicative Intelligence.

Hamlet has a particular fascination for Coleridge because he conceives that the very phenomenon which he himself exemplifies is represented in it. Given the Coleridgean hierarchy of the mental faculties (Reason/Imagination/Understanding//Understanding/Fancy/Sense), Shakespeare is said to have written a play in which the problems of using these powers of the mind are dramatized, and to have chosen as his protagonist a man of genius who fails to accommodate himself to the accidental circumstances or realities of the world in which he lives.

At first sight such an interpretation of Shakespeare's intentions is apt to strike one as fantastic. But if any of Coleridge's statements about the character of Hamlet are to be esteemed at their face value it is worth understanding how and in what context he came to make them. Indeed, if a distinction between Imagination and Fancy derived from the dichotomy of Reason and Sense is regarded as having any validity as a description of the way in which poetry is written, an analysis of one of Shakespeare's major characters in the same terms may not seem a completely useless exercise.

Coleridge's interpretation of the play bears witness to the empirical and realistic foundations of his thought. One senses that he would prefer a Hamlet to a hero more down-to-earth and effectual, but at the same time he is keenly alive to the impracticality of any theorizing and abstraction which cannot be converted into concrete terms. He thought that Shakespeare's play was about the uselessness of such incapacity and he was willing to accept it as a damning if unavailing warning to himself. As he puts it,

> Shakespeare wished to impress upon us the truth, that action is the chief end of existence – that no faculties of intellect, however brilliant, can be considered valuable, or indeed otherwise than as misfortunes, if they withdraw us from, or render us repugnant to action, and lead us to think and think of doing, until the time has elapsed when we can do anything effectually.[9]

The character who emerges from this tragedy, the interest of which Coleridge had described as '*ad et apud intra*',[10] is one in the grip of his interior world, the Reason, one for whom the world of Sense scarcely exists. The consequences of his situation are moral as well as practical; referring to Shakespeare's aims again Coleridge remarks: 'In Hamlet I conceive him to have wished to exemplify the moral necessity of a due balance between our attention to outward objects and our meditation on inward thoughts – a due balance between the real and the imaginary world.'[11]

Coleridge says of Hamlet that 'His mind . . . is for ever occupied with the world within him. . . .'[12] Placed beside the description of poetic and philosophic Method this characteristic seems to be precisely what he has been recommending hitherto. Here is a man preoccupied with the very region of the mind, the Reason or Primary Imagination, from which Ideas or the initiatives of Method are supposed to spring. But although Coleridge has praised reliance on the Reason, he has not claimed that it alone can produce anything worthwhile. Hamlet's plight is a useful reminder of this qualification in the Coleridgean scheme. The world of Reason, as we have noticed, should dominate the world of Sense, but it must be reconciled with it. Hamlet's failure is the result of his inability to reconcile the two.

If Shakespeare, the ideal poet of Imagination, has in fact projected himself into this character and withheld one of his own faculties as Coleridge suggests, it is at this point that the consequent damage becomes apparent. Coleridge refers to Hamlet's 'aversion to externals'.[13] Shakespeare, he contends, '. . . intended to pourtray a person, in whose view the external world, and all its incidents and objects, were comparatively dim, and of no interest in themselves, and which began to interest only, when they were reflected in the mirror of his mind'.[14] Hamlet's mind, he remarks elsewhere, '. . . unseated from its healthy balance, is for ever . . . abstracted from external things. . . .'[15] This state Coleridge describes as an 'overbalance of imagination'.[16]

Here we should recall that in the *Treatise on Method* Coleridge has claimed that '. . . Method results from a balance between the passive impression received from outward things, and the internal activity of the mind in reflecting and generalizing. . . .'[17] If the balance is upset, if, for example, there is a reliance on Reason to the neglect of Sense, disorder will result. According to Coleridge, '. . . if there be an overbalance in the contemplative faculty, man becomes the creature of meditation, and loses the power of action.'[18] He summarizes the desperate situation in which such a person finds himself:

... endless reasoning and hesitating – constant urging and solicitation of the mind to act, and as constant an escape from action; ceaseless reproaches of himself for sloth and negligence, while the whole energy of his resolution evaporates in these reproaches.[19]

If the quotation were given out of context, it would be difficult to tell whether Coleridge is indulging in literary criticism or autobiography. His sympathy for Hamlet's predicament is such that he is tempted to go beyond comment on what the prince does to speculate on what he might have been capable of doing. He allows himself to transgress the limits of the play to discuss the sort of man this 'hero so eminently philosophical' is.[20]

'Hamlet,' he maintains, 'beheld external things in the same way that a man of vivid imagination, who shuts his eyes, sees what has previously made an impression on his organs.'[21] When he explains how it is that a man can feel as Hamlet feels it is the voice of unhappy experience speaking. He refers at one point to the 'reasons why *taedium vitae* oppresses minds like Hamlet's' – '. . . the exhaustion of bodily feeling from perpetual exertion of mind; that all mental form being indefinite and ideal, realities must needs become cold. . . .'[22] But if Hamlet's Fancy is deficient, his Imagination is highly active. Coleridge comments on his 'prodigality of beautiful words', calling them 'the half embodyings of thoughts, that make them more than thoughts, give them an outness, a reality *sui generis*, and yet retain their correspondence and shadowy approach to the images and movements within'.[23]

Hamlet, however flawed his character may be, is what Coleridge calls a 'man of Genius'. The nature of men of Genius is discussed in some detail in the second chapter of *Biographia Literaria*.[24] Hamlet is an extreme example at the opposite pole from men of 'commanding Genius'. 'Such a mind as Hamlet's is near akin to madness,' Coleridge remarks,[25] and one is reminded of his distinction between an excess of Imagination and an excess of Fancy – mania and delirium respectively.[26] One comment recorded in the *Table Talk* is relevant: 'All genius is metaphysical; because the ultimate end of genius is ideal, however it may be actualized by incidental and accidental circumstances.'[27] Hamlet's trouble is that his genius is insufficiently actualized. He has that longing for the indefinite which Coleridge calls elsewhere 'the impulse which fills the young Poet's eye with tears, he knows not why'.[28] It is in this sense that Coleridge interprets the great soliloquy:

> ... in him we see a mind that keeps itself in a state of abstraction, and beholds external objects as hieroglyphics. His soliloquy, 'Oh that this too, too solid flesh would melt', arises from a craving after the indefinite: a disposition or temper which most easily besets men of genius; a morbid craving for that which is not.[29]

He cannot help praising and sympathizing with the man with whom he felt he had so much in common:

> This admirable and consistent character, deeply acquainted with his own feelings, painting them with such wonderful power and accuracy, and firmly persuaded that a moment ought not to be lost in executing the solemn charge committed to him, still yields to the same retiring from reality, which is the result of having, what we express by the terms, a world within himself.[30]

Coleridge cannot find it in himself to criticize; he is content to describe. Men of Reason are too rare in a world of Sense for another man of Reason to refrain from cherishing them.

Coleridge's analysis of Hamlet's character has been described by Professor Raysor as '. . . probably the most influential piece of Shakespearean criticism which has ever been produced'.[31] Its influence must be attributed to such elements of psychological truth as it contains; there is no indication that any of those who praised it in the nineteenth century were aware of the philosophical context from which it emerged. Yet the terms of Coleridge's analysis of the mind of Hamlet turn out not only to have much in common with his analysis of Shakespeare's and his own, but also to be part of the wider discussion of the Communicative Intelligence which has yielded the distinction between Imagination and Fancy and the criticism of Wordsworth. Coleridge's Hamlet may be the product of inspired introspection, but it is introspection developed within the framework of a complicated personal philosophy.

Coleridge's discussion of Milton has never received the praise that has been lavished on his Shakespearean criticism. There is, of course, much less of it,[32] but it differs essentially in being an analysis of Miltonic concepts rather than a study of the poet's characters or situations. Coleridge's treatment of *Paradise Lost* is carried out in terms of abstractions; he seems to have thought of the poem primarily as a vehicle for ideas. Whereas in *Hamlet* his attention is concentrated on the dramatic confrontation of Reason and Sense in a single character, in *Paradise Lost* he is content with scrutiny of the *dramatis personae* as symbolic representations of the various elements in the Reason–Sense struggle in the world as a whole. This sort of criticism is much more limited in its appeal because the interest depends so largely on our interest in the concepts themselves. The detailed illustrations which adorn his criticism of Shakespeare are lacking in his discussion of Milton. There are still a few asides thrown off from the philosophical discussion, but they are comparatively rare.

In *Hamlet*, Coleridge has tried to show, the predicament of the hero is Shakespeare's comment on the hero's mind. In order to fathom what sort of a mind it is, to comprehend it intellectually rather than merely respond to it emotionally, the help of criticism is needed. Only through a crude form of psychoanalysis does it stand revealed. In *Paradise Lost*, however, the different faculties of the mind, which in *Hamlet* are still faculties of one mind, are represented as characters themselves. If Coleridge's *Hamlet* is a play with a message, his *Paradise Lost* is a full-fledged allegory.

Coleridge assumes that Milton, like Shakespeare, is perfectly aware of the meaning of his work, and that he too creates characters out of his own mind; and he describes what he takes Milton to have been doing:

He was, as every truly great poet has ever been, a good man; but finding it impossible to realize his own aspirations, either

156

in religion, or politics, or society, he gave up his heart to the living spirit and light within him, and avenged himself on the world by enriching it with this record of his own transcendant ideal.[33]

Paradise Lost, combining as it does a major part of the Christian mythology with the philosophical problem which most exercised Coleridge's ingenuity, was attractive metal for his criticism to work upon.

His interest is as much theological as literary one feels, for he too is anxious to find a satisfactory resolution to the paradox of the Fall of Man in a universe presided over by a prescient God. The tone of his criticism of *Paradise Lost* is set by his statement that '. . . inasmuch as it represents the origin of evil, and the combat of evil and good, it contains matter of deep interest to all mankind, as forming the basis of all religion, and the true occasion of all philosophy whatsoever.'[34] He wishes to press home the similarities between the predicament of Adam and the situation of every man. His subsequent discussion is divided between the literary character of the poem and its religious content.

In *Aids to Reflection* Coleridge mulls over what is involved in the story of the Fall of Man, and in doing so incidentally provides us with a gloss to his allegorization of *Paradise Lost*. His account is strongly reminiscent of his chart of the mental faculties. Reason and Understanding both appear; Understanding is sub-divided into two manifestations; and the inferior manifestation of Understanding is shown to have to do particularly with the world of Sense. The passage is part of a lengthy footnote:

In the temple-language of Egypt the Serpent was the Symbol of the Understanding in its twofold function, namely, as the faculty of *means* to *proximate* or *medial* ends, analogous to the *instinct* of the more intelligent Animals, Ant, Bee, Beaver, &c. and opposed to the practical Reason, as the Determinant of the *ultimate* End; and again, [it typifies the Understanding] as the discursive and logical Faculty, possessed individually by each Individual – the Logos ἐν ἑκαζῳ, in distinction from the Nous, *i.e.* Intuitive Reason, the Source of Ideas and

ABSOLUTE Truths, and the Principle of the Necessary and the Universal in our Affirmations and Conclusions. Without or in contravention to the Reason (*i.e.* 'the *spiritual* mind' of St. Paul, and '*the Light that lighteth every man*' of St. John) this Understanding (φρονημα σαρκος, or carnal mind) becomes the *sophistic* Principle, the wily Tempter to Evil by counterfeit Good. . . .[35]

The Serpent is represented in this scheme as the personification of Understanding – not in itself bad. It is only when Satan enters into the Serpent, when the Understanding usurps the proper function of the Reason and begins to use its inferior manifestation as a substitute for its superior one, that things go wrong. The consequences of this usurpation are described in the same footnote:

. . . EVE tempted by the same serpentine and perverted Understanding which, framed originally to be the Interpreter of the Reason and the ministering Angel of the Spirit, is henceforth sentenced and bound over to the service of Animal Nature, its needs and its cravings, dependent on the Senses for all its Materials, with the World of Sense for its appointed Sphere. . . .[36]

The resemblance to the broad outlines of the Reason/Understanding/Sense hierarchy is self-evident.

Coleridge's treatment of Milton's rendition of the Fall must be read in the light of this interpretation, even though the passages in *Aids to Reflection* were not published until 1825. They are clearly foreshadowed in the earlier criticism of *Paradise Lost*. His account of the subject-matter of the poem lacks only the philosophical terminology. He begins with a general assertion:

The FALL of Man is the subject; Satan is the cause; man's blissful state the immediate object of his enmity and attack; man is warned by an angel who gives him an account of all that was requisite to be known, to make the warning at once intelligible and awful; then the temptation ensues, and the Fall; then the immediate sensible consequence. . . .[37]

Coleridge insists that Milton, like himself, regards the Fall as an act of Free Will. 'The Calvinists,' he writes, 'took away all human will. Milton asserted the will, but declared for the enslavement of the will out of an act of the will itself.'[38] When he goes on to delineate those characteristics which distinguish human beings from animals, he does so in a way which proves that he was in fact thinking in terms of the mental hierarchy while he was describing *Paradise Lost*. 'There are,' he informs us, 'three powers in us, which distinguish us from the beasts that perish; – 1, reason; 2, the power of viewing universal truth; and 3, the power of contracting universal truth into particulars.'[39] The three powers are evidently those to which he has referred before as Reason (or Primary Imagination); the organ of Reason (Secondary Imagination); and Understanding in its superior manifestation as it gently controls the exercise of the Imagination. Man's free decision to rely upon the world of sensible phenomena as it is ordered by the inferior function of the Understanding constitutes the Fall; it is this decision which Coleridge has attacked as the cause of evil in the world.

The Fall through an act of the will is referred to in 1816 by Coleridge in *The Statesman's Manual*: '. . . in its utmost abstraction and consequent state of reprobation, the Will becomes satanic pride and rebellious self-idolatry in the relations of the spirit to itself. . . .'[40] And he adds, 'This is the character which Milton has so philosophically as well as sublimely embodied in the Satan of his Paradise Lost.' Wilful capitulation to the inferior Understanding and consequent reliance on the world of Sense as a substitute for the Ideas of the Reason is a characteristic of men of Commanding Genius; Milton's Satan is displayed by Coleridge as the superhuman equivalent of such men. 'It is,' he says, 'the character so often seen *in little* on the political stage. It exhibits all the restlessness, temerity, and cunning which have marked the mighty hunters of mankind from Nimrod to Napoleon.'[41] It has recently been pointed out that Coleridge's analysis of Satan's character is related both to his study of 'the relationship between *noumenal* and *phenomenal* worlds' and to his analysis of the career of Napoleon.[42] We have already considered some of the implications which Napoleon's success had for Coleridge[43] – that it represented the power of systematic action carried out in pursuit of a leading idea. In the case of Satan the leading idea is selfishness, and his consistent pursuit of his own ends is what makes him so dangerous and powerful an adversary. It has been maintained that '. . . Coleridge's interpretation of Milton's Satan would have been impossible had Coleridge not been preoccupied with metaphysical and ethical problems.'[44] One need only add that Coleridge's approach to *Paradise Lost* as a whole is an expression of some of his keenest philosophical and theological concerns.

Lest it should be thought that the overtly theological theme of *Paradise Lost* makes it an uncharacteristic example of Coleridge's criticism, it may be worth pointing out that his allegorical interpretation is by no means restricted to such works. It is, however, true that he tends to discuss works which are susceptible of this treatment, and it seems clear that authors who were not open to this approach were likely to be excluded from his canon of the truly great. His descriptions of the characters created by Rabelais, Cervantes and Swift are conducted almost entirely in terms of the mental faculties they represent. 'All Rabelais' personages,' he maintains, 'are phantasmagoric allegories.'[45] Panurge he identifies as '. . . throughout the παvovpγία – the wisdom, that is, the cunning of the human animal, – the understanding, as the faculty of means to purposes without ultimate ends. . . .'[46] Pantagruel is categorized in turn: 'Pantagruel stands for the reason as contradistinguished from the understanding and choice, that is, from Panurge. . . .'[47] Don Quixote, Coleridge represents as a man akin to Hamlet, with Sancho Panza standing for the part of the mind which Hamlet lacks. 'Don Quixote's leanness and featureliness are happy exponents of the excess of the formative or imaginative in him, contrasted with Sancho's plump rotundity, and recipiency of external impression.'[48] He then expands this interpretation in a manner which reminds one forcibly of the analysis of Hamlet's character:

. . . Don Quixote grows at length to be a man out of his wits; his understanding is deranged; and hence without the least deviation from the truth of nature, without losing the least trait of personal individuality, he becomes a substantial living allegory, or personification of the reason and the moral sense, divested of the judgment and the understanding. Sancho is the converse. He is the common sense without reason or imagination; and Cervantes not only shows the excellence and power of reason in Don Quixote, but in both him and Sancho the mischiefs resulting from a severance of the two main constituents of sound intellectual and moral action. Put him and his master together, and they form a perfect intellect. . . .[49]

And even Swift's Yahoos are absorbed into the overriding scheme. According to Coleridge, Swift presents in them 'the disgusting spectacle of man with the understanding only, without the reason or the moral feeling. . . .'[50]

The conclusion is inescapable. Much of Coleridge's admiration of literary works depends upon the extent to which they exemplify what he takes to be the most important issues of philosophy and theology. When he comes to analyse them he has a tendency to do so in terms of these issues – presumably his own attention is so taken up with them that he finds it impossible to direct it elsewhere. His philosophical position provides him with a fairly elaborate structure for psychologizing and he has no hesitation about using it whenever the work in question appears to warrant doing so. It would be tedious to consider every instance in which Coleridge's practical criticism, particularly the more fragmentary parts of it, reflects this habit, but enough evidence has been assembled here to indicate how alive to his philosophical speculations a reader of his criticism must be if he is to avoid mistaking its tendency and sometimes its literal meaning.

III

Coleridge's lecture to the Royal Society of Literature, entitled 'On the Prometheus of Æschylus', says so little explicitly about the play that it is not usually included in discussions of his literary criticism. It was delivered in 1825, considerably later than any of the other examples which we have been considering; and while it will remain something of an anomaly both because of its date and because of its content, it provides us with a highly instructive example of what sort of critic Coleridge might have become had he continued his career as a public lecturer on letters.[51] The lecture has particular relevance for this study, because in it Coleridge gives his philosophical and theological proclivities their head and relegates literature to the role of mere exemplum.

The full title of the original lecture suggests where his interests now lie: *On the Prometheus of Æschylus; an Essay, preparatory to a series of Disquisitions respecting the Egyptian in connection with the Sacerdotal Theology, and in contrast with the Mysteries of ancient Greece*. It will come as no surprise to find that much of the material gathered for discussion under this learned and forbiddingly esoteric title seems familiar. On this occasion Coleridge has undertaken a comparative survey of three different accounts of the Creation, three different archologies, to give them their technical name – the Phoenician, the Greek, and the Hebrew. His immediate object (as usual this lecture is presented as a preamble to a much longer and more comprehensive study) is to demonstrate that there was a connection between the Greek drama and 'the mysteries, or the philosophy, of Greece'.[52] As evidence for this contention he offers Aeschylus's play.

If one disregards the larger context proposed by Coleridge, one is inclined to wonder why he should have been sufficiently interested in the relationship of Greek thought to Greek drama to consider the subject at such length, and why, having done so, he should have felt moved to inflict his considerations on the Royal Society of Literature. The second question can, I think, be answered in much the same terms as the similar one about the motives behind his earlier lectures and critical publications. As Coleridge recognized that his material was inappropriate for a public lecture, and that the lecture which he had given had been obscure, one can most readily explain it as another example of his compromise between necessity and inclination. The society required him to give a lecture; he had been thinking about this subject; *ergo*, he would lecture on it. The real question is, why was he thinking about this subject? what attracted him to it? And here a glance at the preliminary material in the lecture is helpful.

Near the beginning of his essay, Coleridge makes a distinction between 'theism' and 'pantheism'. The relevance of the distinction to what follows is likely to elude the uninitiated, but there is a relevance nevertheless, and one which links the essay as a whole with the major trends in Coleridge's thought which we have been considering. In this instance, he resorts to algebraic equations to explain himself, in which 'W' stands for the world or the 'material universe' and 'G' for God.[53] Both theist and pantheist, he claims, accept the equation 'W − G = 0' – both agree that one cannot conceive of a material universe without God. Where they differ is that while the pantheist believes in the equation 'G − W = 0', that without the material universe one cannot conceive of God, the theist believes that 'G − W = G', or that God's existence precedes and is in no way dependent upon the existence of the world. These equations are offered by Coleridge as part of his sustained attack on beliefs which emphasize the material world as evidence of religious truths rather than as the mere confirmation of them.[54] One supposes that he proposed eventually to demonstrate the separation of the Egyptian pantheism from the theisms (the Hebrew, and, with some qualification, the Greek) which culminated in Christianity.[55] It is the separation which the analysis of the three archologies is designed to emphasize. In theological terms this emphasis may be considered as an attempt to '. . . protect the primacy of the Hebrew culture, and the integrity of the link formed by Greek thought between Hebrew and Christian'.[56] In philosophical terms it is a reiteration of the dichotomy between a Reason-centred and a Sense-centred concept of the universe and an oblique advocacy of the former by a demonstration of its analogy with the Christian theology which Coleridge regarded as being its finest expression.

If one accepts the view of the Communicative Intelligence which Coleridge has put forward, it follows that religion and art are very closely allied. Both draw their inspiration from the same source, and both, presumably, serve the same ends. It will be recalled that Coleridge once divided the Communicative Intelligence into three modes – the 'Natural, Human, and Divine'.[57] He de-emphasized although he did not wholly discount the first of these; he acknowledged the importance of the third; but it was the second which meant most to him personally. As will appear, the three archologies which he discusses in his treatment of *Prometheus* – the Phoenician, Greek and Hebrew – bear a marked resemblance to the Natural, Human and Divine modes respectively.[58] His essay is his most elaborate attempt to argue the close relationship between the Human and Divine modes, between philosophy and poetry on the one hand and revealed religion on the other. His dismissal of pantheism accords with his rejection of the executive function of the Natural mode.

The theological discussion involved is considerably more sophisticated than any we have dealt with so far, and the organization of the essay itself is not calculated to dispel obscurity; it will be necessary, therefore, to deal rather freely with the sequence of its arguments in order to grasp the main outlines of what he is driving at.[59]

Coleridge's description of the three archologies is broadly speaking as follows: The Phoenician and Hebrew are represented as mutually exclusive opposites, and the Greek as occupying a middle place between them. The Phoenician is said to confuse the incomprehensibly various material universe for the incomprehensible Absolute: 'It confounded . . . the multeity below intellect, that is, unintelligible from defect of the subject, with the absolute identity above all intellect, that is, transcending comprehension by the plentitude of its excellence.'[60] The confusion involved is the one which Coleridge has earlier identified as the limiting factor in the Natural mode of the Communicative Intelligence; 'defect of the subject', the inability of the observer to take in the variety of things to be observed, is taken in the Phoenician archology to imply the exaltation of the object, of the variety of the things to be observed. This is the pantheism which Coleridge deplores.

Opposed to it he sets the Hebrew archology, which '. . . imperatively asserts an unbeginning creative One, who neither became the world; nor is the world eternally; nor made the world out of himself by emanation, or evolution; – but who willed it, and it was!'[61] In this account of the origin of things the antecedent Creator remains aloof and separate from the Creation which he has decreed. It falls therefore, within Coleridge's definition of theism.

Between these two rudely sketched extremes Coleridge locates the Greek archology. According to him, 'The Greek philosopheme, preserved for us in the Æschylean Prometheus, stands midway betwixt both, yet is distinct in kind from either.'[62] The compromise is achieved by combining parts of both the other archologies in order to form a third, but it is a third which belongs squarely within the theist camp.

The Greek scheme demands as an antecedent to the material world, an indeterminate something, which corresponds to the Hebrew 'Elohim' or God. 'With the Hebrew or purer Semitic,' Coleridge writes, 'it assumes an X Y Z – (I take these letters in their algebraic application) – an indeterminate *Elohim*, antecedent to the matter of the world, ὕλη ἄκοσμος – not less than to the ὕλη κεκοσμημένη.'[63] The Greek scheme further resembles the Hebrew in regarding this 'antecedent X Y Z' as 'supersensuous and divine'.[64] As Coleridge describes it a little farther on in the essay, the Greek concept of antecedent being is an imprecise one:

> . . . the *Elohim* of the Greeks were still but a *natura deorum*, τό θεῖον, to which a vague plurality adhered; or if any unity was imagined, it was not personal – not a unity of excellence, but simply an expression of the negative – that which was to pass, but which had not yet passed, into distinct form.[65]

The material world is proportionally more important in the Greek scheme, because such identity as the antecedent being has must be inferred from it. The Greeks regard the material universe as being '. . . the occasion and the still continuing substance' of the gods rather than as something caused by them: '. . . to body the elder physico-theology of the Greeks allowed a participation in entity. It was *spiritus ipse, oppressus, dormiens, et diversis modis somnians*. In short, body was the productive power suspended, and as it were, quenched in the product.'[66] This interdependence of the material world and its antecedent, of existence and entity, is what distinguished the Greek archology from its Hebrew and Phoenician counterparts.

Having got so far, Coleridge proceeds to outline some of the particulars of the Greek archology, as it emerges in myth. 'Now according to the Greek philosopheme or *mythus*, in these, or in this identity, there arose a war, schism, or division, that is, a

polarization into *thesis* and *antithesis*.'[67] The original interdependence was lost. In its place were left Ideas and what he
calls *Nomoi*: '. . . the *thesis*,' he tells us, 'becomes *nomos*, or law,
and the *antithesis* becomes *idea*, but so that *nomos* IS *nomos*,
because, and only because, the *idea* is *idea*; the *nomos* is not idea,
only because the idea has not become *nomos*.'[68] (Coleridge's
use of the term law, *nomos*, should not be confused with his
earlier discussion of relations of Law.) The terms Idea and
nomos, then, are used here to express a relationship, not
identities.

Coleridge refines his definition: 'The *nomos* is essentially
idea, but existentially it is idea *substans*, that is, *id quod stat
subtus*, understanding *sensu generalissimo*.'[69] When an Idea is
realized in an object it becomes a *nomos*. But, he continues,
'. . . its productive energy is not exhausted in this product, but
overflows, or is effluent, as the specific forces, properties,
faculties, of the product.'[70] The objects of the material world
do not altogether lack the energy which the ideas of which they
are the realization had. Coleridge suggests that in the world
around us we see evidence that *nomoi*, particularly the higher
forms of *nomoi*, tend towards their original idea. Nature thus
provides an illustration of the original unity. In plants the
tendency is exhausted within the enclosed cycle of plant life.
Coleridge contrasts them with animals: 'In the former, the
productive energy exhausts itself, and as it were, sleeps in the
product or *organismus* – in its root, stem, foliage, blossoms,
seed.'[71] But in the animal the productive energy overflows:
'Here the antecedent unity – the productive and self-realising
idea – strives, with partial success to re-emancipate itself from
its product, and seeks once again to become *idea*. . . .'[72] This
re-emancipation can never be total, but *nomos* can become an
image or analogon of *Idea*. In the lower animals it can progress
from Sensation to Understanding.

In man, the process can continue farther. Idea, like *nomos*,
tends to produce an analogon. *Nomos* produces Understanding;
Idea produces self-consciousness. But the two cannot achieve
identity again. As Coleridge puts it, '. . . as the product can
never become idea, so neither can the idea (if it is to remain
idea) become or generate a distinct product.'[73] The combination of Idea with its analogon of product Coleridge calls

'mind', and he defines it as 'that which knows itself, and the existence of which may be inferred, but cannot appear or become a phenomenon'.[74] He begins to use terms which he has used before when considering the act of self-awareness in *Biographia Literaria*:

> This *analogon* of product is to be itself; but were it indeed and substantially a product, it would cease to be self. It would be an object for a subject, not (as it is and must be) an object that is its own subject, and *vice versa*; a conception which, if the uncombining and infusible genius of our language allowed it, might be expressed by the term subject–object.[75]

He is content to end his analysis of the Greek archology at this point, saying that '. . . the ground work of the Æschylean *mythus* is laid in the definition of idea and law, as correlatives that mutually interpret each the other. . . .'[76] He compares briefly the Platonic and Aristotelian accounts of the correlation, remarking that 'Both acknowledge ideas as distinct from the mere generalizations from objects of sense: both would define an idea as an *ens rationale*, to which there can be no adequate correspondent in sensible experience', and adding, without committing himself for the moment to either view, that the Platonic interpretation holds that the Ideas are constitutive and that the Aristotelean regards them as regulative only.[77]

Apart from the introduction of some new terms drawn from the Greek philosophy, the world picture which Coleridge is describing does not differ substantially from his own one. The poles of Reason and Sense, representing the Communicative Intelligence and Nature respectively, cannot be reconciled by man, but both tend towards reconciliation. Idea and *nomos* do the same. Coleridge maintains that this was 'the philosophy of the mythic poets, who, like Æschylus, adapted the secret doctrines of the mysteries as the (not always safely disguised) antidote to the debasing influences of the religion of the state'.[78] They, like Coleridge, were opposing the capitulation to *nomos* or the world of Sense. By his sympathetic description of their attempts, and by his air of objective comment on them, Coleridge is furthering his own cause.[79]

It is in just this vein that he outlines the allegory of *Prometheus* which expresses these attitudes of the Greek archology. We have already watched him unveil the philosophical implications of Hamlet's character, and the similar implications of the characters created by Milton, Cervantes, Rabelais and Swift. The philosophical implications found in *Prometheus* are not explicitly claimed for his own, but they are so similar that his presentation of them is unmistakably part of his unremitting missionary activity. It is clearly not the *Prometheus* as a work of art which has occasioned his discussion; in this respect his treatment of Aeschylus's play differs from the rest of his literary criticism. And yet only the strangeness of the new terminology divides the results of this later theological excursion into literature from the better-known critical ventures of earlier years. They are patently the products of the same mind and the same process of thought.

Coleridge's analysis of *Prometheus* is a complicated one. The two principal characters involved are, of course, Jove and Prometheus. Coleridge observes that the allegory can be interpreted at several different levels. Accordingly Jove and Prometheus can be thought of respectively as *nomos* and Idea – as the two elements after the schism into thesis and antithesis. They can also be thought of as gods from the pre-schismatic 'τὸ θεῖον', in which case Jove would appear '. . . now as the father, now as the sovereign, and now as the includer and representative of the νόμοι οὐράνιοι κοσμικοί, or *dii majores*' and Prometheus would appear as Jove's former friend and counsellor.[80] A third level of meaning allows them to be thought of in terms of the struggle between the divided gods, in which case Jove emerges as the subjugator and Prometheus as the rebel who successfully prevents the subjugation from being complete; a fourth permits them to be considered as respectively the law of the state (to which Coleridge adds Jove's quarrelsome wife as representative of the church established by law) and the spirit or principle of the law.

Having rung these preliminary changes, Coleridge moves on to the aspect of the allegory which really interests him. He states that 'Both νόμος and Idea (or *Nous*) are the *verbum*. . . .'[81] His meaning is that they are 'verbum' in the sense that both thesis and antithesis are synthesis, the two opposed aspects of reality which, when combined, make up truth. And he goes on to explain that they are respectively 'the Word of the Lord' and 'the Word of the Lord in the mouth of the prophet'.[82] The *nomos*, '*Ζεῦς παντοκράτωρ*' inquires after the secret of his fate (which is that *nomos* is transitory) from the Idea or *Nous*, Prometheus. Coleridge then draws the analogy between Jove as Power and Prometheus as Knowledge, which like the other manifestations of the schism, cannot be reunited.

The schism has made the imparting of the secret impossible. As long as Prometheus remains the representative of Idea he cannot bow to the sway of the representative of *nomos*; if he were to bow, he would cease to be representative of Idea. *Nous*, according to Coleridge, '. . . is bound to a rock, the immovable firmness of which is indissolubly connected with its barrenness, its non-productivity'.[83] To the rock of Prometheus come *Nomizomeni*, deities kindred to Prometheus because of their relationship before the schism but now subject to Jove. They come to offer sympathy, to advise submission, or to tempt. Of these Hermes is the most prominent and Coleridge identifies him as 'the impersonation of interest'.[84] He is the Satan figure of the Greek myth, and like Satan he conjures up for Coleridge all the forces of expedient and shallow if dangerously powerful thinking. He refers to Hermes' 'entrancing and serpentine *Caduceus*', and describes him as impersonating 'the eloquence of cupidity, the cajolement of power regnant', and as 'custom'.[85] Hermes is trying to persuade Prometheus (Reason) to submit himself to the power of Jove (Sense). He represents, therefore, the various inducements which there are for Reason to submit to Sense.

At this point Coleridge interestingly provides an example from Wordsworth to explain what sort of inducements there are. Hermes may like Satan be a genuinely evil force, but many of the minor deities who visit Prometheus are innocent agents of evil. Wordsworth's description in his *Immortality Ode* of Earth's effort to wean her charge away from his childish attributes runs as follows:

> The homely nurse doth all she can
> To make her foster-child, her inmate, Man
> Forget the glories he hath known
> And that imperial palace whence he came:–

Prometheus, then, is identified with the 'glories' once known by the child; he is that spark in man which is Reason, and Jove as a despotic power is trying to bring Reason under the control of the highest manifestation of Sense, the inferior Understanding. The despotism is carried into effect by Custom (Hermes) and necessity, and the mechanic arts and powers (Hephaistos). By these Prometheus is bound. According to Coleridge, 'Nature, or $Zeus$ as the νόμος ἐν νομιζομένοις, knows herself only, can only come to a knowledge of herself, in man!'[86] But even man, as we have seen in the original account of the Human mode of the Communicative Intelligence, cannot quite attain to Reason.

This limitation of human capacity is retained in Coleridge's account of Prometheus. As he puts it here, '. . . even the human understanding in its height of place seeks vainly to appropriate the ideas of the pure reason, which it can only represent by *idola*.'[87] Earlier in the essay, when discussing the Greek account of 'The generation of the νοῦς, or pure reason in man' in more general terms, Coleridge explains that it is infused from above, that it is stolen, that it is stolen from heaven, that it is a spark, and that it is stolen by a god. These characteristics, he explains, signify respectively that the Reason is not evolved from man's other faculties, that it differs from them in kind, that it is superior as well as different, that it is immutable, and that it, like the gods, existed prior to the objects of Sense. The gulf between Reason and Sense, it would seem, is fixed eternally.[88]

But Coleridge is not satisfied to end his treatment of *Prometheus* on a note of pessimism. He remarks rather cryptically at one point in the essay that 'It was the spirit, the *nous*, which man alone possessed. And I must be permitted to suggest that this notion deserves some respect, were it only that it can shew a semblance, at least, of sanction from a far higher authority.'[89] The 'far higher authority' is presumably Christianity. When Coleridge concludes his analysis with the optimistic end of the Greek myth there is more than a hint of a Christian parallel:

Yet finally, against the obstacles and even under the fostering influences of the *Nomos*, τοῦ νομίμου, a son of Jove himself, but a descendent from Io, the mundane religion, as contradistinguished from the sacerdotal *cultus*, or religion of the state, an Alcides *Liberator* will arise, and the *Nous*, or divine principle in man, will be Prometheus ἐλευθερώμενος.[90]

A manuscript reference to Christ as 'the Messiah of the Jews, the *ΗΡΑΚΛΗΣ Ὁ ΕΛΕΥΘΕΡΩΤΗΣ* of the Gentiles', provides further confirmation.[91] One can sense the direction in which his theology is moving. Imagination was to free the Reason from the shackles of Sense and convert them into productive tools; Hercules was to free Prometheus from the bonds imposed by Jove. Christ is to take the place of Hercules and Imagination.

As we have noticed, one of the key features of Coleridge's account of the Communicative Intelligence is that it is communicative. However much his own account of Reason may agree with the Greek one enshrined in Aeschylus's *Prometheus*, however much he may emphasize the dichotomy between Reason and Sense, he does so only in order to argue for attempts to reunite the two. We have considered the development of this aspect of his philosophy, and we have seen the part that it plays in his discussion of poetry. By 1825 his attention seems to have moved away from the Imagination of the creative artist in the direction of a more traditional theological solution. That it should have been possible for it to have done so suggests the extent to which the poetic, the philosophical and the theological were analogous in his mind.

IV

Enough has been said to indicate how closely the leading themes of Coleridge's theoretical and practical criticism are linked to a metaphysical structure of an elaborate and unfamiliar kind. It is time to add a word of caution. It must, I think, be accepted that his criticism can only be understood imperfectly by those who have not scraped an acquaintance with his philosophy. But, as I have tried to suggest in the course of this essay, his philosophy is slippery and by no means static. It is extremely difficult to know how much of it is enough, or, to turn the question around, how little will do. I have not sought to solve the problem, but rather to provide an introduction to some of the materials which will have to be considered if a solution is to be attempted. The greatest hazard of suggesting a new approach to a subject as complicated as Coleridge's criticism is that one is constantly forced to compromise and simplify in order to articulate ideas which Coleridge himself expressed hesitantly because he was aware that he had not yet thought them completely through. Those who have studied his thought themselves know how very treacherous it can be; how a single marginal note can upset a complicated reconstruction, or cause a whole series of apparently unrelated topics suddenly to coalesce. Pleasant as it would have been to offer the reader a handbook to Coleridge's criticism, with all the elements of his theory and practice neatly arranged and confidently awarded praise or blame, the time for that has not yet come.

It is important furthermore that we should avoid mistaking the philosophical background of Coleridge's criticism for his special contribution. This error has naturally given offence to those familiar with the real originators of Transcendentalism, and it has led some of them to try to right the balance by calling him derivative, eclectic, and confused. The truth of the matter is that Coleridge was thoroughly conversant with the prevailing philosophies of his time; he differs from most critics in the English tradition in that he deliberately applies the techniques and conclusions of philosophy to his discussions of literature.

Even his insistence on the power of intuition may be misleading. We must remember that Coleridge's views emerge from his struggle against the over-simplification of thought represented by eighteenth-century empiricism; it is quite possible that he would have struggled just as fiercely against complacent Idealism. Indeed, if his philosophy has any lesson for us today it is not the particular lesson of Transcendentalism, but rather the lesson that answers to philosophical questions are rarely easy and never final.

NOTES

INTRODUCTION

[1] See for example: Alice D. Snyder, *The Critical Principle of the Reconciliation of Opposites as Employed by Coleridge* (Ann Arbor, 1918); A. O. Lovejoy, 'Coleridge and Kant's Two Worlds', in *Essays in the History of Ideas* (Baltimore, 1948), pp. 254–76; Gordon McKenzie, *Organic Unity in Coleridge* (Berkeley, 1939); I. A. Richards, *Coleridge on Imagination* (London, 1934); and for a more general account of such terms, John H. Muirhead, *Coleridge as Philosopher* (London, 1930).

CHAPTER 1

[1] Elisabeth Schneider effectively dissuades one from regarding opium as final cause. See her *Coleridge, Opium and 'Kubla Khan'* (Chicago, 1953), pp. 31–44, and especially p. 37. She does suggest, however, that Coleridge's 'atonic gout' of 1803 was a symptom of his attempt to abstain (p. 63).

[2] *CL*, II, 661–2.

[3] *CL*, II, 814.

[4] *CL*, I, 574, 577, 579, 583, and 587; *CL*, I, 645, 649, 654–5, and II, 661; and *CL*, II, 707.

[5] *CL*, II, 813, 814, 856, 874.

[6] *CL*, II, 856–7.

[7] *CL*, II, 662, 745; *CL*, II, 919 and 950; and *CL*, II, 662, 707.

[8] *CL*, II, 662, and 919; *CL*, II, 919.

[9] *CL*, II, 707; *CL*, II, 707, 776, 787, 927–8; *CL*, II, 820; *CL*, II, 829; *CL*, II, 829–30; *CL*, II, 870 (this plan is inferred from Coleridge's response to a query from Basil Montagu: 'Be under no alarm concerning any other Selections – were there twenty, it would increase not diminish the probable Sale of our's. . . .'); *CL*, II, 877; *CL*, II, 949; *CL*, II, 951, 960; *CL*, II, 1053–4, and *N*, II, 2011, 2458, 2541, 2638, 2648, 3072.

[10] *CL*, II, 729, 759, 760, 776, 856, and 857.

[11] *CL*, II, 889.

[12] *CL*, II, 711.

[13] According to Coleridge the annuity had been reduced in value by the inflation of the currency (*CL*, II, 710).

[14] *CL*, II, 707.

[15] *CL*, II, 710.

[16] *CL*, II, 662.

[17] *CL*, II, 705.

[18] *CL*, II, 714. Cf. *CL*, II, 676: 'Change of Ministry interests *me* not – I turn at times half reluctantly from Leibnitz or Kant even to read a smoking new newspaper such a purus putus Metaphysicus am I become.'

[19] *CL*, II, 877.

[20] *CL*, II, 877.
[21] *BL*, I, 94–135; (Everyman, pp. 54–78).
[22] *CL*, II, 799.
[23] *CL*, II, 707.
[24] *CL*, II, 706.
[25] *CL*, II, 706.
[26] *CL*, II, 927–8.
[27] *CL*, II, 947.
[28] *CL*, II, 952.
[29] *CL*, II, 952.
[30] *CL*, II, 948–9.
[31] *CL*, II, 1053–4.
[32] *CL*, II, 1176–7.
[33] *CL*, II, 1181.
[34] *CL*, II, 1187–8.
[35] *CL*, II, 1188, 1188n; and III, 18.
[36] *CL*, II, 1188.
[37] *CL*, II, 1191.
[38] *CL*, III, 25.
[39] Quoted in *CL*, II, 29n.
[40] *CL*, III, 39; III, 42.
[41] *CL*, II, 1184–5.
[42] *CL*, III, 89.
[43] *CL*, IV, 923. The lack of specific preparation is complained of by Crabb Robinson (*SC*, II, 180–1).
[44] *CL*, IV, 924.
[45] *CL*, IV, 924. Coleridge uses this practice as an excuse for having inadvertently attacked the Unitarians (*CL*, III, 471).
[46] e.g. Collier, cited in *PL*, p. 32. Cf. Crabb Robinson's account of his indolent reliance on 'his old MS. commonplace book' (*SC*, II, 179).
[47] *CL*, III, 111.
[48] *CL*, III, 198.
[49] *CL*, III, 138.
[50] *CL*, III, 159.
[51] *CL*, III, 145.
[52] *CL*, III, 126.
[53] *CL*, III, 131.
[54] *CL*, III, 142.
[55] *CL*, III, 143. Cf. III, 168.
[56] *CL*, III, 153.
[57] *CL*, IV, 551.
[58] *CL*, IV, 551.
[59] *CL*, IV, 552.
[60] *CL*, IV, 560.
[61] *CL*, IV, 561.
[62] *CL*, II, 812.
[63] *CL*, IV, 578–9. Cf. III, 433.
[64] *CL*, IV, 579.

[65] *CL*, III, 433.

[66] The extent of Coleridge's early reviewing has recently been re-examined. To the four reviews identified in 1926 by Garland Greever (*A Wiltshire Parson and his Friends* [London, 1926], pp. 165–7), a number of others have been added. See: George Whalley, 'Coleridge on Classical Prosody: an Unidentified Review of 1797', *Review of English Studies*, n.s. II (1951), 238–47; Charles I. Patterson, 'An Unidentified Criticism by Coleridge Related to *Christabel*', *Publications of the Modern Language Association*, LXVII (1952), 973–88; and David V. Erdman, 'Immoral Acts of a Library Cormorant: the Extent of Coleridge's Contributions to the Critical Review', *Bulletin of the New York Public Library*, LXIII (1959), 433–54, 515–30, 575–87. The suggestion that three of the reviews identified by Greever are not in fact by Coleridge (put forward by Charles I. Patterson, 'The Authenticity of Coleridge's Reviews of Gothic Romances', *Journal of English and Germanic Philology*, L [1951], 517–21) is dismissed by Derek Roper, 'Coleridge and the "Critical Review"', *Modern Language Review*, LV (1960), 11–16. The reviews so far identified show signs of Coleridge's characteristic trains of thought, something of his penchant for moral and theoretical implications, but little, to my mind, of the sustained power which has made him famous. I should attribute the marked difference in quality partly to the lack of an underlying philosophic structure in his early literary discussions. See, however, the contrary opinion of Garland Greever (*op. cit.*, p. 167).

[67] *CL*, II, 709.

[68] The calibre of Coleridge's philosophy is a matter of some dispute. For opposed views, see Muirhead, *Coleridge as Philosopher*, and René Wellek, *Immanuel Kant in England 1793–1938* (Princeton, 1931). Students of literature are understandably reluctant to venture opinions on this issue, and they are inclined to concede that Coleridge was a derivative thinker without discussing their reasons for doing so; but some have defended him stoutly (e.g. Herbert Read, *Coleridge as Critic* [London, 1949], p. 23; and Kathleen Coburn, *PL*, p. 55). The space devoted to Coleridge in Justus Buchler's *The Concept of Method* (New York, 1961) attests to the continuing interest of at least one philosopher in him.

[69] *CL*, IV, 825–6.

[70] *F*, III, 133ff.

[71] *TM*, pp. vii–xxvii, especially pp. xxiv–xxvii.

[72] *CL*, III, 461–2.

[73] *CL*, IV, 776.

[74] *TM*, p. vii.

[75] *TT*, II, 335.

[76] *The Critical Principle of the Reconciliation of Opposites as Employed by Coleridge* (Ann Arbor, 1918), p. 12.

[77] *Coleridge as Critic*, p. 19. See also, Kathleen Coburn, 'Coleridge Redivivus', in *The Major English Romantic Poets*, edd. Clarence D. Thorpe, Carlos Baker, and Bennett Weaver (Carbondale, 1957), p. 120.

[78] Shawcross, I, iv.

CHAPTER 2

[1] *EOHOT*, I, 32–3.

[2] *CL*, III, 531. Cf. the similar claim for his lectures (*BL*, I, 219; Everyman, p. 125).

[3] *EOHOT*, III, 695. See also *F*, III, 98–9 on 'general and long-continued assent, as a presumption of truth'.

[4] *EOHOT*, I, 6–7.

[5] *F*, I, 166–7. Cf. *CL*, II, 720.

[6] *F*, I, 210. Cf. *F* (1809), p. 25.

[7] *F*, I, 261.

[8] *F*, II, 217.

[9] *F* (1809), p. 23.

[10] *EOHOT*, III, 708n–709n. Cf. *F*, I, 189; and *SM*, pp. 19–20.

[11] *F*, III, 130.

[12] *F*, III, 130–2.

[13] *EOHOT*, II, 656–7.

[14] *F*, I, 261. Cf. *F*, I, 186.

[15] *CL*, III, 198. See also, *CL*, III, 131, 141, 147, 168, 197, 202–3; *F* (1809), pp. 11, 22, and 25; and *F*, I, 27, and III, 129. In *Biographia Literaria*, Coleridge delivers an encomium on the proponents of principle: 'If . . . unanimity grounded on moral feelings has been among the least equivocal sources of our national glory, that man deserves the esteem of his countrymen, even as patriots, who devotes his life and the utmost efforts of his intellect to the preservation and continuance of that unanimity by the disclosure and establishment of *principles*.' (*BL*, I, 182; Everyman, p. 104). It clearly applies to himself.

[15a] Note, however, the different sense in which the term 'aphorism' is used in his *Aids to Reflection* in 1825.

[16] *F*, I, 59n.

[17] *F*, I, 206. See also *F*, I, 195–7. For a mystical support of principle, see *SM*, p. 29.

[18] *CL*, II, 709. Commenting on Bacon's use of the term '*Idols*', Coleridge declared it synonymous with Plato's ' "*Opinion*" (δόξα), which the latter calls "a medium between knowledge and ignorance" ' (*TM*, p. 43).

[19] *EOHOT*, III, 707. In a speech delivered in 1795, Coleridge had argued that attention to the 'consequences' of an opponent's opinions, to the neglect of his train of thought, was characteristic of the unsatisfactory level of contemporary political discourse (*EOHOT*, I, 25). In *The Watchman*, he had suggested that '. . . the very act of dissenting from established opinions must generate habits precursive to the love of freedom' (*W*, p. 4). He was later to become more conservative, however, although he continued to hold that false opinions could, by exciting opposition, breed true ones (*CL*, III, 127; and *F*, III, 57–8).

[20] *F*, II, 145.

[21] *F*, II, 148–9. Cf. *F*, I, 13–14: '. . . an author's harp must be tuned in the hearing of those, who are to understand its after harmonies; the foundation stones of his edifice must lie open to common view, or his friends will hesitate to trust themselves beneath the roof.' See also *F*, I, 47–8; and III, 130. Coleridge condemns the arrogance of those who neglect to make themselves informed before presuming to come before the public as instructors (*F*, I, 45).

[22] *F*, III, 98–9.

[23] *PL*, p. 290. Coleridge praises Spinoza's 'iron Chain of Logic' (*CL*, IV, 548) and Kant's 'adamantine chain' (*BL*, I, 145; Everyman, p. 84); and he contrasts the evolutionary styles of Hooker, Bacon, Milton and Taylor, with the style of Seneca, '. . . where the thoughts, striking as they are, are merely strung together like beads, without any causation or progression' (*MC*, p. 217).

[24] *EOHOT*, II, 657.

[25] *EOHOT*, II, 657. Cf. *SM*, Appendix, p. x, where Coleridge connects this power with the achievements of 'COMMANDING GENIUS'—a term more loosely employed in *Biographia Literaria* (*BL*, I, 31; Everyman, p. 17). He praises Burke (*BL*, I, 183; Everyman, p. 105) and abuses Pitt (*EOHOT*, II, 324 and 325) for their respective possession and lack of system.

[26] *EOHOT*, II, 648.

[27] *F*, I, 202–3.

[28] *F*, I, 204–5.

[29] *EOHOT*, II, 613.

[30] *CL*, III, 147.

[31] *CL*, III, 131. Coleridge, comparing his favourite, Sir Alexander Ball, with Nelson, remarks that his 'excellence was more an affair of system' (*F*, III, 313–14).

[32] Cf. Coleridge's account of his early distaste for the '*conjunction disjunctive*' of the epigrams of Pope (*BL*, I, 18; Everyman, p. 9).

[33] *F*, I, 181–2. Cf. *EOHOT*, III, 922–3.

[34] *F*, I, 25–6, and 191. This was a conviction of long standing. In 1796, Coleridge had declared his faith that '. . . the final cause of all evils in the moral and natural world is to awaken intellectual activity' (*W*, p. 101). And in 1800 he had stated that 'The whole faculties of man must be exerted in order to noble energies; and he who is not in earnest, self-mutilated, self-paralysed, lives in but half his being' (*EOHOT*, I, 230).

[35] *CL*, III, 253. Cf. 253–4 and 255; British Museum MS, Egerton 2825, fol. 20; and *SC*, II, 35–6. As Alice D. Snyder has remarked, 'Coleridge's whole life may be looked upon as the story, the drama, of the born thinker trying to prove that thought mattered' (*Coleridge on Logic and Learning* [New Haven, 1929], pp. 31–2).

[36] *F*, III, 132. Cf. *MC*, p. 220. Coleridge had long before adverted to the dangers of stating truths to those who were incapable of understanding them. (*EOHOT*, I, 30). As he put it in *Biographia Literaria*, 'Veracity does not consist in *saying*, but in the intention of *communicating* truth . . .' (*BL*, I, 147; Everyman, p. 85). Coleridge may, perhaps, justly be charged with paternalism here, but not, I think, with disingenuousness. Cf. also his praise

of Hume, British Museum MS, Egerton 2826, fols. 299–300; *NOED*, I, 110; Coleridge's coinage 'Minimifidianism' for watered-down religion (*A to R*, p. 207); and *SM*, p. 47. Coleridge comments on Donne's endorsement of Gregory Nazianzen's statement that the Christian religion is '*simplex et nuda*': 'A religion of ideas, spiritual truths, or truth-powers, – not of notions and conceptions, the manufacture of the understanding, – is therefore *simplex et nuda*, that is, immediate; like the clear blue heaven of Italy, deep and transparent, an ocean unfathomable in its depth, and yet ground all the way. Still as meditation soars upwards, it meets the arched firmament with all its suspended lamps of light. O, let not the *simplex et nuda* of Gregory be perverted to the Socinian, "plain and easy for the meanest understandings"!' (*NOED*, I, 89).

[37] *F*, I, 85–6. Coleridge compared himself to a chamois-hunter as early as 1803 (*CL*, II, 916). He was aware of what an uncomfortable guide he could be, and how likely he was to overestimate the agility of those who were trying to follow him. (See *F*, I, 24–5; and II, 301–2).

[38] *F*, I, 191. Cf. *F*, I, 35. He opposes the use of easy illustrations in books of mathematical instruction on the ground that '. . . it ought to be our never-ceasing effort to make people think, not feel. . . .' (*SC*, II, 45). Also, on pictures for the instruction of the poor, see *N*, II, 2420.

[39] *F*, I, 17. Cf. *F*, II, 68.

[40] *CL*, III, 282. Coleridge expressed disillusionment with French thought in 1802 (*EOHOT*, II, 492, and 502). I am in agreement with Huw Parry Owen's statement: 'In assessing Coleridge's linguistic peculiarities and aphoristic method of presentation one has to remember that he does not offer a finished system of thought, after the manner of St. Thomas Aquinas or Calvin. He is searching after truth at the same time as he is stating it. Moreover, he intends his readers to share his search, and so to share also his experience of ever-increasing mental growth' ('The Theology of Coleridge', *Critical Quarterly*, IV [1962], 59).

[41] *F*, III, 153. Cf. his description of the 'tree of false knowledge' in *The Statesman's Manual* (*SM*, Appendix, p. xliv).

[42] *F*, III, 177–8. Cf. *TM*, pp. 37–8. In his MS 'Treatise on Logic', Coleridge maintains that '. . . that alone is truly knowledge, in relation to the individual acquirer, which reappears as power. . . .' (British Museum MS, Egerton 2825, fol. 78); cf. also, fol. 86: '. . . not *what* we understand nor – how *much* – but simply *how* we understand'.

[43] Cf. Coleridge's criticism of neo-Kantian treatment of Kant's arguments as a 'compleat system of Metaphysics' (MS note, in end-papers, to Wilhelm Gottlieb Tennemann, *Geschichte der Philosophie* [Leipzig, 1798], I, 216. British Museum copy: C. 43.c.24.)

[44] *F*, I, 25. Coleridge expresses the belief that in the setting forth of his ideas in *The Friend*, '. . . a duty was performed in the endeavour to render it as much easier to [his readers], than it had been to [him], as could be effected by the united efforts of [his] understanding and imagination' (*F*, I, 16). As Miss Snyder has pointed out, Coleridge's interest in the problems of teaching was lifelong. (*Coleridge on Logic and Learning*, p. 45.)

[45] *F*, I, 10.

[46] *F*, I, 8.

[47] *F*, I, 19. See also his anxiety over the necessity of beginning with the most difficult part. (*F*, I, 23.)

[48] *F*, I, 17.

[49] *F*, I, 23.

[50] *F*, III, 157.

[51] *TM*, pp. 1–2.

[52] *F*, III, 135–6. Cf. *TM*, pp. 3, 12, and 14; and *F*, III, 213–14.

[53] *F*, III, 129–30.

[54] *F*, III, 150. Cf. *TM*, p. 2.

[55] *F*, III, 150–1.

[56] *TM*, p. 2.

[57] *F*, III, 151.

[58] *TM*, p. 2.

[59] For Coleridge on the unsatisfactory nature of 'arrangement', see *CL*, II, 956 (an attack on alphabetically arranged encyclopaedias), *TM*, p. 10 (on dictionaries), and *TM*, p. 3. In 1801, he had used the term to mean 'Method' (*CL*, II, 727).

[60] *F*, III, 151.

[61] *TM*, p. 2.

[62] *F*, III, 205–6. Cf. *TM*, p. 42; *F*, III, 249; and *PL*, p. 331.

[63] And because, as will appear in Chapter Four, such hunches had divine sanction.

[64] *TM*, p. 2. Coleridge compares the Method based on an initiative to the process of an educated man's mind (*F*, III, 134–5; *TM*, pp. 13–14), and its converse with the thought of the ignorant. (*F*, III, 135 and 248; and *TM*, pp. 52–3).

[65] *TM*, p. 2.

[66] *TM*, p. 7. Cf. *Vorlesungen*, p. 13.

[67] *TM*, p. 7.

[68] *TM*, p. 7.

[69] *F*, III, 181–2. Cf. *TM*, p. 17, where Coleridge admits the part played in 'Experimental Philosophy' by accidental discoveries, but asserts that these discoveries would be without value if they did not 'excite some master IDEA'. Cf. Schelling's comments on Lichtenberg's success. (*Vorlesungen*, pp. 43–4). Coleridge traces the classical use of the term 'Idea' (*BL*, I, 99n–100n; Everyman, p. 57n).

[70] *TM*, pp. 2–3. Coleridge cites the authority of Warburton (*F*, I, 192), and gives credit to Proclus. (*CL*, III, 279).

[71] *TM*, p. 6. For further discussion, see *TM*, pp. 8, 9, and 10. For a more general identification of 'Ideas' with 'Genius', 'Totality', 'predilection for *noumena*', etc., see *F*, III, 89n.

[72] *TM*, p. 11.

[73] *TM*, p. 4.

[74] *F*, III, 164.

[75] *F*, III, 153–4. The text contains the misprint, 'It gives its very existence'.

[76] *F*, III, 158.

[77] *TM*, p. 4.

[78] *F*, III, 154.

[79] *F*, III, 154.

[80] *F*, III, 154-5.

[81] Coleridge offers a mystical criterion of the presence of 'ultimate principles'. (*SM*, pp. 28-9) For an earlier declaration of his wish to achieve unconditional principles, see *CL*, III, 146.

[82] Coleridge discriminates similarly between *Metaphysical* and *Physical Ideas*, and appears to define them by their subject-matter: 'We distinguish Ideas into those of essential property, and those of natural existence; in other words, into Metaphysical and Physical Ideas. Metaphysical Ideas, or those which relate to the essence of things as possible, are of the highest class. Thus, in accurate language, we say, the *essence* of a circle, not its nature; because, in the conception of forms purely Geometrical, there is no expression or implication of their actual existence: and our reasoning upon them is totally independent of the fact, whether any such forms ever existed in Nature, or not. Physical Ideas are those which we mean to express, when we speak of the *nature* of a thing actually existing and cognizable by our faculties, whether the thing be material or immaterial, bodily or mental. Thus, the laws of memory, the laws of vision, the laws of vegetation, the laws of crystallisation, are all Physical Ideas, dependent for their accuracy, on the more or less careful observation of things actually existing.' (*TM*, pp. 9-10).

[83] *TM*, pp. 4-5. Cf. *F*, III, 163; and *TM*, p. 55.

[84] *F*, III, 183. Cf. Coleridge's comments on this process as practised by students of electricity (*F*, III, 186-8, and 191). Coleridge quotes Bacon to the effect that '. . . all science approaches to its perfection in proportion as it immaterializes objects'. (*PL*, p. 334).

[85] *PL*, pp. 360 and 361. Coleridge's rejection of 'general consequences' as a criterion of right and wrong is analogous. See *F*, II, 218-20.

[86] *F*, III, 98.

[87] *F*, III, 162. Coleridge had begun to ponder this question by 1801 (see *CL*, II, 672), and he refers to it again in 1806 (*CL*, II, 1194-5).

[88] *F*, III, 162.

[89] *EOHOT*, III, 692-3.

[90] *PL*, p. 359.

[91] *F*, II, 38.

[92] *F*, I, 355-6.

[93] *PL*, pp. 364-5. Cf. the scepticism expressed in 1796: 'You deem me . . . an Enthusiast, I presume, because I am not quite convinced with yourself and Mr. Godwin that mind will be omnipotent over matter. . . .' (*W*, p. 159). And again, apropos of political theorists, see *F*, 11, 20-21; and of political abstractions, *EOHOT*, III, 693. For scepticism about attempts to attain certainty and suspicion of '*supposed discoveries*' in metaphysics, see *CL*, II, 673, and 675. Even Aristotle is cited as evidence that '. . . the greatest of men have too great a love for systems of their own creation' (*PL*, p. 188). See also Herbert Read, *Coleridge as Critic*, p. 31. As Margaret L. Wiley has pointed out, 'Coleridge's thinking follows closely the pattern of scepticism traceable in many seventeenth-century men whom he

admired. . . .' ('Coleridge and the Wheels of Intellect', *PMLA*, LXVII [1952], 101).

[94] *PL*, p. 153.

CHAPTER 3

[1] *CL*, I, 224.

[2] *CL*, I, 227.

[3] *CL*, I, 263, 270, 273, and 318. For a discussion of Coleridge's early reviews, see above, Chapter 1, n. 66.

[4] *PW*, II, 962.

[5] *CL*, II, 912.

[6] *CL*, II, 936.

[7] *CL*, II, 953.

[8] *CL*, II, 953.

[9] *The Letters of William and Dorothy Wordsworth: The Middle Years*, ed. Ernest de Selincourt (Oxford, 1937), I, 165 and 168.

[10] *CL*, III, 58–9 and n.

[11] *CL*, III, 117.

[12] *CL*, III, 148–9; 124–5.

[13] *CL*, III, 135–6.

[14] *CL*, III, 272. For a later but more detailed account of his feelings towards Jeffrey's revisions, see *UL*, II, 407–8.

[15] *CL*, III, 275. Cf. 316–17; and *SC*, II, 75.

[16] *SC*, II, 33.

[17] *SC*, II, 33. Cf. British Museum MS, Egerton 2800, fol. 89r: 'It is too certain, that the grievances here enumerated have been rendered both more diffusive and more intense by the nature, number, and prodigious circulation of Reviews and Magazines, which with Newspapers, and a Shelf or two of Beauties, Extracts, and Anas, form nine tenths of the Reading of nine tenths of *the reading Public*. . . .'

[18] *SC*, II, 33.

[19] *SC*, II, 34.

[20] *SC*, II, 38. Cf. *CL*, III, 107; and *F*, I, 318n.

[21] *CL*, IV, 564. By this time he had begun to feel the critical lash himself. See *CL*, III, 433 and 532. In a letter to Stuart, Coleridge mentions a cabal of notables which he and Bowles had talked over as being capable of running a review in opposition (*CL*, III, 539).

[22] Reckoning without the interpolations. See Everyman, p. xviii.

[23] See A. L. Strout, 'Knights of the Burning Epistle', *Studia Neophilologica*, XXVI (1953–4), 79–80. In a letter written to John Murray in 1816, Coleridge mentions the characteristics he considered appropriate for a review (*CL*, IV, 648). Cf. the conditions he tried to impose on *Blackwood's Magazine* in 1819 (*CL*, IV, 976). See also British Museum MS,

Egerton 2800, fol. 84r. The financial return must have been the principle motive. (Cf., for example, *CL*, IV, 665). The restraint shown in *Biographia Literaria* concerning the *Edinburgh Review* (*BL*, II, 117–18; Everyman, pp. 237–8) is the more remarkable when Coleridge's real feelings are known.

[24] *F*, I, 41.

[25] *SC*, II, 23.

[26] *SC*, II, 74–5.

[27] *TM*, Appendix, p. 86.

[28] *BL*, II, 116; (Everyman, p. 237).

[29] 'It will be found, that the least of what I have written concerns myself personally. I have used the narration chiefly for the purpose of giving a continuity to the work, in part for the sake of the miscellaneous reflections suggested to me by particular events, but still more as introductory to the statement of my principles. . . .' (*BL*, I, 4; Everyman, p. 1).

[30] *CL*, II, 707.

[31] *TM*, Appendix, p. 88.

[32] *BL*, II, 123; (Everyman, p. 241).

[33] *BL*, I, 63; (Everyman, p. 36).

[34] *W*, pp. 5–6.

[35] *SC*, II, 48. Cf. *CL*, III, 29; and *SC*, II, 38 and 62.

[36] Shawcross, II, 248–9.

[37] *BL*, I, 22; (Everyman, p. 11).

[38] *CL*, IV, 598.

[39] *CL*, IV, 591.

[40] *BL*, I, 92; (Everyman, p. 53).

[41] *BL*, II, 181; (Everyman, p. 277). Cf. George Watson's recent statement: 'Coleridge . . . is essentially a critic who practises descriptive criticism only as an illustration' (*The Literary Critics: A Study of English Descriptive Criticism* [Harmondsworth, 1962], p. 113).

[42] *BL*, II, 116–17; (Everyman, p. 237).

[43] *BL*, I, 53–4; (Everyman, p. 30).

[44] *BL*, II, 181; (Everyman, p. 277).

[45] *SC*, II, 35–6.

[46] *CL*, II, 1039.

[47] *SC*, II, 33.

[48] *SC*, II, 33.

[49] *SC*, II, 35.

[50] *SC*, II, 36.

[51] *SC*, II, 35.

[52] *SC*, II, 82.

[53] *BL*, I, 237; (Everyman, p. 135).

[54] *BL*, I, 240; (Everyman, pp. 136–7).

[55] *BL*, I, 241–3; (Everyman, pp. 137–8).

[56] *BL*, I, 264; (Everyman, p. 149).

[57] *BL*, I, 293; (Everyman, p. 166). As Alice Snyder points out: 'With regard to actual performance, the case for Coleridge is stronger than it appears when one thinks, for instance, of the twelfth chapter of the *Biographia*. Unpublished manuscript material gives striking evidence of the

patience with which Coleridge tried to practice what he preached, in the way of leading the student on, simply and naturally' (*Coleridge on Logic and Learning*, p. 47).

⁵⁸ For an account of contemporary hostility, see René Wellek, *Kant in England*, pp. 25ff.

⁵⁹ *BL*, I, 291; (Everyman, pp. 164–5).

⁶⁰ *BL*, I, 293; (Everyman, p. 166).

⁶¹ On 'landing-places' as a means of 'bribing' the reader's attention, see *F*, I, 324–5. George Whalley has drawn attention to the similarity of technique in *Biographia Literaria*: 'The Integrity of *Biographia Literaria*', *Essays and Studies*, n.s. VI (1953), 99.

⁶² *BL*, II, 85; (Everyman, p. 217).

⁶³ *SC*, II, 37.

⁶⁴ *BL*, I, 158–9; (Everyman, p. 92).

⁶⁵ *BL*, I, 250; (Everyman, p. 142).

⁶⁶ *BL*, I, 250; (Everyman, p. 142).

⁶⁷ *BL*, I, 251; (Everyman, pp. 142–3).

⁶⁸ *BL*, I, 251; (Everyman, p. 143).

⁶⁹ *BL*, I, 251; (Everyman, p. 143).

⁷⁰ *BL*, I, 252; (Everyman, p. 143).

⁷¹ *BL*, I, 253; (Everyman, p. 144). I have removed the comma which stands after 'inward organ' and replaced it after 'for it' as the sense demands.

⁷² *PL*, p. 153.

⁷³ *BL*, I, 254; (Everyman, p. 144).

⁷⁴ Watson rightly excuses the perplexity of the Victorians: '[They] could not be expected to understand what he was talking about: some of his texts had not been printed, most had not been edited, and his criticism was nearly all of an order that would respond only to close and concentrated exegesis' (*The Literary Critics*, p. 113).

⁷⁵ *BL*, I, 255; (Everyman, p. 145).

⁷⁶ *BL*, I, 256; (Everyman, p. 145).

⁷⁷ *BL*, I, 257; (Everyman, p. 146).

⁷⁸ *BL*, I, 257; (Everyman, p. 146).

⁷⁹ e.g. *PL*, pp. 360 and 361.

⁸⁰ *F*, III, 183.

⁸¹ *BL*, I, 257–8; (Everyman, p. 146).

⁸² *BL*, I, 258; (Everyman, p. 146).

⁸³ *BL*, I, 259; (Everyman, p. 147).

⁸⁴ *BL*, I, 259; (Everyman, p. 147).

⁸⁵ *BL*, I, 260; (Everyman, p. 147).

⁸⁶ *BL*, I, 260; (Everyman, p. 147).

⁸⁷ *BL*, I, 260; (Everyman, pp. 147–8).

⁸⁸ *BL*, I, 261; (Everyman, p. 148).

⁸⁹ *BL*, I, 261; (Everyman, p. 148).

⁹⁰ *BL*, I, 261; (Everyman, p. 148).

⁹¹ *BL*, I, 263; (Everyman, p. 149).

⁹² *BL*, I, 264; (Everyman, p. 149).

⁹³ *BL*, I, 264; (Everyman, pp. 149–50).

[94] *BL*, I, 265; (Everyman, p. 150).

[95] *BL*, I, 266; (Everyman, p. 150).

[96] *BL*, I, 266; (Everyman, pp. 150-1). Cf. British Museum MS, Egerton 2826, fols. 77-8.

[97] *BL*, I, 267; (Everyman, p. 151).

[98] *BL*, I, 267-8; (Everyman, pp. 151-2).

[99] *BL*, I, 270; (Everyman, p. 153).

[100] *BL*, I, 270; (Everyman, p. 153).

[101] *BL*, I, 270; (Everyman, p. 153).

[102] *BL*, I, 271; (Everyman, p. 153).

[103] *BL*, I, 271; (Everyman, p. 153).

[104] *BL*, I, 272-3; (Everyman, p. 154).

[105] *BL*, I, 275; (Everyman, p. 156).

[106] *BL*, I, 275; (Everyman, p. 156).

[107] *BL*, I, 282; (Everyman, p. 159).

[108] Christopher North seems to have been the first to express his impatience publicly. See, 'Some Observations on the "Biographia Literaria" of S. T. Coleridge, Esq. – 1817', *Blackwood's Magazine*, II (1817), 16-17.

[109] *BL*, I, 295; (Everyman, p. 167).

[110] *TM*, p. 2.

[111] *TM*, p. 4.

[112] *TM*, p. 7.

[113] *F*, III, 158.

[114] *BL*, I, 92; (Everyman, pp. 52-3).

[115] *TT*, II, 335.

[116] *Organic Unity in Coleridge*, p. 1. Cf. Frederick Denison Maurice, *The Kingdom of Christ* (London, 1842), 2nd ed., I, xi, where Coleridge's writing is given credit in that '. . . it shews us what we have to seek for, and that it puts us into a way of seeking'.

[117] *Coleridge as Critic*, p. 18. Cf. Coburn: '. . . the principles of Method are the principles of literary criticism' ('Coleridge Redivivus', p. 120).

[118] *PL*, pp. 191-2. Kathleen Coburn's speculation (*PL*, p. 192n) that 'generalization' is perhaps an erroneous substitution for 'organization' seems to me too to be consistent with Coleridge's usage. Cf. also *PL*, pp. 148-9; *F*, II, 88-9; and III, 314.

CHAPTER 4

[1] Shawcross, I, lxxff.

[2] *CL*, I, 354.

[3] See for example, Wellek, *Kant in England*, pp, 67-8 and 80.

[4] *EOHOT*, I, 7 (Republished in *The Friend* [1818], *F*, II, 242). Cf. Coleridge's description of himself, *Inquiring Spirit: A New Presentation of*

Coleridge from His Published and Unpublished Prose Writings, ed. Kathleen Coburn (London, 1951), pp. 33–4.

[5] *BL,* I, 136; (Everyman, p. 79).

[6] *BL,* I, 136–7; (Everyman, p. 79).

[7] *BL,* I, 144; (Everyman, p. 83).

[8] *BL,* I, 247–8; (Everyman, p. 141). The suggestion that Coleridge adopts rather than evolves his philosophy (e.g. Claud Howard, *Coleridge's Idealism,* p. 29) is an over-simplification. As Kathleen Coburn points out, '. . . Coleridge borrows only when his own thinking has reached almost the same point as his creditor's, so that he feels able fully to enter into the other's thought, indeed more fully than the propounder very often; he sees its further implications and applications and makes it his own by loading it with his own accumulated knowledge.' (*PL,* p. 55). Some German students of Coleridge have made a point of the way in which he mastered German thought for his own purposes. See for example, Enrico Pizzo, 'S. T. Coleridge als Kritiker', *Anglia,* XL (1916), 210–11 and 219; and Helene Richter, 'Die philosophische Weltanschauung von S. T. Coleridge und ihr Verhältnis zur deutschen Philosophie', *Anglia,* XLIV (1920), 320ff.

[9] *PL,* pp. 347–8.

[10] *CL,* II, 685–6.

[11] *CL,* II, 671–2.

[12] *CL,* II, 688–9.

[13] *CL,* II, 688.

[14] *BL,* II, 6; (Everyman, p. 171).

[15] *CL,* II, 947–8.

[16] *CL,* IV, 591; 589–90; and 585.

[17] *CL,* III, 533.

[18] For a more general account, see J. A. Appleyard, *Coleridge's Philosophy of Literature: The Development of a Concept of Poetry 1791–1819* (Cambridge, Mass., 1965).

[19] 'Kant and the English Platonists', in *Essays Philosophical and Psychological in Honor of William James* (New York, 1908), p. 291. Cf. *Vorlesungen,* p. 17.

[20] *F,* III, 154. Cf. *TM,* p. 4.

[21] *F,* III, 154–5.

[22] British Museum MS, Egerton 2826, fol. 192v.

[23] *CL,* II, 1195.

[24] *CL,* II, 1197.

[25] *CL,* III, 483.

[26] *TM,* p. 9.

[27] *PL,* p. 390. The original reading of 'man' for 'wings' would, I think, make just as good sense, if less pleasing sound.

[28] *F,* I, 181.

[29] *EOHOT,* II, 653–4.

[30] *BL,* I, 252; (Everyman, p. 143).

[31] *BL,* I, 272; (Everyman, p. 154).

[32] *BL,* I, 273; (Everyman, p. 154). There is a curious parallel between this idea of a higher consciousness and the speculations indulged in by

Coleridge after his tale of the young woman in the Catholic town in Germany. (See *BL*, I, 112–16; Everyman, pp. 65–7).

[33] *CL*, II, 688.

[33a] When talking about pre-Freudian psychology it is difficult to find terms which have not been pre-empted by the associations of post-Freudian usage. Encouraged by the example of Lancelot Law Whyte (*The Unconscious before Freud* [London, 1960]), I shall use the term 'unconscious' to refer to what Coleridge describes as 'that which lies *on the other side* of our natural consciousness' (*BL*, I, 246; Everyman, p. 139).

[34] *TM*, pp. 37–8. Cf. *F*, III, 177–8.

[35] British Museum MS, Egerton 2826, fol. 6.

[36] British Museum MS, Egerton 2826, fol. 68.

[37] British Museum MS, Egerton 2826, fol. 59.

[38] British Museum MS, Egerton 2826, fol. 60.

[39] *CL*, II, 709.

[40] *CL*, III, 172.

[41] *BL*, I, 99n–100n; (Everyman, p. 57n).

[42] *SC*, II, 113.

[43] *SC*, II, 10. For a useful discussion of Coleridge's opinions on the value of 'obscure ideas', see Lucyle Werkmeister, 'Coleridge on Science, Philosophy, and Poetry: their Relation to Religion', *Harvard Theological Review*, LII (1959), 85–118.

[44] *CL*, III, 482.

[45] *CL*, II, 1198.

[46] *PL*, pp. 194–5.

[47] *CL*, III, 533.

[48] *CL*, III, 533. Cf. Shawcross, II, 230.

[49] See, for example, *CL*, IV, 631–3.

[50] *NOED*, I, 218.

[51] *SM*, p. 63.

[52] *N*, II, 2445n. Cf. also Coleridge's plaintive note: 'O . . . that my mind may be made up as to the character of Jesus, and of historical Christianity, as clearly as it is of [Christ] the Logos and intellectual or spiritual Christianity – that I may be made to know either their especial and peculiar Union, or their absolute disunion in any peculiar sense' (*N*, II, 2448).

[53] G. A. Wells has pointed out that Coleridge objected to Herder's contention that man learned everything from nature. See 'Man and Nature: an Elucidation of Coleridge's Rejection of Herder's Thought', *Journal of English and Germanic Philology*, LI (1952), 321.

[54] *CL*, III, 146.

[55] *TM*, p. 8. Coleridge recognizes Jacobi as a predecessor: 'Jacobi, who, slighting or rejecting all supernatural evidences of an historical and outward nature, finds the only sure ground of all religious convictions in inward revelation, in an instinctive Fore-tokening of the Conscience and in Faith as a *sentiment*. . . .' (British Museum MS, Egerton 2801, fol. 7). Cf. W. Schrickx, 'Coleridge and Friedrich Heinrich Jacobi', *Revue Belge de Philologie et d'Histoire*, XXXVI (1958), 812–50, especially 827.

[56] *TM*, p. 10.

⁵⁷ *NOED*, I, 2. This is the reason for Coleridge's disapproval of the practice of regarding miracles as proof of the divinity of Christ. See for example: 'Just look at the answer of Christ himself to Nicodemus, *John* iii. 2, 3. Nicodemus professed a full belief in Christ's divine mission. Why? It was attested by his miracles. What answered Christ? "Well said, O Believer?" No, not a word of this; but the proof of the folly of such a supposition. *Verily, verily, I say unto thee; except a man be born again, he cannot see the kingdom of God,* – that is, he cannot have faith in me' (*NOED*, II, 286). Coleridge speaks out elsewhere against '. . . that fashion of modern theologists which would convert miracles from a motive to attention and solicitous examination, and at best from a negative condition of revelation, into the positive foundation of Christian faith' (*NOED*, I, 46–7).

On nature as evidence of God, Coleridge seems to have wavered. In *The Statesman's Manual*, he speaks of '. . . a revelation of God – the great book of his servant Nature. That in its obvious sense and literal interpretation it declares the being and attributes of the Almighty Father, none but the *fool in heart* has ever dared gainsay' (*SM*, Appendix, p. xiii). On the following page of Gillman's copy in the British Museum (Ashley 2850), Coleridge has written: 'At the time, I wrote this Work, my views of *Nature* were very imperfect and confused.' The confusion lies, I think, in his not having qualified his description of the book of nature by stressing our inability to read it. His position is better represented by his comment on Donne's remarks on St. Cyril's suggestion that 'the light that lighteth' is the light of nature: 'The error here, and it is a grievous error, consists in the word "nature". There is, there can be, no light of nature: there may be a light in or upon nature; but this is the light that shineth down into the darkness, that is, the nature, and the darkness comprehendeth it not. All ideas, or spiritual truths, are supernatural' (*NOED*, I, 91).

⁵⁸ *NOED*, II, 322. Coleridge is aware of the potential danger of misconstruing or misapplying the Ideas *ab intra*. See for example his account of alchemy: 'The potential (Λόγος θέανθρωπος) the ground of the prophetic, directed the first thinkers (The Mystae) to the metallic bodies, as the key of all natural science. They then actually blended with this instinct all the fancies and fond desires, and false perspective of the childhood of intellect. The essence was truth, the form was folly; and this is the definition of alchemy. Nevertheless, the very terms bear witness to the veracity of the original instinct' (*NOED*, I, 121).

⁵⁹ On the possibility of analytic and synthetic judgements in God, see British Museum MS, Egerton 2826, fols. 270–271: '. . . in God's conceptions, if we dare attribute the term at all in reference to God, or in the conceptions of spiritual beings superior to man, tho' still like himself finite, the distinction of Analytic & synthetic may not exist or each conception might actually contain all other conceptions.'

⁶⁰ *A to R*, p. vi.

⁶¹ *NOED*, I, 28.

⁶² *NOED*, II, 280.

⁶³ *NOED*, I, 90. Cf. Coleridge's comment on Waterland's interpretation of the text, 'But God's thoughts are not our thoughts': 'That is, as I would

interpret the text; – the ideas in and by which God reveals himself to man are not the same with, and are not to be judged by, the conceptions which the human understanding generalises from the notices of the senses, common to man and to irrational animals, dogs, elephants, beavers, and the like, endowed with the same senses. Therefore I regard this paragraph . . . as a specimen of admirable special pleading *ad-hominem* in the Court of eristic Logic; but I condemn it as a wilful resignation or temporary self-deposition of the reason. I will not suppose what my reason declares to be no position at all, and therefore an impossible sub-position' (*NOED*, II, 185–6).

[64] *PL*, p. 312.

[65] *BL*, I, 240; (Everyman, pp. 136–7).

[66] *TM*, p. 6.

[67] *SC*, II, 50.

[68] *BL*, I, 246; (Everyman, p. 139).

[69] *BL*, I, 246; (Everyman, p. 140). Cf. Thesis II, *BL*, I, 264; (Everyman, p. 150).

[70] *SM*, Appendix, pp. viii and vii.

[71] *SM*, Appendix, p. v.

[72] *SC*, II, 107.

[73] *SC*, II, 36.

[74] *BL*, II, 51; (Everyman, p. 197).

[75] *F*, III, 263.

CHAPTER 5

[1] *SC*, II, 12.

[2] 'Some Observations on the "Biographia Literaria" of S. T. Coleridge, Esq. – 1817', *Blackwood's Magazine*, II (1817), 5.

[3] M. H. Abrams provides a useful account of the Romantics' predecessors. See *The Mirror and the Lamp: Romantic Theory and the Critical Tradition*, 2nd ed. (New York, 1958), pp. 184ff.

[4] *W*, p. 100.

[5] *MC*, p. 195.

[6] *SC*, II, 111.

[7] *SC*, II, 112.

[8] *SC*, II, 53.

[9] *CL*, IV, 545.

[10] *CL*, II, 810.

[11] See *BL*, I, 8; (Everyman, p. 3). Cf. Coleridge's mention of Young's comments on Pindar (*CL*, II, 864).

[12] *TM*, p. 25.

[13] *TM*, p. 25.

[14] *TM*, pp. 35–6.

[15] Coleridge unfortunately reserved the relevant theology for discussion in *The Friend*, while the greater part of his treatment of the Method of the Fine Arts appears in the *Treatise* only. Read's suggestion that Coleridge rejected the identification of artistic and absolute truth (*Coleridge as Critic*, p. 31) seems to me to be more relevant to his religious thinking of a later period. Cf. James D. Boulger, *Coleridge as Religious Thinker* (New Haven, 1961), p. 106: '. . . the sudden falling-off in allusions to the myth-making power and the imagination in his later writings leads one to the belief that the role of the imagination in the higher reason was reduced by a thinker fully conscious of the implications such contradictions held for a truly Christian point of view.'

[16] *TM*, p. 5.

[17] *F*, III, 163–4.

[18] *F*, III, 164.

[19] *TM*, p. 62.

[20] *TM*, pp. 62–3.

[21] *BL*, II, 41n; (Everyman, p. 192n).

[22] *SC*, II, 98.

[23] *SC*, II, 98.

[24] *NOED*, I, 2.

[25] Coleridge offers a variation on this analogy in his 1818 essay 'On Poesy and Art': '. . . nature itself is to a religious observer the art of God. . . .' (Shawcross, II, 254). And again, '. . . nature itself would give us the impression of a work of art, if we could see the thought which is present at once in the whole and in every part; and a work of art will be just in proportion as it adequately conveys the thought. . . .' (Shawcross, II, 255).

[26] *BL*, I, 246: (Everyman, p. 139).

[27] *TM*, p. 11.

[28] *F*, III, 148.

[29] *CL*, II, 812.

[30] *SC*, II, 63.

[31] *SC*, II, 107.

[32] *BL*, II, 91; (Everyman, p. 221).

[33] *BL*, II, 11; (Everyman, pp. 173–4).

[34] *F*, III, 163–4; and *TM*, pp. 62–3.

[35] *BL*, I, 295–6; (Everyman, p. 167).

[36] Shawcross, I, lx–lxxvii.

[37] Shawcross, I, lxvii.

[38] Shawcross, I, lxviii.

[39] Shawcross, I, lxviii. The interpretation advanced by M. H. Abrams follows the same general lines, and differs mainly in being more specific. His statement that '. . . the primary and already creative act of perception yields the "inanimate cold world" of the ever-anxious crowd', and that 'The subsequent and higher act of re-creation . . . transforms the cold inanimate world into a warm world united with the life of man, and by that same act, converts matter-of-fact into matter-of-poetry' (*The Mirror and the Lamp*, p. 68) seems to me mistaken.

[40] Shawcross, I, lxix.

[41] Shawcross, I, lxix. Cf. D. G. James, *Scepticism and Poetry: an Essay on the Poetic Imagination* (London, 1937), p. 15; Clarence D. Thorpe, 'Coleridge as Aesthetician and Critic', *Journal of the History of Ideas*, V (1944), p. 403; R. L. Brett, 'Coleridge's Theory of the Imagination', *Essays & Studies*, n.s. II (1949), 79; Frederick B. Rainsberry, 'Coleridge and the Paradox of the Poetic Imperative', *English Literary History*, XXI (1954), 133; James Volant Baker, *The Sacred River; Coleridge's Theory of the Imagination* (Baton Rouge, 1957), p. 119.

[42] *Coleridge on Imagination.*

[43] e.g John Livingston Lowes, *The Road to Xanadu* (London, 1930), p. 103.

[44] *The Use of Poetry and the Use of Criticism* (London, 1933), p. 77.

[45] In *Perspectives of Criticism*, ed. Harry Levin (Cambridge, Mass., 1950), pp. 125–59.

[46] 'Coleridge on the Function of Art', p. 145.

[47] 'Coleridge on the Function of Art', p. 146. Bate's account of Secondary Imagination, however, seems to me to be misleading. He states that the '. . . appointed task of the "secondary" imagination is to "idealize and unify" its objects. . . . Indeed, its field is explicitly stated to consist of "objects" which (*as objects*) are essentially fixed and dead' (pp. 145–6). But Coleridge does not say that Secondary Imagination struggles to 'idealize and unify' objects, but only that it struggles to 'idealize and unify'. In fact, he makes an oblique contrast between it and objects in the next sentence: 'It is essentially *vital*, even as all objects (*as* objects) are essentially fixed and dead.' The view that Secondary Imagination is directed towards the world of material phenomena seems to me an erroneous one. J. V. Baker's account of the contribution of the unconscious is, I think, relevant to Fancy alone, and not, as he supposes, to Imagination. (See *The Sacred River*, pp. 152–63).

[48] 'Coleridge on the Function of Art', p. 146.

[49] Although he is sometimes ambivalent. See for example, *F*, I, 270: 'The Sense, (vis sensitiva vel intuitiva) *perceives*. . . .'

[50] *A to R*, p. 73. Cf. his glossary in *The Statesman's Manual*: 'A conscious Presentation, if it refers exclusively to the *Subject*, as a modification of his own state of Being, is = SENSATION. The same if it refers to an OBJECT, is = PERCEPTION. A PERCEPTION, immediate and individual is = INTUITION' (*SM*, Appendix, p. xlvii). Cf. also a passage in Coleridge's MS, 'On the Divine Idea': 'As rationally might I assert a Tree to be a Bud, as B[isho]p Berk[e]ley Perception to be Sensation, which is itself but the minimum, lowest grade, or first manifestation of Perception' (Huntington Library MS, HM 8195, p. 10.) A. O. Lovejoy refers to the currency of this notion of perception in German thought of the period. See his *The Reason the Understanding and Time* (Baltimore, 1961), pp. 20–1 especially.

[51] Cf. *NOED*, I, 59: 'In all proper faith the will is the prime agent. . . .'

[52] *BL*, I, 293–4; (Everyman, p. 166).

[53] British Museum copy (C.43.c.24), VIII, ii, 960n. This note can be dated with some confidence as belonging to the period between the beginning of July, 1818, and the end of March, 1819. The set of Tennemann belonged to J. H. Green: Coleridge sent him a letter on 3 July 1818 asking

if he might borrow it 'two Volumes at a time' (*CL*, IV, 870), and used it when he was preparing for his series of philosophical lectures which ended on 29 March 1819. (See *PL*, pp. 18ff.) As Coleridge did not admire Tennemann's work and used it merely as a convenience, it is unlikely that he continued to annotate it after the lecture series was over.

[54] *F*, I, 266. Cf. Boulger's account of the 'higher reason'. (*Coleridge as Religious Thinker*, pp. 65–93).

[55] *F*, I, 266.

[56] *F*, I, 266.

[57] *F*, I, 266–7. Cf. a passage in one of Coleridge's manuscripts: 'The Reason and it's Objects do not appertain to the World of the Senses, outward or inward – i.e. they partake neither of Sense nor of Fancy. Reason is *Supersensuous*: and here th' Antagonist is the *Lust of the Eye*.' (British Museum MS, Egerton 2801, fol. 218v.)

[58] *SM*, Appendix, p. xii.

[59] *F*, I, 266. Cf. *NOED*, I, 17–18.

[60] In a note to her edition of *Biographia Literaria* – (London, 1847), I, 297 – Sara Coleridge mentions that Coleridge later struck out the phrase '. . . a repetition, &c.' in a copy of the book which he had annotated. It is suggested by James Benziger that Coleridge saw the damaging implications of making an unconscious human act analogous with the creative act of God, which would be represented as a result as '. . . some dim *Spiritus Mundi* which directs the evolution of the world without really knowing what it is doing. . . .' ('Organic Unity: Leibniz to Coleridge' *PMLA*, LXVI [March 1951], 42). The correction, then, seems relevant to Coleridge's later dissatisfaction with Schellingian theology, and not to the definition of Primary Imagination itself. Cf. Rainsberry, 'Coleridge and the Paradox of the Poetic Imperative', p. 134, for another interpretation.

[61] *CL*, III, 172.

[62] *BL*, I, 246; (Everyman, p. 140). Cf. *SM*, Appendix, p. xxi–xiii.

[63] Cf. the statement in 'On Poesy and Art' that '. . . there is in genius itself an unconscious activity; nay, that is the genius in the man of genius' (Shawcross, II, 258).

[64] *BL*, I, 273; (Everyman, p. 154).

[65] British Museum MS, Egerton 2826, fol. 56.

[66] British Museum MS, Egerton 2826, fols. 59–60.

[67] *BL*, I, 296; (Everyman, p. 167).

[68] *BL*, II, 11; (Everyman, p. 174). Cf. *A to R*, p. 153: 'Therefore, not *by* the Will of man alone; but neither *without* the Will.' Cf. the moral counterpart – 'a habit of distinct consciousness' (*A to R*), p. 12.

[69] Coleridge toys with a paradox in *Aids to Reflection* (p. 216): 'Reason indeed is far nearer to SENSE than to Understanding: for Reason . . . is a direct Aspect of Truth, an inward Beholding, having a similar relation to the Intelligible or Spiritual, as SENSE has to the Material or Phenomenal.'

[70] *TM*, p. 62.

[71] *TM*, p. 63.

[72] *BL*, II, 11–12; (Everyman, p. 174).

[73] *TM*, p. 62.

[74] See, for example, *SC*, II, 102: '. . . there is a language not descriptive of passion, not uttered under the influence of it, which is at the same time poetic, and shows a high and active fancy. . . .' In a marginal note in Daniel Stuart's copy of *Aids to Reflection* (British Museum copy: C. 134. c. 10), Coleridge connects the inappropriate use of Fancy with idolatry: 'When the Invisible is sought for by means of the Fancy in the World *without*, and the Awe < is > transferred to imaginary Powers (Dæmons, Genii, &c) or to sensible Objects (*Fetisches*, *Gris gris*, Saints' Images, Relics, &c) the Man becomes a Phantast in the one case and superstitious in the other. The *Idea* of God is contained in the Reason: and the *Reality* of this Idea is a Command of the Conscience. Yet by placing even this *out of* ourselves, as if it existed in Space, we change it into an Idol' (pp. 98–9).

[75] *BL*, I, 110–12; (Everyman, pp. 63–5).

[76] *BL*, I, 112; (Everyman, p. 64).

[77] *BL*, I, 126–7; (Everyman, p. 73).

[78] It might be interesting to compare this with Wordsworth's 'emotion recollected in tranquillity'. Cf. also the remark made by Coleridge in 1830: 'A poet ought not to pick nature's pocket: let him borrow, and so borrow as to repay by the very act of borrowing. Examine nature accurately, but write from recollection; and trust more to your imagination than to your memory.' (*TT*, I, 205).

[79] *CL*, II, 706.

[80] There is, I believe, a basic confusion in J. V. Baker's objection to this aspect of Coleridge's theory. According to him, 'The weakness of Coleridge's theory is using "fancy" as a name for the associative power and assuming that the associative power is "mechanical" ' (*The Sacred River*, p. 217). Coleridge does neither. Association for him provides the materials for fancy; the associative power (as Baker is clearly aware when he is discussing it specifically – e.g. pp. 35–9) is not in Coleridge's view mechanical, in fact this is the point of his quarrel with the Hartleyan account.

[81] For example, see *MC*, p. 38. I am obliged to dissent, therefore, from the interpretations of Fancy given by F. R. Leavis, who dismisses it as 'merely an ancillary concept' ('Coleridge in Criticism', *Scrutiny*, ix (1940), 63); R. L. Brett, who describes its products as 'purely the result of an associative and not a creative process' – the two are not incompatible in Coleridge's scheme – ('Coleridge's Theory of the Imagination', p. 79); J. V. Baker, who asks, 'Why does Coleridge block off fancy from imagination and assign to fancy exclusively the tricks of association, which he regards at best as poor mechanical shuffling?' – again, I think an unnecessarily unsympathetic view of Fancy (*The Sacred River*, p. 248; cf. p. 225); and Walter Greiner, who states that although Fancy is *'eine Dichterkraft'*, it is incapable of working that '. . . *Verwandlung* . . . *welche nur im Bereich der* "secondary imagination", *des echten Dichtungsvermögens, möglich ist.*' – Coleridge, as I have tried to show does not contrast Imagination and Fancy as respectively *'echt* 'and *'unecht'*. ('Deutsche Einflüsse auf die Dichtungstheorie von Samuel Taylor Coleridge', *Die neueren Sprachen*, n.s. II [1960], 60; cf. 63).

[82] *CL*, II, 1198.

[83] *SM*, Appendix, p. v. Cf. Boulger, *Coleridge as Religious Thinker*, pp. 96–7.

[84] *BL*, I, 86–7; (Everyman, p. 50). It is worthwhile to compare this much-maligned statement with Kant's on the distinction between understanding and the senses: 'These two powers or capacities cannot exchange their functions. The understanding can intuit nothing, the senses can think nothing. Only through their union can knowledge arise. But that is no reason for confounding the contribution of either with that of the other; rather it is a strong reason for carefully separating and distinguishing the one from the other.' (*C of Pure R*, p. 93).

[85] *BL*, II, 12; (Everyman, p. 174). I omit the phrase 'MOTION its LIFE', because I do not understand it in any technical sense. Coleridge does not seem to have left any trace of a developed theory for it, and it does not receive much attention in the *Biographia*. Possibly the phrase, '*move & impress motions*', which occurs listed as a fifth class of psychological facts in an 1804 notebook entry may provide a clue (*N*, II, 2382).

For a parallel use of the 'body', 'drapery' image, see Coleridge's account of the Phoenician theology as manifested in 'popular and civil worship' (*LR*, II, 339–40).

CHAPTER 6

[1] Lest this emphasis should give the misleading impression that Coleridge ignored ur underestimated the conscious element in art, it should be said that his philosophical preoccupation with the nature, source, and validity of the unconscious may be attributed to his realization that the mysterious challenged explanation more than the obvious, and to his belief that the extra-rational was being under-estimated by his contemporaries. While he does take issue with what he thinks to be over-simplified theories of poetry, his whole impulse seems to be towards rational explanation of his dissatisfaction. In the end, far from denying the part played by the rational in art, he affirms that 'GOOD SENSE is the BODY of poetic genius', and insists on the additional presence of a higher form of Reason which can be accommodated to the Christian persuasion. In Coleridge's account, without the Imagination there can be no great poetry, but without the Will and Understanding there can be no poetry at all. For a sane, brief discussion of this matter, in the course of which the 'anti-Romantic' accusations of F. L. Lucas and Irving Babbitt are directly met, see Clarence D. Thorpe, 'Coleridge as Aesthetician and Critic', pp. 388 and 408–14.

[2] *BL*, II, 13; (Everyman, p. 175).

[3] Cf., for example, T. M. Raysor's estimate (*SC*, I, xxviii and n).

[4] *SC*, II, 125.

[5] *SC*, II, 86.

[6] *SC*, II, 125.

[7] *TM*, p. 27. (Italics Coleridge's.)

[8] For his exploitation of the paradox, see *TM*, p. 26.

[9] *TM*, p. 36.

[10] *SC*, II, 98.

[11] *MC*, p. 43.

[12] *SC*, II, 76.

[13] *SC*, II, 96.

[14] *SC*, II, 58-9.

[15] *SC*, II, 58.

[16] *SC*, II, 66.

[17] *BL*, II, 21; (Everyman, pp. 179-80). Cf. Coleridge's comparison of Shakespeare and Henry More. (*NOED*, I, 128.)

[18] *TM*, p. 62.

[19] *TM*, p. 38.

[20] Shawcross, II, 254-5.

[21] *BL*, II, 41n; (Everyman, p. 192).

[22] *SC*, II, 102.

[23] *SC*, II, 99.

[24] *SC*, II, 101.

[25] *SC*, II, 53-4.

[26] *CL*, II, 810.

[27] David Hartley, *Observations on Man, His Frame, His Duty, and His Expectations* (London, 1791). Note to I, 81, written in pencil on the end-papers of the British Museum copy (C.126.1.2).

[28] *SC*, II, 53.

[29] *SC*, II, 85.

[30] It is worth noticing the similarity of this thinking to Kant's discussion of things-in-themselves (e.g. *C of Pure R*, p. 24).

[31] *SC*, II, 250.

[32] *MC*, pp. 43-4. Cf. *N*, II, 2086: 'Poetry a rationalized dream dealing [? about] to manifold Forms our own Feelings, that never perhaps were attached by us consciously to our own personal Selves. – What is the Lear, the Othello, but a divine Dream/ all Shakespere, & nothing Shakespere. – O there are Truths below the Surface in the subject of Sympathy, & how we *become* that which we understand[?ab]ly behold & hear, having, how much God perhaps only knows, created part even of the Form.' Cf. Coleridge's comment on *Venus and Adonis*: 'It is throughout as if a superior spirit more intuitive, more intimately conscious, even than the characters themselves, . . . were placing the whole before our view. . . .' (*BL*, II, 15-16; Everyman, p. 176).

[33] *SC*, II, 140.

[34] *SC*, II, 125.

[35] *SC*, II, 110.

[36] Shawcross, II, 158.

[37] Shawcross, II, 159.

[38] See J. R. de J. Jackson, 'Coleridge on Dramatic Illusion and Spectacle in the Performance of Shakespeare's Plays', *Modern Philology*, LXII (1964), 13-21.

[39] *SC*, II, 56-7.

[40] *SC*, II, 130.

[41] *SC*, II, 123.

[42] *SC*, II, 135.

[43] *SC*, II, 103–4.

[44] *SC*, II, 103.

[45] *F*, I, 247.

[46] *SC*, II, 50–1.

[47] *CL*, IV, 641.

[48] *CL*, IV, 641.

[49] *CL*, IV, 642.

[50] *SC*, II, 65.

[51] *MC*, p. 194.

[52] *MC*, pp. 194–5. Note the coupling of memory with Imagination; Fancy ('a mode of Memory') is also relevant as one of the two poetic faculties.

[53] For further thoughts on the involuntary nature of children's intellection, see *BL*, II, 154–5; (Everyman, pp. 260–1).

[54] *NOED*, I, 235.

[55] *BL*, I, 4; (Everyman, p. 1).

[56] *CL*, II, 1034.

[57] *BL*, II, 172; (Everyman, p. 271).

[58] *BL*, II, 173; (Everyman, p. 271).

[59] *BL*, II, 178; (Everyman, p. 275).

[60] *BL*, II, 36; (Everyman, p. 189).

[61] *BL*, II, 37–8; (Everyman, p. 190).

[62] *BL*, II, 38; (Everyman, p. 190).

[63] *BL*, II, 40; (Everyman, p. 191).

[64] *BL*, II, 49; (Everyman, p. 196).

[65] *BL*, II, 49–50; (Everyman, pp. 196–7).

[66] *BL*, II, 51; (Everyman, p. 197).

[67] *BL*, II, 51; (Everyman, p. 197).

[68] *TM*, pp. 27–30.

[69] *BL*, II, 57–8; (Everyman, p. 201).

[70] *BL*, II, 59–60; (Everyman, p. 202).

[71] *BL*, II, 60; (Everyman, p. 203).

[72] *BL*, II, 65–6; (Everyman, p. 206).

[73] *BL*, II, 66; (Everyman, p. 206).

[74] *BL*, II, 66; (Everyman, p. 206).

[75] *BL*, II, 66; (Everyman, p. 206).

[76] *BL*, II, 66; (Everyman, p. 206).

[77] *BL*, II, 68; (Everyman, p. 207).

[78] *BL*, II, 71; (Everyman, p. 209).

[79] *BL*, II, 84; (Everyman, p. 217).

[80] *BL*, II, 86–7; (Everyman, p. 218).

[81] *BL*, II, 131; (Everyman, p. 246).

[82] *BL*, II, 132; (Everyman, p. 246).

[83] *BL*, II, 60; (Everyman, p. 202).

[84] *BL*, II, 136–9; (Everyman, pp. 249–50).

[85] *BL*, II, 139; (Everyman, p. 251).

[86] *BL*, II, 141; (Everyman, p. 252).

[87] *BL*, II, 141–2; (Everyman, p. 252).
[88] *BL*, II, 142; (Everyman, p. 252).
[89] *BL*, II, 142; (Everyman, pp. 252–3).
[90] *BL*, II, 148; (Everyman, p. 256).
[91] *N*, II, 2057.
[92] *CL*, IV, 574–5.
[93] *BL*, II, 1–2; (Everyman, pp. 168–9).
[94] *CL*, II, 830.
[95] British Museum Add. MSS. 41325, fol. lllv

CHAPTER 7

[1] *MC*, p. 170.
[2] *SC*, I, 16.
[3] Made in 1827 (*TT*, I, 69).
[4] See, *SC*, I, xliv–xlv.
[5] *SC*, II, 173. Cf. *SC*, II, 181–2.
[6] *SC*, I, 34.
[7] *SC*, II, 150.
[8] *SC*, II, 150. It is worth noticing that Coleridge does not advocate interpretations of literature which go beyond the intentions of the author. His comment on the allegorization of the Bible is pertinent: '. . . I readily acknowledge, that allegorical *applications* are one thing, and allegorical *interpretation* another: and that where there is no ground for supposing such a sense to have entered into the intent and purpose of the sacred Penman, they are not to be commended' (*A to R*, p. 254n). And again, 'To retain the literal sense, wherever the harmony of Scripture permits, and reason does not forbid, is ever the honester, and, nine times in ten, the more rational and pregnant interpretation' (*A to R*, p. 90).
[9] *SC*, II, 154–5.
[10] *SC*, I, 18.
[11] *SC*, I, 34.
[12] *SC*, II, 224.
[13] *SC*, I, 35.
[14] *SC*, II, 150.
[15] *SC*, II, 224.
[16] *SC*, II, 224.
[17] *TM*, p. 29.
[18] *SC*, II, 223.
[19] *SC*, II, 150.
[20] *SC*, II, 98.
[21] *SC*, II, 150. Coleridge seems to approve of this habit in a poet; indeed it is close to the procedure which he regards as typical of the activity of Fancy. He refers at one point to Hamlet's '. . . thoughts, images, and fancy

[being] far more vivid than his perceptions . . .,' – by which he clearly means 'sense perceptions' (*SC*, I, 34). There is a parallel in his description of Fancy in *Biographia Literaria* as 'no other than a mode of Memory emancipated from the order of time and space', but Hamlet's mental process is insufficiently '. . . blended with and modified by that empirical pheno-menon of the will, which we express by the word CHOICE' (*BL*, I, 296; Everyman, p. 167). This half-conscious mental activity, however essential it may be to the writing of poetry, is evidently a liability when one is forced to deal practically with the world of Sense.

[22] *SC*, I, 35.

[23] *SC*, I, 35.

[24] Chapter II, *passim*.

[25] *SC*, II, 152.

[26] *TT*, II, 330–1.

[27] *TT*, II, 87.

[28] *TM*, p. 6.

[29] *SC*, II, 224.

[30] *SC*, II, 152.

[31] *SC*, I, xliv.

[32] See, *Coleridge on the Seventeenth Century*, ed. Roberta Florence Brinkley (Durham, North Carolina, 1955), pp. 541–612.

[33] *MC*, p. 165.

[34] *MC*, p. 161.

[35] *A to R*, p. 251n, corrected according to the errata sheet, p. xvi.

[36] *A to R*, p. 253n.

[37] *MC*, p. 161.

[38] *MC*, p. 163.

[39] *MC*, p. 163.

[40] *SM*, Appendix, p. ix.

[41] *MC*, p. 163.

[42] Benjamin T. Sankey Jr., 'Coleridge on Milton's Satan', *Philological Quarterly*, XLI (1962), 505.

[43] See above, p. 29.

[44] Sankey, p. 508.

[45] *MC*, p. 127.

[46] *MC*, p. 127.

[47] *MC*, p. 128.

[48] *MC*, p. 100.

[49] *MC*, p. 102.

[50] *MC*, p. 128. Cf. Coleridge's comment on 'The unimportance of mere exterior' in Books I and II of *Gulliver's Travels* (*MC*, p. 114).

[51] For a discussion of the circumstances surrounding the lecture, see George Whalley, 'Coleridge on the *Prometheus* of Aeschylus', *Proceedings and Transactions of the Royal Society of Canada*, Third Series, LIV (1960), Section II, 13–16.

[52] *LR*, II, 331.

[53] *LR*, II, 328–9.

[54] Cf. pp. 90–2 above.

[55] As Professor Whalley has pointed out. ('Coleridge on the *Prometheus* of Aeschylus', p. 19).

[56] *Ibid.*, p. 18.

[57] *CL*, III, 533.

[58] It is a case of similarity and not identity, however. The Phoenician and Greek archologies are acceptable examples of the Natural and Human modes but Coleridge criticizes the Hebrew archology in a way which would not have been appropriate for the Divine mode. (Cf. *TM*, pp. 48–9, for an earlier treatment of the same subject-matter). One becomes aware of the different weight placed on the New Testament as an account of revelation; as will become apparent, Christianity, particularly the phenomenon of God as man in Christ, has affinities with the Greek scheme as Coleridge describes it. There may be an inconsistency here; if so, it is one to which we have already had occasion to refer. Coleridge was brought back to orthodox Christianity '. . . through the Logos, not the Gospels, a metaphysical rather than a historical approach'. (*N*, II, 2445n and above, p. 90). He would probably have argued that the New Testament was the only adequate example of the Divine mode; nevertheless, he allows the Old Testament to approximate it in its relationship to Greek and Phoenician accounts. As it is, he concentrates on the Greek. By doing so he is able, intentionally or not, to speculate much more boldly than he could if Holy Writ were in question.

[59] For an outline of the formal structure of the essay, see Whalley, 'On the *Prometheus* of Aeschylus', p. 17.

[60] *LR*, II, 339.

[61] *LR*, II, 340.

[62] *LR*, II, 340.

[63] *LR*, II, 340.

[64] *LR*, II, 340.

[65] *LR*, II, 342.

[66] *LR*, II, 341.

[67] *LR*, II, 343.

[68] *LR*, II, 343.

[69] *LR*, II, 343.

[70] *LR*, II, 343.

[71] *LR*, II, 344–5.

[72] *LR*, II, 345.

[73] *LR*, II, 346–7.

[74] *LR*, II, 347.

[75] *LR*, II, 347. Cf. *BL*, I, 254–9; (Everyman, pp. 144–7).

[76] *LR*, II, 348.

[77] *LR*, II, 348.

[78] *LR*, II, 348.

[79] See, for example, his disclaimer: 'Not that I regard the foregoing as articles of faith, or as all true. . . .' (*LR*, II, 349).

[80] *LR*, II, 350.

[81] *LR*, II, 354.

[82] *LR*, II, 354.

[83] *LR*, II, 355.
[84] *LR*, II, 355.
[85] *LR*, II, 355–6.
[86] *LR*, II, 358.
[87] *LR*, II, 358.
[88] *LR*, II, 336–7.
[89] *LR*, II, 338.
[90] *LR*, II, 358.
[91] British Museum MS, Egerton 2801, fol. 231v.

Index